Frank N. Thomas, PhD
Thorana S. Nelson, PhD
Editors

Tales from Family Therapy
Life-Changing Clinical Experiences

Pre-publication
REVIEWS,
COMMENTARIES,
EVALUATIONS . . .

More pre-publication
REVIEWS, COMMENTARIES, EVALUATIONS . . .

"**A**s the authors tell their tales about life-changing clinical experiences, they take you into the world of being a therapist, sharing the joys, the doubts, the struggles, the failures, the mishaps, and the unintentional, sometimes unexplainable successes. Their stories are about the human side of being a therapist—not about the theories underlying therapists' work nor the techniques used to intervene—but about those moments when something occurs in therapy that lingers long past the therapeutic encounter in the memories, perhaps the souls, of therapists. You may find yourself learning about what good therapy really is from these therapists' experiences.

Many of the tales are touching due to the authors' frank and honest discussion of the ways in which clients and the work they do affects them. There are stories about working with families, couples, and children. There are stories about humorous times in therapy, about difficult times in therapy, and about challenging times of learning therapy. Many stories are about remarkable clients and what appear to be therapeutic moments that were life-altering for them. Many of these moments occurred even though their therapists weren't sure what to do.

As in any collection of short stories, different readers will find that certain tales resonate with them more than others. You may even find some stories rekindling memories of your life-changing clinical experiences and have an uncontrollable impulse to tell your tale to a colleague!"

Cheryl L. Storm
Professor and Chair,
Department of Marriage
and Family Therapy,
Pacific Lutheran University,
Tacoma, WA

"**I**t is rare that one can say that a book about therapy is charming, but this one is. And while you are being charmed, you may learn a great deal."

Bill O'Hanlon
Co-Author, *In Search of Solutions: A Brief Guide to Brief Therapy*

The Haworth Press, Inc.

Tales from Family Therapy
Life-Changing Clinical Experiences

HAWORTH Marriage and the Family
Terry S. Trepper, PhD
Senior Editor

Tales from Family Therapy

Life-Changing Clinical Experiences

Frank N. Thomas, PhD
Thorana S. Nelson, PhD
Editors

The Haworth Press
New York • London

The Haworth Press, Inc., 10 Alice Street, Binghamton, NY 13904-1580

Cover design by Monica L. Seifert.

Library of Congress Cataloging-in-Publication Data

Tales from family therapy : life-changing clinical experiences / Frank N. Thomas, Thorana S. Nelson, editors.
    p. cm.
Includes bibliographical references and index.
ISBN 0-7890-0450-X (alk. paper).
1. Family psychotherapy—Case studies. I. Thomas, Frank N. II. Nelson, Thorana Straver.
[DNLM:1. Family Therapy—case studies. 2. Life Change Events—case studies. WM 430.5.F2 T143 1998]
RC488.5.T343 1998
616.89'156—dc21
DNLM/DLC
for Library of Congress
                                                    97-28202
                                                       CIP

CONTENTS

ABOUT THE EDITORS

Frank N. Thomas, PhD, is Associate Professor and Clinical Graduate Faculty in the Family Therapy Program in the Department of Family Sciences at Texas Woman's University in Denton, Texas. Also an Adjunct Faculty member at Texas Christian University's Brite Divinity School, he teaches masters and doctoral students and supervises a wide range of mental health professionals, including family therapists, psychiatrists, psychologists, social workers, counselors, and ministers. For ten years, he directed the annual Conference for the Texas Division of the American Association for Marriage and Family Therapy (AAMFT), which over 1,000 mental health professionals attend every year. The co-author of *Strength Upon Strength: Brief Competency-Based Approaches,* Dr. Thomas has published and presented recently in the areas of client perspectives of therapy, solution-oriented therapy and supervision, and cultural sensitivity in training therapists. He also writes and presents on contextually sensitive approaches in the areas of brief therapy, eating disorders, ethnography and therapy, storytelling, multicultural supervision, social constructionist theory and practice, family wellness, and training for frontline practitioners. Dr. Thomas is a licensed marriage and family therapist and is Secretary to the Board of AAMFT.

Thorana S. Nelson, PhD, is Director of the Marriage and Family Therapy Program in the Department of Family and Human Development at Utah State University in Logan. She has taught in accredited marriage and family therapy programs since 1986. The co-editor of *101 Interventions in Family Therapy* (The Haworth Press, 1993), her scholarly interests include training in marriage and family therapy; gender, class, and culture; and family therapy stories and interventions.

CONTRIBUTORS

Tom Andersen, MD, is Professor, University of Tromso, Tromso, Norway.

Steven L. Barnett, MD, is Clinical Senior Instructor, University of Rochester Department of Family Medicine, Rochester, New York.

Jerome Bercik, MSW, is Adjunct Professor, Purdue University Calumet, Hammond, Indiana.

Adrian Blow, MMFT, is a doctoral student in the Family Therapy Program, Purdue University, West Lafayette, Indiana.

Rudy Buckman, EdD, is a family therapist with the Salesmanship Club Youth and Family Centers, Dallas, Texas.

Brian Cade, BA, CSW, is a brief and family therapist in private practice, Sydney, New South Wales, Australia.

A. Elaine Crnkovic, MS, is a family therapist with the Mesilla Valley Hospital, Las Cruces, New Mexico.

Robert L. DelCampo, PhD, is Professor, New Mexico State University, Las Cruces, New Mexico.

Shannon B. Dermer, MS, is a doctoral student in Marriage and Family Therapy, Kansas State University, Manhattan, Kansas.

David C. Dollahite, PhD, is Assistant Professor, Brigham Young University, Provo, Utah.

Michael Durrant is Director, Eastwood Family Therapy Centre, Epping, New South Wales, Australia.

Douglas G. Flemons, PhD, is Associate Professor, Nova Southeastern University, Fort Lauderdale, Florida.

Lisa Aronson Fontes, PhD, is Visiting Scholar, University of Massachusetts, Amherst, Massachusetts.

Justyna Ford, MS, is a doctoral student at Nova Southeastern University, Fort Lauderdale, Florida.

J. Scott Fraser, PhD, is Associate Professor, School of Professional Psychology, Wright State University, Dayton, Ohio.

Donald K. Granvold, PhD, is Professor, University of Texas at Arlington, Arlington, Texas.

Shelley Green, PhD, is Associate Professor, Nova Southeastern University, Fort Lauderdale, Florida.

Jürgen Hargens, Dipl-Psych, is with project: system, Meyn, Germany.

Bruce P. Kuehl, PhD, is Associate Professor, University of Wisconsin-Stout, Mennomenie, Wisconsin.

Susan B. Levin, PhD, is Executive Director, Houston Galveston Institute, Houston, Texas.

Laurie B. Levine, PhD, is a marriage and family therapist in private practice, Atlanta, Georgia.

Grace Luther, PhD, is a retired Professor, St. Mary's University, San Antonio, Texas.

Geddes Macallan, JD, is an attorney in Fort Worth, Texas.

Linda Metcalf, PhD, is Adjunct Professor, Texas Christian University, Fort Worth, Texas.

Scott D. Miller, PhD, is Director, Brief Therapy Training Consortium, Chicago, Illinois.

Leslye King Mize, PhD, is Assistant Professor, University of Houston/Clear Lake, Houston, Texas.

James Morris, PhD, is a family therapist in independent practice, Mason, Texas.

Thorana S. Nelson, PhD, is Director of the Marriage and Family Therapy Program, Utah State University, Logan, Utah.

Victor Nelson, STM, is Director, Evergreen Family Therapy Center, Logan, Utah.

Raeline M. Nobles, MS, is an adjunct faculty member, Our Lady of the Lake University, San Antonio, Texas.

Janet L. Osborn, PhD, is Assistant Professor, The Family Institute at Northwestern University, Chicago, Illinois.

Phoebe Snover Prosky, MSW, is Director, A Center for the Awareness of Pattern, Freeport, Maine.

Silvia Echevarria Rafuls, PhD, is Assistant Professor, University of Florida, Gainesville, Florida.

Jamie Raser, LMSW-ACP, is a faculty member, Houston Galveston Institute, Houston, Texas.

Kathleen M. Rhodes, MS, is a marriage and family therapy intern, Nova Southeastern University, Fort Lauderdale, Florida.

Marjorie Roberts, PhD, is a psychologist in private practice, Salem, Massachusetts.

Lucille Marmolejo Romeo, PsyD, is a psychologist and a marriage and family therapist in independent practice, El Paso, Texas.

Joellyn L. Ross, PhD, is a Clinical Associate, Penn Council for Relationships, Philadelphia, Pennsylvania.

Mallika Ruth Samuel, MS, is a human resource development consultant in Bangalore, India.

Monica Scamardo, MS, is an intern therapist, Our Lady of the Lake University, San Antonio, Texas.

Kent Slayton, MA, is a psychotherapist in private practice, San Antonio, Texas.

Debra W. Smith, MSW, is Program Coordinator, Rutgers University School of Social Work, Continuing Education Program, New Brunswick, New Jersey.

Catherine E. Ford Sori, MS, is a doctoral student in Marriage and Family Therapy, Purdue University, West Lafayette, Indiana.

Jenny Speice, PhD, is Fellow, Primary Care Institute of Highland Hospital, Rochester, New York.

Sally A. St. George, PhD, is Associate Professor, Lindsey Wilson College, Columbia, Kentucky.

Howard W. Stone, PhD, is Professor, Brite Divinity School, Texas Christian University, Fort Worth, Texas.

Frank N. Thomas, PhD, is Associate Professor and Clinical Graduate Faculty, Family Therapy Program, Texas Woman's University, Denton, Texas. He is also Adjunct Faculty, Brite Divinity School, Texas Christian University, Fort Worth, Texas.

Tina M. Timm, MSW, is a doctoral student, Marriage and Family Therapy Program, Purdue University, West Lafayette, Indiana.

Tracy Todd, PhD, LMFT, is President of the Brief Therapy Institute of Denver, Inc., Westminster, Colorado.

Karl Tomm, MD, is Director, Family Therapy Program, University of Calgary Medical School, Calgary, Alberta, Canada.

Edward J. Weiner, MD, is a physician in private practice, Fairview Hospital, Great Barrington, Massachusetts.

Joseph L. Wetchler, PhD, is Director, Marriage and Family Therapy Program, Purdue University Calumet, Hammond, Indiana.

Jonathan Wilks, MSW, is a clinical supervisor at Youth Shelters and Family Services, Santa Fe, New Mexico.

Carol Williams, MS, is a crisis counselor, Our Lady of the Lake University, San Antonio, Texas.

Kristin A. Wright, MA, is a doctoral candidate, Nova Southeastern University, Fort Lauderdale, Florida.

Daniel Wulff, PhD, is Assistant Professor, Kent School of Social Work, University of Louisville, Louisville, Kentucky.

Series Editor's Comments

When therapists go to conferences, their favorite activity—well, maybe their *second* favorite activity—is to discuss among themselves their experiences "in the trenches." I am not speaking necessarily of clinical interventions, although they do of course chat about those as well. They talk about those weird, wild, life-changing experiences that make doing therapy the most wonderful and enlightening, if not frightening, job there is.

Frank Thomas and Thorana Nelson's *Tales from Family Therapy* is not only a chronicle of those rich experiences that surround therapy, but is also a tribute to our wonderful chosen career. The book's contributors, all of whom are practicing clinicians, share the joys, the miseries, the embarrassments, and the breakthroughs of doing therapy. You can certainly tell that these people love their work and love the families they treat.

Drs. Thomas and Nelson should be proud of compiling this book. It was a difficult task because they never were completely sure how it would turn out. They conceived the idea of a book of shared experiences among clinicians, but beyond that, the actual format was not known until the manuscripts started coming in. Once they did, however, we all knew that this would be a totally unique collection—a book that really had not been done before.

Tales from Family Therapy is one of those books that will truly be of interest to a broad range of readers. It will be a delight for professionals, who will immediately identify with the stories, as well as glean ideas for expanding their own clinical horizons. It will be of great interest to clinical students, who may come to realize how complex yet fulfilling being a therapist is. This book will also be of interest to the general public, who will get an unparalleled "peek behind the scenes" of what being a family therapist is *really* like.

This is a wonderful book. I literally could not put it down. I feel proud to be a therapist, and proud to have been associated with this groundbreaking book. No therapist will be able to resist the stories, and no therapist will go unchanged after having read them.

Terry S. Trepper, PhD
Executive Editor
Haworth Marriage and the Family

Foreword

"Everybody has at least one!"

—*Michael Durrant*

We all have at least one story we can share about a clinical situation that triggered an unexpected emotion or learning experience. Some of these emotions include sadness, excitement, feelings of accomplishment, despair, humor, or even regret. Often, we bury these stories away, possibly forgetting them. Maybe, on some occasion, we will share them with some close and trusted colleagues. Frightened, insecure, or possibly too embarrassed to say to others, "I did a great job helping those clients," we operate in a world where successes are minimized, and failures are recognized.

Recalling and telling success stories is not what clinicians do. We attend "clinical staffings" to describe those clinical situations that were unsuccessful or had a bad occurrence. While such a context is needed, therapists, like other humans, need to have an opportunity to discuss successes and the challenges they overcame.

The authors in this compilation respectfully share the tales of their encounters. Each clinician humbly, and appropriately, gives credit to the clients for the change that occurred. However, to co-create a relationship for change, the clinician's role must also be considered. These authors describe what they had to do to create this change.

Storytelling has always been a form of education and identification. This collection of tales, written by some exceptional storytellers, will stimulate the interests of all readers. Depending upon your need, these authors share ideas, techniques, interventions, and personal emotions for us to ponder. Maybe you will take away from the story a great idea for an intervention or a new strategy. Possibly, you will reaffirm a value or belief about the inherent strengths that our clients possess, and can use if we allow them to do so. Stories also allow us to identify with the storyteller. While reading these stories, there will be times when you may reflect upon some of your own experiences, and shed a tear, deeply feel for the predicament the client and therapist are experiencing, or even smile and chuckle over a situation that you can find humor in because of its similarity to your own experience. Since we tend to work in isolation, it is refreshing to learn that we share similar struggles and experiences and, at the same time, can learn some useful methods to deal with clinical situations.

Without a doubt, you can learn some "how to's" and gain insight in creating interventions and strategies. This book contains a plethora of tactics to engage and create change when working with a wide array of clients. This information will benefit the reader greatly, and satisfy many clinicians' perpetual question: "What do you do with. . . . ?"

The strategies range from beautiful simplicity to head-scratching complexity. These strategies will stimulate all clinicians to think about how to approach the varying clinical situations. Additionally, this book becomes an resource to identify possible methods of working with families. Refreshing to the reader is the diversity of approaches and considerations made by the authors. This work does not represent a model or style of therapy, but rather unique caveats of client-therapist constructed realities.

Merely focusing on the craft of these skilled clinicians, however, would be erroneous. It would be very easy to loose the essence of these stories by focusing one's attention on their creativity. The constructed *relationships* highlighted here are also an important focal point. Each story masterfully accents the nuances and approaches used to create a cooperative and empowering client-therapist relationship. The authors reclaim the notion that the relationship we co-create with our clients and how we behave in that relationship is the important variable in therapy, not the model or technique we choose to use.

Remindful that therapy is not simply a "how-to" craft in which we follow the script of a fashionable style of therapy, these authors stress how our own definition of "self in therapy" constructs a therapy style that signifies humanity and respect. The relationships discussed here are encouraging. These authors have defined for themselves the types of relationships they want to create with their clients. This creation reflects the value and intrapersonal ethic of each clinician.

Reflected, yes, are the strategies. However, the more I read, the more I realized the strategies paled in comparison to the values shared by these storytellers. The authors have moved beyond simply writing about what it is they do and the interventions they use. The recitals humanize the clinician, reflecting how each clinician's values and intrapersonal ethic impacts the therapy process. These stories bare the author's soul. Each tale reflects a value, turmoil, sadness, exultation, or achievement experienced within the client-therapist relationship. Some narratives will remind us to rely on our own inner strengths as therapists when dealing with those challenging clients, while others will simply put in perspective the struggles of a contemporary therapist. Many authors I know—all I have grown to respect. The vulnerability that is represented gives faith that in an era of practicing what is vogue without demonstration of effectiveness, there are clinicians attempting to remain true to their clinical values, beliefs, and methods.

Tracy Todd, PhD, LmFT
President, Brief Therapy Institute of Denver, Inc.

Preface

What is it that keeps us doing our work as therapists? Sheldon Kopp, the guru of anti-gurus, states that he will quit doing therapy when it ceases to be fun for him (or when he ceases to learn, or something—I will look it up). For most (if not all) of us, therapy is not always fun or rewarding. However, it often *is* fun and rewarding and we do not always talk about that.

Recall those times when a client family left your office, and you smiled to yourself or even gave yourself a mental high-five? When therapy seemed to get unstuck, or the clients came up with a wonderful twist to their homework that made the difference? Or when, with tears in your eyes, you sat with someone who was accepting something difficult with sadness and healing?

Recall the amusing times: when the "perfect" metaphor came to mind and fell with the thud of a water balloon. When a child innocently made the covert overt, and the parents squirmed just a wee bit. When a couple *really* began to communicate and you thought maybe you should leave the room.

Recall the embarrassing times: when you forgot your clients' names, yawned, belched, passed gas, or even, horror of horrors, nodded off. Whitaker could recover from such gaffs, most of us turn red.

Recall the angry times: when clients *refused* to cooperate and improve the way you knew they could. When you did not feel like doing therapy, but did. When family members or other professionals seemed to insist on making things worse. When you had to admit to yourself that, sometimes, you really did not know what you were doing.

This book is about those times. Frank T. and I ('Rana—Frank added the apostrophe) wanted to work on a project together, and we wanted it to be fun. Each of us, at separate times, had thought about a collection of therapists' stories—amusing, embarrassing, angry, meaningful stories. Stories from therapy that helped us remember why we do what we do and for whom we do it. Stories that would help us know why others stay in this crazy, wonderful business, that would make us laugh, ponder, or simply gather the courage to go on.

We had a lot of fun setting the project up for gathering and publishing the stories. We had no idea what was in front of us: not the soliciting, cajoling, and editing—we already knew about that—but the wonderful things that would come from the therapists'—and, sometimes, the clients'—pens and keyboards. People have emphatically shared their joys, triumphs, laughs, and hearts with us—and with you. The stories speak to us. Read them, savor them, learn from them, laugh with them, sit in awe of them, and, most of all, enjoy them. We certainly have!

Thanks must be given to our authors, colleagues, and friends, for their courage in writing for us and to you. Thanks also to Terry Trepper and The Haworth Press for giving us all the opportunity to appreciate these stories. I want to thank Frank for taking me on this journey with him. He has done most of the work and should get most of the credit. I also want to thank Vic for having more faith in me than I have in myself, and to Taylor for smiling at me *all* the time.

Acknowledgments

Thorana and I cannot begin to thank every person who contributed to this project. First, we must express our thanks to the authors. Every writer cooperated beyond our wildest expectations, and we are grateful for their efforts. Very few of us realized how different the writing for this book would be, mostly because we had to move from an academic form of writing to a more accessible style. Some struggled . . . some gave up . . . and we are indebted to those who stuck with us.

We wish to thank Terry Trepper, the editor of this book program, for his optimism and encouragement. He has been our cheerleader, fan, and drum major, and we appreciate his never-ending confidence.

A special note of gratitude goes out to Susan Trzeciak Gibson, Peg Marr, Devon Murphy, and the staff of The Haworth Press for their patience and exceptional editing.

Also, we are grateful for the support of our spouses, Lori and Victor. They knew this project needed our care and feeding for many months, and their generosity and patience moved this book from an idle comment to a reality . . . thank you, thank you, thank you.

Let me be Frank:

This book would never have been written without the encouragement of Tom Chancellor, Patrick O'Malley, Steve Brachlow, Nancy Kingsbury, Sara Wright, Howard Stone, Leslye Mize, Kristi Brown, Bill Lawrence, Brian Cade, Lori Carraway, Jack Cockburn, Tracy Todd, Bruce Burkland, Karen Forbis, Ed Weiner, and Lillian Chenoweth. Some know why . . . others can only guess.

To the great storytellers I have known personally—Heinz von Foerster, Richard "A Living Eccentric" Gunnarson, Ralph Powell, the late Carl Whitaker, Valborg "Mrs. B" Biery, Jim Groves, Tom Milholland, b.f. maiz, Bill Anderson, George Pulliam, Ben Furman,

Joe Strano, Jeff Myers, Rob Becker, Deb Corley, Charlie Fishman, Bill O'Hanlon, Dennis Liesch, Glenn Loy, Judy Swint, Neil Newfield, Thom Schultz, Sensei Bill Sosa, Tommy Smith, Scott Hensley, Tom Andersen, and Dennis Thum—you fueled the fire that burns in the belly.

To Brad Keeney, who helps me create future stories: Our laugh-per-minute ratio is higher than in any other relationship I have. Apart, we are creative; together, we are . . . too weird. Thanks for the ever-improvisational moments and your hard-to-understand faith in me.

To Michael Durrant, whose rapier wit and phenomenal storytelling has kept me in stitches for years. Ten thousand miles' distance has not kept us from the phone conversations, rapid fax and e-mail exchanges, and occasional leisurely talks in North America that have kept me somewhat sane.

Also, to all my clients, students, and the therapists I have supervised through the years: I am a composite of our work together. Thank you for enlightening me and creating the desire I have to learn.

Of course, "'Rana" moved our rough idea to a reality with her knowledge of publishing, people, and politics. I could not ask for a more cooperative partner in crime.

To my mom, who allowed me to grow up without hyperactivity-counteracting medication, preserving my bizarre sense of humor and irrepressible curiosity: thanks for giving me plenty of rope.

I am also grateful for my daughter, Allison, who lets my strangeness go by with only a roll of the eyes.

And finally, I salute my dad. He died too soon to spin them all, but he left me a boatload of stories that seem to come up every day.

THERAPY WITH FAMILIES

Courting the Unknown in a Cross-Cultural Context

Jonathan Wilks

Convincing thunder galloped overhead and I looked out my window expecting to see a herd of horses disappear in the sky over the mountains. The summer rains were late and so were my clients. I imagined the storm, clouds as gray as horse's hooves, passing over their pueblo down south, the brown adobe walls darkening in the rain and the roads playing hide-and-go-seek as they passed through the flooding arroyos. I wished I were home with my wife and baby, and the last line from a Randall Jarrell poem repeated in my mind as it had all summer: "All that I've never thought of—think of me!" I was nervous about meeting the Tafoyas, a Pueblo Indian family.

They arrived thirty minutes late. Devin was hard to see in his baggy clothes and baseball cap; his small waist kept his sagging jeans up, daring gravity the way only a fifteen-year-old can. Devin's father, Martin, was a handsome man. Maybe he was forty; his work boots were broken in and he had a thick mustache that descended on either side of his mouth, meeting across his chin. I'd often wished I could grow a goatee like that. Devin had been ordered to therapy by his Juvenile Probation Officer when he told her he wanted to kill himself. He was put on probation when he was caught with his father's loaded .45 automatic on campus—evidently he had been threatened by some gang members the day before. He settled into my office and looking out the window, spoke about their drive up in the rain.

"We made pretty good time, huh," Martin said to Devin as he pointed to the window with his chin.

"Yeah," replied Devin.

"I'm glad you could make it . . . roads OK?" I inquired.

"I don't know; we slept all the way," Martin said, laughing. Devin joined him, rubbing his eyes. We talked like this for a while. Throughout our ten months of work together, Martin and Devin often showed up late or without an appointment. The amazing thing was that almost without exception, I was free whenever they appeared. Donna, the receptionist at the agency, would lean in my office doorway and say, "Martin and Devin are here and your three o'clock just canceled." I'd look at my clock—2:55.

Even now, I'm not sure whose story I'm telling. Much of what I know about Devin, such as how he came to no longer hear voices in the shower and why his depression departed like a weather front, I've imagined myself—so it could very well be my story. And if this *is* the therapist's story, then it's about how I came to learn that while I can lay claim to the knowable details of a family's life, the mystery of change belongs only to the family itself.

Devin had a small garden in which he grew gourds for making ceremonial rattles. I found out about it because Martin admired a rattle that hung on my office wall, which I had received as a wedding gift.

"He started growing them about two years ago when I stopped drinking and came back," Martin said.

"No," responded Devin. "I thought about growing them the year before, when Mom left."

Martin reconsidered. "That'd make it three years then, huh?"

During our first five meetings, Martin did most of the talking, and I was often spellbound by his speaking. He was eloquent and loved his son deeply. He would tell Devin that gangs and drinking were "white people's ways." During one of his talks, he put forth the notion that Devin could choose to do what he wanted, but that he would be buried on the reservation and "you should live where you will die." Devin listened in silence, but I felt compelled to question Martin here. "If your son had his way, he might be dead already. He wanted to kill himself awhile back. How come?" Martin became silent and looked down. He said that he'd once wanted to kill himself when "the bad feelings were all that I had left in me."

"Have you asked Devin if the bad feelings are with him?"

"No, not really," Martin responded, turning to Devin.

A lengthy conversation in Tewa ensued between father and son. I did not interrupt. Nor did I ask, when it ended, what had been said. Though I was curious, I had to believe that if they wanted me to know, they would tell me. While they talked, I recalled my trips to the reservations with my father when I was young.

My father, a tribal attorney, often took me with him when he traveled to Northern Arizona for tribal council meetings. Once, some white developers came with graphs and charts and made a presentation to the council. The developers, a man and a pretty woman who said she was half Sioux, told the council that they needed approval for the project that day in an attempt to force the council's hand. The council members, who had been dead quiet during the presentation, began to talk in the Hualapi language with each other. They spoke for about twenty minutes before the developers sat down. After another twenty minutes, the head of the council turned to the developers, who stood up, and said, "After much talk, the council has decided to hold a rodeo in April." The developers left looking confused, and the council took a lunch break that was accompanied by a great deal of laughter.

And so, sitting with Martin and Devin, I decided not to demand that they put an end to my curiosity—I simply had to believe that they knew what needed to be said. After a while, Martin turned the conversation back to English and spoke to Devin, "Tell Jonathan about the voices."

"I hear them mostly in the shower and I thought they were my aunts or cousins, but they were still asleep. It scared me, you know."

"I didn't know it was that bad." Martin shook his head and looked out the window. "He feels so bad that he wants to kill himself sometimes."

"What do you think is causing them?" I asked.

"He's sad about his mother . . . and so . . . well, I think I know who is doing it," Martin said and turned to his son.

"Devin, do you know what your Dad is talking about?" I asked.

Devin nodded yes, and suddenly I felt unsure of myself. I didn't know what to ask next. I asked Martin if he could keep Devin from hurting himself. Martin agreed to lock up the rifles until Devin felt better or they went hunting.

"Look, Martin," I said, "do you know how to help your son with this?"

"Yeah. I know who can help him. His grandfather is in a society. He knows lots of our ways. He's real powerful. You know, the clown dancers."

"Koshari?" I asked.

"Hey," Devin said, "how'd you know that?" and he almost laughed aloud. I had no idea where I learned the Pueblo name for the black-and-white-striped dancers. Perhaps I picked it up as a child during my travels with my family through the pueblos or from my wife, who teaches at the Institute of American Indian Arts. "So Martin," I continued, "you know who to ask to take care of these voices and bad feelings . . . will you do it?" Martin nodded and Devin said that he and his grandfather were close, that he had kept his grandfather's name instead of his own parents'. The father and son left my office that day to consult Devin's maternal grandfather.

I remember that sometime during that hour-and-a-half session, Martin said he liked coming to my office because I "wasn't too curious." But I was very curious. I could only imagine the rest of the story. Devin's gourd field was on his grandfather's land; his grandfather was a dancer. I imagined ceremonial rattles and songs, pollen being thrown in a dark field near the grandfather's house. I thought that Devin might need to be put on medication for the voices, and I worried that my failure to get a no self-harm contract from him could be viewed as negligence. I felt profoundly confused by my role during the session; was I being deceitful by not asking the questions that stuck in my throat? Was I negligent in not suggesting a psychiatric evaluation? Martin and Devin reminded me of how little I know sometimes. The Tafoyas and I live in the same region, and yet we occupy worlds that can only be reconciled by the unknown. Almost everything we know about each other can only be spoken about in the language of difference, but these details lie to us if we give them dominion over our relationships. However, the unknown, just like faith, is redemptive; it allows us to participate in each other's lives with the trust and respect that obviates the particular differences manifested by the known world. When the Tafoyas departed, I felt bereft of words, as if my voice had been swallowed by darkness.

I drove home that night and the dark outside matched the darkness inside me. As I drove, I remembered the summer before, waking up at four in the morning to the sound of a gunshot outside my window. I bolted out of bed and went for my gun and the phone to call 911. Half way to the phone, I realized that my wife, child, and dog had not stirred. The neighborhood was quiet. No one else had heard the shot. I could not go back to sleep and later that morning, feeling slightly melancholy, I called my father in Phoenix. He told me that Karen, his associate, had shot herself with her brother's service revolver that morning. In fact, Karen had been helping me for the past year with my search for my birth mother. Driving home with this memory, I felt strangely comforted. The world speaks in ways I don't always understand: just like the Tewa that Martin and Devin spoke that afternoon in my office; I didn't understand, but they did and that would have to be enough.

A week later, Martin and Devin showed up unannounced. We met for a while, and Devin said he felt better—no more voices. His father had taken him to his grandfather and they had had "a long ceremony." I fought back the urge to ask just how long. Three months later, Devin still reported no voices or bad feelings. I worked with Martin and Devin until the probation period ended. Sometimes weeks would pass without my hearing from them and then they would arrive either a day late or an hour early and we would talk about their latest hunting trip, about Devin's new school, about family, or about Ford F-150 trucks. Over time, our conversations created a context of trust and forgiveness. Returning fathers need their son's forgiveness, and Devin came to trust his father. They missed their last session, but it was raining pretty hard that day.

I haven't seen the Tafoyas in a few years now, and have come to realize that I remain attached to them not by what I know, but by all I do not know. I often imagine their lives, allowing my past and theirs to mingle in my mind; then I imagine Devin now, standing in his gourd field or cruising in a low-rider, being held not by me or his father, not by the rain or the leather seat of his car as it slows down at a traffic light, but by all that I've never thought of—Devin, think of me.

A Game of Snakes-and-Ladders

Brian Cade

One of the metaphors that I perhaps use the most in my work and that many clients have found to be particularly helpful in anticipating the future as they struggle to deal with the difficulties in their lives is one that was provided, at least in embryo form, by an eight-year-old girl. Melinda had been severely neglected and sexually abused as a small child and, although now adopted and living in a secure environment, she was still struggling with the aftermath of both the abuse and of the various moves between different relatives and a succession of foster homes that had predated the final move to her current family. She had been placed with the present couple about two years earlier.

Her adoptive parents had told Melinda that she was coming to see me so that I could help her to like herself more. They called me "the happy doctor." She was continually picking at spots and scabs on her face and on her stomach, such that they often looked most unsightly and sometimes became infected. She frequently masturbated until she became extremely sore and it became too painful to continue. She also had genital warts. She continually told lies both at home and at school. Although her relationship with her adoptive father was usually steady and affectionate, with her new mother she was, in her own words, like the girl from the children's rhyme with the curl in the middle of her forehead: When she was good she was very very good, but when she was bad she was horrid.

Much of our communication was through the medium of a whiteboard. I invited her to draw a picture of herself that showed the way she felt about herself now and then a picture of how she would look when she really liked herself. She drew first an ugly, distorted figure in brown and black, covered with spots and with a decidedly miserable-looking mouth. The second picture was of a much prettier girl with brightly colored clothes and a big smile. She drew some flowers around the feet and a sun in the sky.

As I struggled to find a way of expressing a scale that would be meaningful for her to help her envisage and measure her progress from being the girl in the first drawing to the girl in the second, Melinda came up with a wonderful insight which also provided us with an evocative scale. She said that getting better was a bit like being in a game of snakes-and-ladders. As you moved forward, you sometimes went up a ladder and felt that you were beginning to get there. Then, every now and then, you would slip down a snake. Some days you would feel that you had gone up one of the big ladders and things were really good. "Then you slide down that bloody big snake and feel you've gone right back to the beginning again." She put a hand over her mouth realizing she had cussed. I told her that it was alright, that I used to be a truck driver and was not easily shocked. She went on to say, "But you mustn't let yourself get too upset because, if you keep on going and don't let sliding down the snakes upset you too much, everyone gets to the finish in the end."

From that time on, each session I would draw a snakes-and-ladders board and Melinda would indicate what her position was on the board that represented how good she felt about herself on that particular day. She agreed with me that the difference between snakes-and-ladders and real life was that, in real life, you could often make your own mind up about how you wanted to act and react, although sometimes it was difficult not to "slide on down that snake." I suggested, both at school and at home, that she keep a watch out for any time that she could easily have slipped down a snake but didn't and did something else instead.

The sessions with this young girl were often very moving. There were times she was keen to tell me how things were going, and times when she didn't want to talk about anything personal. I would always respect her wishes. She was never prepared to talk about the masturbation, but was always prepared to indicate where she was on the board with "the thing that we don't talk about." Over a period of about a year (the gap between sessions widening as time passed), she moved on steadily up the board.

Melinda is now twelve years old. I have seen her again recently to help her and her adoptive parents negotiate the somewhat tricky process of her (and them) meeting up with her natural mother who, at the time I am writing this, is still in prison at the end of a long sentence for drug-related offenses. Melinda could not remember much about us drawing the snakes-and-ladders board and, anyway, is now old enough to understand the idea of a regular scale using zero to ten. I certainly remember it though, and I have used it regularly both with children and adults, all of whom find that it certainly fits with their experience of the ups and downs in their lives. Many of them find it a useful metaphor to help them deal with the realities of the unevenness of the process of change. As I did with Melinda, I often make the suggestion that they keep a watch out for any time that they could easily have slipped down a snake, but didn't and did something else instead.

From Not Knowing, to Knowing, to Not Knowing, to Shared Knowing

Marjorie Roberts

In recent years, I have described the focus of my clinical work as collaborative. My approach includes an emphasis on conversation and shared expertise with my clients. Within this perspective, my role is often that of an inquirer, while the role of my clients is often one of informer.

Several years ago, I was involved in therapeutic meetings with a family of adult sons and their mother. The meetings were initiated by the oldest son, who was planning to marry a woman who was an outsider to his religious tradition of Judaism. This possibility was viewed by the other family members as similar to a death in terms of the loss of their religious and cultural traditions to the next generation. The mother in this family was angry and vocal in terms of her efforts to prevent this marriage from happening.

In the course of our meetings, I learned that the members of this family had little opportunity to unite in their grief concerning the death of the husband and father sixteen years earlier. The dying father had asked his wife not to tell his young sons of his impending death. By accident, the oldest son learned of his father's impending death from relatives, but was instructed not to tell anyone and to keep his knowledge a secret. During our meetings, the oldest son said that the secrets surrounding his father's death and the unspeakableness of them made him uncomfortable and separated him from his family and friends. He felt like an outsider in his family and with his friends, all of whom had living fathers. He did not find a comfortable niche until he left home and went away to college. His family stated that they viewed his distance from them and preference for his new lifestyle as yet another loss or death.

I became increasingly aware of the unspoken grief related to the past, to include the father's death and loss of a close family connection, and related to the future, as the family anticipated the possible loss of their Jewish tradition. As I inquired, the family explained to me that in their Jewish tradition, it is a mother's role to teach Jewish customs to the children. They feared that if this young man married a non-Jewish woman, their traditions would not be shared with possible children.

As we spoke, I began to recall bits of information that I as a non-Jewish woman had learned from friends, colleagues, and other clients about Jewish mourning customs and traditions. I had already begun to think of our therapy meetings that took place weekly or biweekly as a therapeutic approximation of sitting shivah, a Jewish tradition in which mourners gather together at intervals for seven days following the death of a loved one. I felt comfortable as a witness to their tears and expression of anguish related to the past and fears of anticipated loss. This metaphor of sitting shivah further helped me understand my role of witness and inquirer.

However, in my efforts to learn more about other Jewish traditions that might be useful to this family, I stepped out of my role of inquirer. In retrospect, I remember feeling uncomfortable as an outsider to their tradition. I had listened to the mother and another son speak about their fears that they would lose their tradition from outside non-Jewish influence. Instead of identifying my outsider's "not knowing" position to the family and exploring this dilemma with them, I sought outside consultation with a friend who is of Jewish background and teaches world religion courses. As I write, I am aware that at this point in our work, I missed an opportunity for openness rather than the secrecy that had silenced this family, for the family and I to discuss the outsider-insider dilemma that existed in our work together which was also such a large part of this family's experience.

In my consultation with my friend, I learned about the Jewish practice of saying Kaddish prayers in a synagogue in honor of a deceased person on the anniversary of his or her death. Even at this writing, I question the accuracy of my understanding of this tradition. However, at the time of my consultation, my certainty was greater.

In subsequent meetings, secure in my newfound wisdom, I explored my developing notion of writing a series of their own

Kaddish prayers to honor their father. My idea was that these personal prayers would make their grief and fears speakable within a comfortable tradition. Initially, the family members seemed to ignore or not hear these ideas. When I persisted and clarified my thinking, the family members looked at me curiously. Finally, they explained the prescribed, formalized, and ritualistic nature of the prayer. In retrospect, my proposal was perhaps similar to a suggestion of rewriting the Scripture, but more significantly, revealed the limits of my "knowing position."

At this point, I humbly explained my discomfort and dilemma as an outsider to their religious tradition and identified my own religious tradition as Catholicism. I further shared with them that in my efforts to be helpful to them, I had sought outside consultation to better understand their traditions. They laughed at what a poor learner I had been and enthusiastically responded that they could teach me about both Judaism and Catholicism since the sons had attended a Catholic school as well as a Hebrew school.

When I returned to my position of genuine "not knowing" and to shared inquiry, our work moved forward comfortably. In subsequent work with other clients of Jewish background, I continue to want to learn more about their traditions and am especially curious about the varied meanings of certain Yiddish words. I am always surprised that my interest and questions somehow convey to my clients that "I know" about their traditions. Several clients have asked me if I am of Jewish background. I smile, remember my teachers, and say how much I admire their traditions and always want to learn more.

Interesting Moments in Psychotherapy

Joellyn L. Ross

Moments when a session shifts emotional gears, when you realize you have reached the heart of the matter, are rare and wonderful events. They haunt the heart and human core of the therapist for days with feelings of strong connection and recognition of the small miracles generated by these emotionally significant moments.

After a session such as this, I bask in the generated emotions while at the same time questioning the timing and asking myself, "Could this have happened sooner? What circumstances, relational and psychotherapeutic, are necessary for such moments to occur?"

My connection with the C family always was good, although therapy limped along for a year, with minimal progress and no breakthroughs. I liked them a lot, and they appeared to find our work helpful, but I felt that real change was always elusive.

The Cs brought their youngest child and only daughter, sixteen-year-old Nancy, who was very obese, as well as sullen and seemed somewhat depressed. The parents were very concerned about her weight, as they felt it interfered with her social life and her enjoyment of her high school experience. They also complained about her poor grades, back talk, and generally negative attitude. They said they had tried everything—diet, exercise equipment, encouragement—to get their daughter to lose weight, with no results. They said they had spoken to her repeatedly about her attitude, also with no results.

During the first session, I spoke to the parents, while occasionally making eye contact with Nancy, and told them that since their efforts were not working, they should cease. "If your daughter wants to commit suicide with doughnuts," I said, "it's her choice. You need to let her handle it." As for her attitude, I said I needed to see what would happen once the parents stopped pressuring Nancy about her weight.

The parents responded to my recommendation and they stopped nagging Nancy about her weight, which endeared Nancy to me, but didn't result in any weight loss. Over the course of eight months, we dealt with Nancy's grades, her problems with her friends, her attitude, and, after many, many months, her weight. Mostly, I met with Nancy and her mother, as they seemed to have more difficulty dealing with each other than the father had dealing with either of them. Small changes were made, most significant of which was the mother and Nancy joined a local health club together and started working out several times a week. It seemed to help their relationship, and both lost a few pounds and toned up. One of the best sessions I had with the two of them, although not life changing, was one in which I asked Mrs. C about her own upbringing and life experiences, much of which Nancy heard for the first time. It seemed to help Nancy see her mother as a real person, and also cemented my connection with mother and daughter much better, even though they drove each other crazy a lot of the time.

Mr. C started attending sessions eight months into therapy, as both parents were alarmed with Nancy's increasingly vulgar and provocative back talk. Adding to the family's stress was Mr. C's being at a career crossroads when he was approached for a promotion which would necessitate the family's moving again. Over the course of their thirty-year marriage, the Cs had lived in five different states, and both mother and father were ambivalent about whether he should accept the promotion, if offered. Meanwhile, Nancy's obstreperousness kept escalating as she got closer to her seventeenth birthday and the ability to get a driver's license.

Over the four-month course of meeting with the mother, father, and Nancy, I empathized with the parents' not liking their daughter's disrespectful behavior, while I continuously commented on their unwillingness to assign consequences to Nancy for her behavior. No matter how obnoxious Nancy was, she still got rides and other favors; the parents said that if they refused, they would have to endure more of her tantrums and invective. At one session, about a month before Nancy's birthday, the father did try to set a consequence by telling her that he wouldn't take her for driving practice because she was being so nasty in the session; Nancy walked out of my office in a huff.

Ten days before Nancy's seventeenth birthday, the family came into my office looking terribly dispirited. The Cs had gone away for a weekend and Nancy had taken the car out with a friend (of course, I thought: standard teenage behavior, especially in southern New Jersey). Wisely, they had checked the car's mileage before they left and had caught Nancy. She was grounded until her birthday. I applauded the parents' setting consequences, and questioned why they were taking her misbehavior so personally.

The father said that very morning, he had told Nancy he would not be able to take her for her driver's test the morning of her birthday as they had planned, but would be able to take her when he got home from work on her birthday. He was upset that when he had told her of this change, she had responded with "more of her cursing." "I don't understand you," he said, turning to his daughter, "it's not like I told you I won't take you at all."

"I don't believe you'll take me when you get home," Nancy yelled. "You'll find some excuse . . . I don't trust you!"

Initially, I misinterpreted Nancy's upset to be more of her bratty behavior. I told the parents that if Nancy were my daughter, she would have to not curse at me for at least a month before I would take her for her driving test, etc., etc. However, Nancy's words to her father, "I don't trust you!", stayed in my head. I knew they meant something, that she was saying something significant.

The session continued with Nancy arguing with her father, who repeatedly complained he didn't want to deal with this anymore, saying he wanted Nancy out of the house, and that he hated coming home to all this upset. My brain finally clicked into gear as the mother started to interrupt the battle between the father and daughter. "The fight is with him, not you," I told her. "I know she drives you crazy too, but her real fight is with her father."

The father stopped and looked at me with a quizzical expression.

"I know you are a trustworthy person, but your daughter has said she doesn't trust you," I said to him. "I know she goes about it all backward, but I think she wants something from you . . . maybe your approval?"

The father looked stunned for a moment, then his expression shifted; he looked as if he understood. "I know I'm very critical," he said. "It's hard for me to show affection." Tears ran down Nancy's face as he spoke. "She said she didn't trust you," I said to the father. "She meant something important. You need to find out why she doesn't trust you." "I know," he said, "I know."

Why was I surprised? Moments such as these, when sessions literally shift gears into an emotional hyperspace we rarely experience, still amaze me. Mostly, they occur when I'm in a state of "flow," when I'm not actively cogitating, but am allowing my words to emerge in response to the moment. Later, I tell myself I should have known, should have been able to predict, but regardless of my self-criticism, I remain in awe of and humbled by the process, however bumbling I judge myself to be.

I don't remember exactly how, but the father then started talking about his own upbringing and his tumultuous life in assorted homes. "Does your daughter know all this?" I asked. The mother interrupted, ever protective, saying they didn't talk about these things because they were so painful. I pressed on, saying that it was his history, and that it helped explain who he is and why he values what he does. "Your daughter needs to know these things about you. The two of you need to talk about your history," I said to the father. Nancy was still crying. She needs to know her father, I thought, to connect with him as she was connected with her mother.

This session truly did change the course of therapy. At the next meeting, Nancy bragged about getting her driver's license and, when I asked her about her grades, she pulled out an appointment book and read off the list of grades, all significantly better than they had been for a long time. The parents reported fewer outbursts and less cursing, and said that Nancy was being very responsible with the car. Six months later, the family continues to make improvements. The father and mother went on a long overdue vacation, and left Nancy at home so she would be able to go to her job. There were no problems. Nancy's grades still need improvement, but her overall behavior is acceptable.

Psychoanalytic thinkers might analyze this case as demonstrating the resolution of an Electra problem between father and daughter. Systemic thinkers might describe the case as a realignment of appropriate generational boundaries and reestablishment of the parents' executive functioning. I think, regardless of theoretical persuasion, that a significant emotional experience enabled the family to mobilize its strengths and to function more effectively.

Hysterical or Historical?

Sally A. St. George

> . . . that little space of quiet that always separates a story from
> ordinary events.
>
> —Michael Dorris, *Guests*

Family therapy is a unique blend of intentional and well planned interventions, along with unplanned or unexpected events. The following is a story of family therapy that has this blend of planned help and serendipitous occurrences. It is the sequence of those unanticipated events that serve as the heart of this story.

I was working as an in-home family therapist at the time, and had been working with this particular family for about one month. This family had six members who lived in the home. There was a single mother and five children: three girls aged fifteen, ten, and four years, and two boys aged twelve and three years. Shortly after I arrived at the family's home for a scheduled meeting, the mom and adolescent son erupted into an argument. Actually, it was a discussion that had gone awry. During the day, one of the son's teachers had called the mother to report uncooperative behavior and a backlog of assignments that were not completed. This situation was not new with the family, but we had been working steadily on getting the son to behave in a respectful manner toward his teachers.

With the whole family seated in the living room, the mom (Michelle) and the adolescent son (Terry) began by talking about the phone call. Michelle had been calm and collected and asked for her son's understanding/explanation of the situation by using some of the skills that she and I had devised. To her credit, I observed her asking questions that required her son to clarify his thinking rather than supplying his mother with her own interpretations. She was practicing her new kind of listening, but then Terry's answers seemed to sound like a familiar refrain, not taking any responsibility for his misbehavior and placing the blame for the trouble on the teacher. I chimed in at that time, cuing Michelle with suggested questions *and* cuing Terry with ways he could answer so that his mom could take him seriously and he could be understood accurately. In spite of our best efforts, the discussion was transposed into an argument.

The volume was swelling into a crescendo at the same time that the tone was becoming sharp and the rhythm off the beat. Michelle became more accusing and critical of Terry's immaturity. She said to me that she was "sick of his irresponsibility" and was sure "he was involved with a gang and would end up being shot to death." She began to include issues unrelated to the school phone call, complaining that he had not taken out the garbage or done the dishes for days, but that he still expected privileges to go out with his friends. The family referred to this part of the performance as "talking junk," meaning that they got off-key by introducing past offenses and transgressions into the current discussion, with the effect of never returning to the measures that needed the attention and rehearsal. We were all familiar with this song, so when I saw them warming up to play that arrangement, I turned to Michelle and softly said, "Now, don't go historical on me; we are getting somewhere." That is exactly the time when the music turned into a noisy blast.

Michelle turned to me and declared that "nothing had changed," that "this therapy program was not working at all," and that Terry was just as unruly as he had ever been. She retreated to the bathroom and slammed the door. Terry accused his mother of never believing him and always blaming him for everything, and he fled upstairs to his bedroom. I was left to count rests; we were all feeling offended, misunderstood, and discouraged.

The older daughter/sister had been with us the whole time, and in the quiet interlude, I congratulated her on not being drawn into the argument. Her tendency was to intervene in a way she intended to be helpful, but which would often aggravate rather than relieve the situation. However, this time she let her brother and mom do the work of discussing and resolving. I tried to speak to Michelle through the bathroom door, but I received no response. I tried calling upstairs to Terry, but he did not answer either. It seemed to me that no one was ready to talk. I was also feeling hurt and angry by Michelle's remarks that criticized my ability to help this family. The little kids went back to their playing and the older daughter started cleaning. I asked the older daughter if she would please call me if mom and son resumed their arguing, and I left the home feeling dejected and doubtful.

The next day when I arrived to talk with just the mom, I found the atmosphere rather chilly. Michelle seemed aloof, irritated, and uninterested in talking with me. The intensity of her reaction caught me off guard. I was baffled, and in trying to figure this out, I replayed the conversation from the previous evening. Yes, the argument did represent some backpedaling given our concerted efforts, but both Michelle and Terry had orchestrated some really fine talking and listening too. Perfection was not a goal, arguments were not exactly new behaviors, anger was no stranger, so this was perplexing. Was her mood due to my decision to leave last night? Every vibe in me said something was wrong, so I was persistent in my efforts to have Michelle explain to me what was going on with her.

She said that she had talked with her older daughter last night and perhaps if I could answer a question for her she might feel better, but she was hesitant because it was touchy, and she wasn't sure what to expect. I urged her to say what she needed. We had a solid relationship and straight talks were part of the deal; I assured her I could take it. Her question was, "In the middle of the argument, what did you say to me? I thought you said, 'Don't go hysterical on me,' but my daughter said you said 'historical.' Which was it?"

How clear things were becoming to me! Bells were sounding in my head. I recalled previous talks where I learned how sensitive Michelle was to any intimation that she was less than capable mentally or emotionally. My hypothesis was that this woman was insulted and betrayed by what she though I had said. Mom was relieved when she found out that I did not say "hysterical." We sat down and processed the havoc wreaked by this word. This is the way I understood the mom's explanation of her reaction: first of all, she was angry at me. She had interpreted my calling her hysterical as criticism of her mothering, something that she said she had resented with other workers, but which she had not experienced between us. She said she was comfortable when I would challenge her to think about things differently, but anything that she would interpret as outright criticism was an injury to our growing trust and caring. She was ready to fire me, that is, until her daughter cast some doubt on what mom thought she had heard the night before. I had been on the correct intuitive track.

In further processing, Michelle revealed that she was afraid to tell me how angry she was because if she was wrong or had misheard me, she feared it would damage our relationship and/or that I would get mad and become critical. Actually, this turned out to be a good experience for both of us; we talked about the difficult feelings and reactions associated with misunderstandings, rather than stuffing them or assigning one right truth and one wrong truth. Furthermore, we listened to each others' stories without trying to correct them—exactly what I had been coaching her to do with her children. I felt validated and told her so—and so did she. This whole mess was the perfect experience to illustrate the things that we had been talking about, only our talking had been rather distant and abstract. This much more personal experience came complete with nervousness, fear, sweat, and relief.

Oddly enough, "hysterical" and "historical" became significant words in our vocabulary. We could laugh at the times we would catch ourselves, either becoming hysterical (which we defined as quick to judge, failing to listen, not able to get that repetitious tune out of our heads) or going historical (defined as bringing unhelpful, past, and irrelevant "junk" into the conversation, which promoted hopelessness). The discord in these words dissipated and their usefulness and playfulness became a humorous shorthand for us, a kind of language that led to all the privileges of holding exclusive membership—specialness, humor, investment, closeness, and understanding. I wouldn't take back those two days for anything!

Those two days illustrate two things. First, as I indicated before, the unexpected occurrences in therapy can be most helpful. Second, it illustrated that good therapy comes in stereo. As I now recall this experience with this family, I find that the unexpected in therapy is exciting. Because of its uncertainty and lack of precedence, the family and I are afforded maximum freedom to improvise. This improvisation happens not because one of us assumes the role of conductor, but because we are all players creating newness.

A quick coda: What goes around comes around. Several weeks later, I arrived at this family's home wearing a weary, beleaguered look on my face. They were curious about what was wrong; I briefly told them that I had just emerged from a rather arduous, disagreeable argument with my adolescent son and daughter. Mom's perceptive comment was, "Did you get hysterical with them, or did you go historical?" She was playing our song!

Clients Do the Craziest Things . . . Like Prove Therapists Wrong

Shannon B. Dermer

Almost every therapist starts his or her training with delusions of grandeur. They believe that they can help anyone get through his or her problems. And I, alas, was no exception to the "delusional rule." I believed that armed with only my good intentions, intelligence, and wit, I could convince clients to behave in ways more congruent with their goals. Of course, I hit a few bumpy points in the beginning of my clinical work, but it was not until I met *them* that I felt like I hit a brick wall.

Them consisted of a mother and daughter team with powers greater than any family therapy modality. Faster than an automatic thought, more powerful than a paradoxical intervention, able to leap family centers in a single bound—look up in the sky; it's a bird; it's a plane; it's *them*! I felt as if they had superpowers with which no human therapist could contend, and I certainly did not have any kryptonite to slow them down.

Mom (Christina) and daughter (Jo) walked into my office with matching grimaces and balled up fists as accessories. Each took a chair in a neutral corner and alternated between glaring at each other and glaring at me. I greeted them each with a toothy grin and an outstretched hand. After the introductions, Christina started explaining how Jo was out of control and that something had to be done or she was sending Jo to the nearest foster home. She went on to list a series of transgressions ranging from Jo fighting with her younger brother and sister to breaking curfew, refusing to help around the house, talking back, cursing, and spending hour after hour on the telephone. Christina's story was interrupted by the occasional "She's not fair," "What a liar," "Oh, please," and the odd grunt or sigh from Jo's corner. After Christina's complaints (or maybe during—it is all a blur to me now), Jo listed the atrocities her mother perpetrated against this innocent teenager. Her list included everything from excessive restrictions to her mother trying to ruin her life.

Slightly stunned, but with good intentions still intact, I asked what each wanted for herself and from the other person. To make a long story somewhat shorter, each felt that she deserved what she wanted without having to give an inch to the other person. I began to feel more frustrated as my time to talk became increasingly shorter due to their arguments. We made an appointment for the following week, and I asked them to think about what they wanted and in what areas they were willing to negotiate.

The next session was worse than the first. Jo came in with her fingernails painted black and her bangs dyed black. Christina, needless to say, was not thrilled with her daughter's fashion choices. Christina demanded that I change her daughter and Jo demanded I change her mother. Christina was an overworked single mother who did not have the time or patience to deal with her daughter's "nonsense." Jo was an angry adolescent who felt as though her mother "just didn't understand." I was a therapist in over her head, who did not have a clue how to intervene in the stalemate between mother and daughter.

Predictably, Christina and Jo did not show for their next appointment and decided to discontinue therapy for the time being. I felt relief and pangs of failure at the same time. Part of me wanted them to come back, and part of me thought, "Good riddance!" I thought that was the last I would hear of *them*. However, (as is known to happen from time to time) I was wrong.

Approximately every two months, Christina called in the middle of a crisis. The first time she called because she wanted to know how to put her daughter in a foster home. The second time, Christina had gone back to school and was having an even harder time getting Jo to follow the rules. The third time she called because she and Jo and gotten into a physical fight.

After hearing the details of the fight, I decided that social services had to be called and the incident reported. We decided that I would make the call and let Christina know what social services said about the incident. Because this was the first report, Christina had called for assistance, and the fight had "only" left red marks on Jo's face, social services asked me to pass along the message that they would mark down the details of the fight, but would not do anything if Christina continued counseling. If, on the other hand, Christina refused to go to counseling, I was to call them back and they would pursue the report. Christina was relieved; she agreed to come back to counseling.

At this point, it had been about six months since I last met with Christina and Jo. Now that I had some experience under my belt, I decided to approach things a bit differently. In addition to some experience, I had also learned more about strategic and solution-focused therapy. I decided to combine the two approaches in working with *them*. Despite being a convert of solution-focused therapy, I had my doubts about whether this family could really change.

Christina came in with the familiar grimace and balled up fists, but sans her sparring partner. When they reached the parking lot of my office building, Jo had refused to come into the session, and was willing to walk the several miles home rather than attend. Christina gave up arguing the point with her daughter and let her walk home. I congratulated Christina on not letting her daughter sidetrack her from attending the session. I told her that she should offer to bring her daughter again, but if Jo refused, Christina was not to push the point. However, if Jo asked about what went on in session Christina was to reply, "That's between me and the therapist. If you want to know, you'll have to come in and find out what we're talking about."

As before, Christina listed all her woes, including not doing well in school; having to deal with her own mother; and trying to balance children, a job, and a long-term relationship all at once. I commiserated with the hardships and took every opportunity to move Christina from focusing on the negative to exploring goals and the positive aspects. In order to give the reader an idea of how difficult this task was, I will share a small part of one session:

Therapist: Let's say that Jo was here in session and I asked her what her goals and wants were. What would she say?
Client: She wouldn't say anything. She wouldn't answer.
Therapist: Pretend you are Jo and answer how she would answer.
Client: [Crosses her arms and will not reply.]

Therapist: Okay. What if I held her down and tickled her with a feather until she answered?

Client: She's too stubborn; she still wouldn't say anything.

Therapist: You're absolutely right. She is very strong willed. Okay. Okay. How about if I held her down and injected her with truth serum so she had to answer? She doesn't have any choice but to tell the truth!

Client: Hmm. She would tell you that she wants to stay at the same school, wants me to be nicer to her . . .

As the reader can tell, getting Christina to see her daughter in anything but a negative light was like pulling teeth. She continued to jump from catastrophe to catastrophe during our sessions. One day I said, "Christina, you keep describing all of these bonfires and we keep jumping from fire to fire trying to put them out. We can either jump from bonfire to bonfire and see small bits of success slowly emerge or we can concentrate on one fire for a while and probably see big changes faster. Which do you prefer?" Christina chose to focus on one fire, so we began to prioritize her bonfires.

Of course Christina's relationship with her daughter was like the great Chicago Fire of 1871. The kicker was that Mrs. O'Leary's clumsy cow continuously knocked over the lantern in this family. Fortunately, opportunity knocked at the barn door with an extinguisher. Christina conversed with a valued friend who extracted from various Oprah Winfrey shows (I often find that Oprah has more power in the therapy room than I do) and parent meetings the idea of "warm fuzzies." Everyone, especially children, needed warm fuzzies. A warm fuzzy is anything that makes a person smile or feel good and is not harmful. We spent the rest of the time discussing what kind of warm fuzzies Christina could give Jo.

We decided during our discussions that although it appeared as though Jo did not care about Christina, Jo actually cared very much and would rather her mother yell at her than not pay attention to her at all. Christina resolved to give her daughter more positive attention. The problem was that every time Christina tried to compliment her daughter, the interaction ended up in a fight. We decided that face-to-face warm fuzzies were not going to work at this time, but we thought Jo still needed positive attention. As an alternative,

Christina was to leave her daughter Post-It notes around the house with only positive statements.

In two weeks, Christina came back not only having done the notes, but also had several pleasant conversations with Jo and implemented a chore schedule. During the two weeks, Christina and Jo had several pleasant contacts. Jo had been rummaging through some old papers in the garage and had come across a letter that Christina had written to Jo when Christina was pregnant with her. The letter detailed how much she was looking forward to having a child and that she wanted for her child all the things that she never had. In addition, there were also papers in the same box outlining who the children were to go to if anything ever happened to Christina and what possessions each of the children were to get. Jo was stunned to learn that her mother really did think about her welfare and after discussing the letter, Christina explained to Jo how much she loved her and she would always care about her welfare.

At the next session, Christina reported things were going well. She actually laughed during our meeting. (I thought the woman had lost control of her smile muscles in some horrible accident.) The great thing was that she laughed about her daughter getting in trouble. That weekend, Christina came home to find that Jo shaved her younger sister's hair off. The girl was completely bald! Jo argued that Kelly asked her to do it, so she should not get in trouble.

"I was so angry I could hardly speak," Christina reported, "but I know that Kelly probably did ask her to do it; besides, Kelly sat there and let Jo do it. I also know that Jo should know better than to do such a thing. So I grounded them both from the television for two weeks." Christina laughed and said, "That girl looks so ridiculous with no hair, but it will grow back."

My jaw almost hit the ground and I sat speechless for a while. I followed up my impression of a deer caught in headlights with an onslaught of statements of empathy, compliments, and awe at the composure Christina demonstrated. We spent the rest of the session discussing her handling of the "hairy" incident.

Christina continued to amaze me until the day we terminated our sessions. In that time, the younger children had stopped doing their chores and Jo asked her mother if she could take over their responsibilities in order to earn more money. Excuse me, let me state that again. Jo asked her mother if she could take over the others' chores! In addition, I watched a woman who had repeatedly grounded her children for a year, and then let them off the hook in less than a week, give appropriate consequences for misbehavior and stick to the punishment.

Also, Christina began to like complimenting Jo and giving attention for appropriate behavior. In fact, in our last session, Christina explained to me how she enjoyed praising Jo. Jo stayed over at a friend's house on the previous Friday night and had plans to go shopping on Saturday morning. Knowing that Jo might want some extra money for shopping, Christina drove over to the friend's house with muffins for Jo and her friend, dropped off the allowance money, and then went home. Christina took great pleasure in describing the look of surprise and delight on Jo's face when she dropped off breakfast and the money.

Although I have seen many families since *them*, I will always remember Jo and Christina. They proved to me that I should never underestimate the power of families to change. I fell into the trap of believing that Christina and Jo were not capable of breaking their patterns of interaction. I have rarely been so happy to be proved wrong. Whenever I get frustrated by a case or begin thinking clients will never change, I think about *them*. Instead of envisioning Mrs. O'Leary's cow kicking over a lantern, I picture the cow kicking me in the rear to get me back on track.

Well, I have enjoyed sharing this story and I guess I have milked it (pun intended) for all its worth. I hope the reader takes from this story what I learned. Never underestimate the ability of families to prove you wrong or their ability to change.

The Courtship of Eddie's Grandfather

Daniel Wulff

This is my story about an introductory phase of doing family therapy in a family's home. It highlights the importance of the first client contact and the decisions made by the therapist in the earliest moments of that interaction. Decisions regarding how to start and how to respond to clients in the initial interchanges (when there hasn't been enough time to analyze and think everything through) are crucial and are oftentimes pivotal in working with those clients.

This example also illustrates the importance of the underlying premises or assumptions upon which we base our work as therapists—how we conceptualize a person to be a client, how we understand the process of change in people, and how we envision our roles as therapists. What happens if a client *immediately* rejects our helping efforts? If a client initiates an argument with us, will we enjoin them in this way? Working with clients never follows a smooth and predictable path. Our best guesses as to how clients will respond to our presence and our efforts to help need to be continuously modified during the course of therapy.

Ten years ago, I worked as a therapist for an in-home family therapy agency in a Midwestern city. My agency worked with families who were referred to us by the local social service department to deal with serious issues of neglect and abuse. Parents in these families were on the verge of having their children placed in a foster home or a residential treatment center due to imminent concerns for the safety and well-being of one or more children. The families participated voluntarily in the sense that they had the right to refuse to work with us, but in reality, failure to work with us was typically interpreted by social services and the juvenile court as an unwillingness on the part of the client(s) to make what was considered to be necessary changes. Our agency assigned two therapists to each case, and we had broad professional discretion as to how often we worked with clients, what we chose to address, and the strategies we incorporated. Our central objective was to reduce or eliminate the potential for neglect and/or abuse that was present. If we were unsuccessful, the probable outcome would be placement of the children out of the home.

The case that I will discuss here concerns the serious neglect and potential abuse of a two-year-old boy (Eddie) by his eighteen-year-old mother (Stacey). Stacey was unmarried and had been living with her mother (Ruth) and stepfather (Pete) for one month prior to our introduction to the family. Pete was a sixty-three-year-old self-employed housepainter; Ruth was a fifty-eight-year-old homemaker who worked part-time as a waitress. They lived in a modest house and finances were tight.

A month prior to our involvement, Stacey and her parents decided to live together again, albeit for somewhat different reasons. Pete and Ruth were not only concerned about Stacey's decisions to leave Eddie with very questionable caretakers while she socialized with friends or went to school or work, but also with Stacey's long-standing pattern of using illegal drugs and dating men who were abusive and involved in criminal activities. Their fear for Eddie's safety and well-being, coupled with their concern that social services might take custody of Eddie if his living environment did not improve, led them to see Stacey's move back into their home as a positive step. Ruth was more of a proponent of her daughter moving back than was Pete, but he went along with it out of a deference to his wife's worries and wishes.

Stacey had been struggling financially when she was on her own, and social services was monitoring her parenting closely; she decided that living with her parents would appease social services and keep her child with her, which she very much wanted. Ruth's taking care of Eddie when Stacey needed to be gone would be viewed favorably by the social services department.

When the referral came to my agency, my co-therapist and I made a phone call to the family to arrange for an initial visit. I spoke with Ruth, who was very cordial and arranged a time for us to meet them. Everything at this point seemed normal and fine.

When we arrived at the appointed time, Pete answered the door. I introduced myself and as I extended my hand to shake his, he coldly turned away, leaving my co-therapist and me standing at the door. This felt like a clear snub; both my co-therapist and I were taken aback. We both looked at each other as if to say, "What is going on here?" Given that we had just met this man, we did not have a ready response for this. Ruth had witnessed this and hustled into the picture, trying to smooth over this awkward situation by welcoming us into their home. Pete was already sitting in his easy chair as Ruth escorted us into the living room and invited us to sit down. Ruth told us that Eddie was sleeping and that Stacey was not at home. She said that Stacey knew about our coming today and she (Ruth) was puzzled as to why Stacey was absent.

There was obvious tension in the room among everyone, centering around Pete's clearly unhappy demeanor, but we proceeded as we normally did at any initial meeting. As my co-therapist began explaining our program, I was progressively aware of Pete bristling in his chair. He wasn't saying anything, but he looked as if he was on the brink of exploding. I was unsure of whether to focus on him or to try to ignore this situation. This was all happening so fast and we didn't know what was going on with Pete. In my mind, it seemed reasonable to conclude that he was angry with our presence, but I couldn't exactly figure out why. After a couple of minutes of proceeding as if nothing was wrong, I decided to interrupt my co-therapist in order to directly address Pete's apparently hostile mood. Looking for an appropriate way to approach Pete (hopefully not making matters worse) I asked, "Maybe we have come by at a bad time?" This seemed to me to be nonaccusatory and gave him an opportunity to explain himself. I was hoping that his upset was due to something that was unrelated to our presence. If this were the case, he could clear it up and proceed or we could come back at a better time. He curtly said, "No." Now I was left as clueless as before, but having opened up the concern directly, I decided to continue. I asked "Does your mood have something to do with our being here?" He said very abruptly and loudly that our coming into their home was "a waste of time, a misuse of taxpayer's money," and "you can't help Stacey anyway—only she can do it herself." This opened up the issue and we were then faced with how we should respond. Do we argue these points? Do we ask him to give us a fair chance to prove him wrong? Do we ask his wife her views? Do we walk out?

Without much deliberating and without caucusing with my co-therapist, I responded to Pete by saying that our involvement with their family was *optional*. He seemed surprised by this statement and I reiterated that if he did not want us to work with his family for the reasons he gave, he could simply ask us to leave and we would honor his wish. With little hesitation, he forcefully and rather rudely said, "Well then get out!" Now, when I had told Pete that he could ask us to leave, my hunch was that he would back off his position and engage with us in a discussion of his frustration which would lead to a working relationship. His statement surprised both my co-therapist and myself. I felt somewhat obligated to follow through with what I had said; I needed to stand by my word. Ruth looked shocked. My co-therapist looked shocked as well, but she smoothly followed my lead on this. We wished them well and quietly exited.

Our experience had been that very few families rejected our help, so we were a little shaken by this unanticipated turn of events. We notified the social service worker of the family's decision to not work with us. He too was surprised by this situation, but thanked us for trying anyway.

I thought that this was the end of the story with this family, but three days later, Pete telephoned me to ask why I had not informed him that his refusal of our services would get him into serious trouble with the juvenile court judge. (When we had left Pete's house a few days before, I had given no thoughts to what might transpire with the judge as a result of our not working with this family. Our leaving Pete's house was *not* part of a deliberate strategy in which we conspired with the juvenile judge to orchestrate this family's motivation level. We were not anticipating Pete's call, so we were once again spontaneously feeling our way with this family). I asked Pete to explain what had happened. At a court review hearing a few days after our meeting, the judge (who was unaware of the family's refusal of service or chose to not acknowledge it) asked Pete how the therapy with our agency was going. Pete told the judge that he had refused our services. In response, the judge launched into an angry tirade about how the therapy was essential for Eddie's well-being. Pete was told by the judge in no uncertain terms that he had better reinitiate therapy with us—or else.

Even though Pete called to request therapy, the meeting where he "threw us out" so to speak, was still vivid in my mind and I was not convinced that the judge's stern lecture had substantively reversed Pete's hostile position toward us. As we talked, Pete sounded more conciliatory and cooperative than I would have expected, given all that had happened between us.

He explained that he was unhappy with the judge's coercing of him into therapy, but he also felt that under these circumstances, the only prudent course for him was to cooperate with the judge and work with our agency. I was torn between thinking that Pete was really willing to give working with us a try and thinking that after a while, his motivation would decrease and evaporate, leaving us once again fighting for our legitimacy to work with the family.

It was at this time that I thought that we had real leverage with him and we could be quite challenging and provocative with him without risking his withdrawal from us. He really felt the pressure from the court to coax us back. I then thought of "playing a little hard to get." I took a "devil's advocate" position by stating that I felt the reasons he gave for refusing therapy were still valid and I urged him to hold his ground with the judge. By my essentially assuming his earlier posture of rejecting therapy, Pete found himself in the uncomfortable position of refuting each of his previous claims that therapy was a waste of time, a waste of money, and ineffective because the changes needed to come from Stacey herself. By Pete personally dismissing each objection to therapy, I had hoped that he would begin the process of really changing his views on working with us.

I believed that he still privately disagreed with therapy, even though he was now talking in favor of therapy for his family. As long as the judge factor was active, I believed that Pete would maintain a positive position toward therapy. I was concerned that if that factor ever faltered, so would Pete's cooperation with the therapy. We seemed to have a window of opportunity to begin with this family. If we could establish a solid rapport, perhaps the coercive influence now so necessary may not be required.

I explained to Pete that my past experiences in working with clients who had been forced to work with us usually turned out to be frustrating for both the clients and myself. I said that when clients felt coerced, their motivation only lasted a short time, inevitably giving way to anger about the coercion, a resumption of the attitude that counseling was useless, and in the end, withdrawal. I hedged by saying that this process was not inevitable, but that I was fearful that it could happen with he and our agency. I suggested that both he and I should take a few days to think this situation over in order to make absolutely sure that we both felt that we were doing a wise thing by trying to work together. He felt this was unnecessary, but I insisted upon it.

The next day, Pete called me and said he had no doubts about the therapy with us. I told him that I was still a little shaky about this, but on the strength of his assurances of success, we would agree to work with his family. I carefully stated that we should all remain alert to those old feelings of "therapy cannot work" in case they resurfaced. He agreed.

We worked collaboratively with this family for five months, at the end of which we reached a successful termination. Periodically throughout our time together, Pete made some disparaging comments about the process or progress of therapy, to which I responded by suggesting that an appropriate response to his concerns might be a cessation of services. These comments always evoked a smile from Pete, and we were always able to work through whatever impasse was before us.

I think this case illustrates how fast moving therapy can be. Pete's instantaneous challenge to our presence put us in a position to have to make important decisions that fundamentally affected our work without sufficient time or information to make those decisions. We had to decide whether to press him to accept our services or to back away and let him determine the outcome. In the heat of the moment, we chose to let him make that call. The mandate to work with us came from the judge and I believe we would have been in a very different (and strained) relationship had we tried to convince Pete that he *had* to work with us. In fact, my opinion is that we had no authority to insist or demand that he work with us. Despite how dire the consequences might have been, Pete and his family had the right to refuse therapy with us. Allowing the judge to be the coercive agent allowed us to avoid being the oppressor of this family. Sidestepping the role of forcing the family into therapy with us was without question, a more advantageous position for us as therapists.

Although I could have portrayed our work outlined in this example as being deliberately designed and calculated, I wanted to show how we had to decide things abruptly and spontaneously without much confidence in the outcome at that time. We were largely leaping into the dark. I see what happened as having a good resolution, but while it was occurring, we were not at all confident that things would turn out successfully.

Our instincts told us to not fight with Pete to get him to accept our services. This was a strongly held belief in our work with clients. Despite whatever we as therapists might think to be the appropriate way for our clients to act, we believe that the client must be afforded the right to choose their behavior for themselves. This fundamental premise about clients was operative at the time of this case and remains a cornerstone of my therapy today.

A Healing Ritual for Pseudocyesis

Karl Tomm

About ten years ago, I had the opportunity to work with a young family in which the thirty-year-old mother reported an unusual experience. Despite having had her fallopian tubes tied five months earlier, this woman was convinced that she was pregnant. She described herself as having morning sickness with nausea and vomiting. She also had a sensation of quickening in her lower abdomen. Repeated physical examination and lab testing did not confirm any pregnancy. Although she was informed about these negative findings and was told that she was not pregnant, she continued to insist that she was. Consequently, her family physician suggested that she consult me as a psychiatrist about these feelings. Traditional psychiatric nosology would describe her condition as *pseudocyesis,* which refers to the development of classic signs and symptoms of pregnancy in a nonpregnant woman.

The woman's husband provided me with a long history of major psychiatric problems that his wife had had prior to this presentation with pseudocyesis. She had at least six hospitalizations with episodes of hypomanic behavior and psychotic symptoms including auditory hallucinations and delusions of persecution. The various diagnoses she was given included schizophrenia, bipolar disorder, schizoaffective disorder, multiple personality disorder, and borderline personality disorder. When she was having extreme psychiatric symptoms, she seemed to respond fairly well to treatment with major tranquilizers. In light of this history, the temptation to disqualify her current experience of being pregnant as psychotic was quite strong. I tried to avoid this explanatory path because it would reify the psychiatric labeling with which she had already been burdened. Furthermore, my assessment of her experience as psychotic would be a major disqualification that would be "crazy making" in itself. Instead, I oriented myself to try to understand what could be coherent about what she was experiencing. For one thing, it seemed important to obtain some information about her obstetric history and not allow myself to be overly influenced by her psychiatric history.

This woman actually had a great deal of experience with confirmed pregnancies. She was also quite knowledgeable about the biological details involved. She had three pregnancies with her first husband. The first came to term and she delivered a girl (who was eleven years old when I first met the family). Her second pregnancy ended with a spontaneous abortion. The third was terminated medically because of recurrent bleeding that required blood transfusions. Following the break-up with her first husband, she became pregnant as a result of a transient relationship and had another miscarriage. She subsequently got involved with and married the man who accompanied her to the consultation with me. With this second husband, she had brought a fifth pregnancy to term and delivered another girl (who was three when I met the family). About a year prior to our initial meeting, she had become pregnant for the sixth time. Interestingly, she reported having had difficulty convincing her doctor of this. He didn't believe that she was pregnant at first, and tried to convince her otherwise. Eventually he did a urine test and the pregnancy was confirmed. However, at about five months' gestation, she aborted spontaneously. Both she and her husband saw the stillborn fetus and noticed that it was male. She was quite upset about this loss because she would have liked to have had a boy. Following the stillbirth, on the recommendation of her physician, she had her tubes tied. Her physician felt that she might not be able to handle it mentally if she had a third child.

When I first met this woman, her thoughts were clear and her speech was coherent. She did, however, convey a considerable amount of anxiety. While inquiring about her symptoms and history, I found it noteworthy that she often referred to her "son" who had been lost at five months' gestation. She described recurrent episodes of feeling that she was pregnant ever since his abortive delivery. Of all her pregnancies, these feelings were most similar to those that she experienced when she was pregnant with the boy. I asked whether the couple had given the boy a name or any kind of a burial. They had not. It seemed to me that this child was still very much alive for this woman on a psychological and emotional level. I speculated that her thoughts and feelings in relation to the boy were contributing to her symptoms of pseudocyesis on the physical level. I wondered whether a structured experience through which she could be clearly affirmed in a consensual reality of the boy having existed, having been born, and then having died, might make it possible for her current pregnancy to come to a natural end.

With this in mind, I raised the possibility of planning a burial ritual to simultaneously accept the son as a full member of the family and to acknowledge his loss. I indicated that the participation of the whole family in such a ritual would probably contribute to making the birth and death of the boy more legitimate and real for the mother. It seemed especially important that the husband participate, since he had been a material witness to the boy's existence. Both the husband and wife welcomed the idea, so I proceeded to outline various aspects of a possible ritual for them to carry out together. Since the couple had not given the boy a name, I suggested they do so. I encouraged them to imagine what psychological and physical characteristics he could have had. I suggested that they identify some objects that might represent the son for them and also write out on paper the kinds of thoughts that leave them with negative feelings concerning his death. I suggested that they collect these items and writings and, together with the girls, organize a funeral ceremony so that they could recognize the boy as a full member of the family, acknowledge his death, and place him to rest.

Because the mother favored cremation while the father preferred burial, I suggested that they burn the objects that reminded them of their son and bury the ashes. I proposed that they do this in a beautiful place in the countryside which they could visit in the future if they wished. I also suggested that they clearly define which thoughts about the boy they wanted to keep alive and continue to carry inside themselves. The validity of these memories was emphasized because the mother believed that her son's spirit continued to exist somewhere, perhaps in some other life form. I asked them to spend at least one hour each Sunday over the following six weeks discussing the boy, the specific memorial arrangements they wanted to make, and how to include the two girls. Following these preparations, they could proceed and carry out a ceremony if they felt comfortable doing so.

I saw them again in follow-up two months later, together with their daughters. They all seemed quite excited about what had happened. The couple had taken the proposed ritual very seriously and proceeded to make quite elaborate preparations. The mother made a small doll to represent the boy and a cradle to place him in. She built an altar and the father took photographs. After a brief ceremony, they burned the small doll along with envelopes that contained the negative memories they had written out. They then placed the ashes in an urn that the mother's father had brought back from South America. The memorial service included the four family members as well as the mother's sister, who happened to be visiting from out of town. The following weekend, the family arranged an outing during which they threw the ashes into a local river.

The woman reported that her feelings of being pregnant had intensified as they prepared for the ritual. However, her symptoms disappeared after the family enacted the memorial service. She no longer had any feelings of nausea or quickening. She acknowledged that she sensed some deeper sadness which had not yet come to the surface, but she felt confident that she could cope with these feelings should they arise. Everyone was pleased with the outcome. The woman subsequently expressed a great deal of gratitude to me for having suggested the ritual. It had created a special occasion on which her husband was fully affirming in relation to a significant life experience for her, and had helped make the existence of her son and his death more real for the whole family. In the ensuing months, the feelings of pregnancy recurred occasionally at times of stress, but to a minor degree. After a year and a half, she no longer mentioned them.

Unfortunately, the overall therapy was not as successful as the outcome of the ritual. I do not want to leave the reader with the impression that the couple "lived happily ever after." I continued to work with them over the next couple of years, trying to help unravel some ongoing conflict in the marriage. The husband turned out to have a chronic habit of disqualifying his wife and her experience in various ways. This confused her at times, frustrated and annoyed her at others. He tended to respond to her attempts at protest with further disqualification. For the most part, I supported her protest and tried to help him acknowledge and accept her experience whenever possible. I worked hard to help them develop general patterns of consensual validation and mutual affirmation along the lines of what had occurred with the memorial service.

However, increasing marital conflict arose as the woman struggled to find her own voice. Problems concerning sexuality emerged and the woman eventually left the home to live with her parents. She accused her husband of sexually abusing the girls. Child Protection Services conducted an investigation and interviewed both girls, but found no evidence to support their mother's allegations. During one session, she angrily accused me of molesting her daughters as well. She subsequently apologized for this accusation, but it left me with less confidence in supporting her reported experiences. She began focusing more and more on divorce. The husband construed his wife's desire to stay away and end the marriage as part of her unrealistic confusion. He managed to recruit various family members and professionals, including myself, to share this perspective. Consequently, my interventions became overly biased toward a reunion. This turned out to be a major mistake in that subsequent to this, the woman perceived me as being on her husband's side. I thought I was being neutral at the time, but in retrospect, can see that her intuition was correct. My vulnerability to being recruited into his perspective may have been enhanced by the success of the ritual. It had led me to become embedded in seeing the four of them as an intact family. After six months of further therapy, the woman did return to the home, mainly for the children. She remained in the household for another two and a half tumultuous years, but then left again. This time, she decided to stop the family therapy because she saw me as aligned with her husband's preference for remaining together as a couple. In effect, I had drifted away from my original orientation of strongly affirming her preferences and experience, and had inadvertently contributed to further disqualification of her by questioning her desire to separate.

In preparing to write up this ritual, I called them to ask about what had transpired in the seven years since I had last seen them. The woman was living alone on a disability allowance. She had resumed treatment by other professionals, who were more individually oriented, but she continued to have major problems with suicidal episodes and repeated hospital admissions. Despite her concerns about possible sexual abuse, she left both girls for the husband to raise. She did obtain a divorce, and subsequently remarried. However, the third marriage only lasted about a year. At the time of my call, she indicated that she now regarded the second husband as a reasonably reliable resource for herself, and the two of them were trying to cooperate in parenting the girls. Unfortunately, the older daughter developed serious problems during her adolescence with suicidal behavior, drug abuse, running away, and sexual promiscuity. The father and younger daughter were still together and appeared to be doing quite well. He had maintained his work and she was committed to her schoolwork.

I asked the woman and her ex-husband to give me any constructive feedback they could about my earlier work with them. The woman did not express any negative feelings about the family therapy. Her recollection of the ritual for the feelings of pregnancy continued to be very positive. The ex-husband indicated that he wished he could have had more help to escape the tendency to see his ex-wife as psychiatrically ill, which he could now see as so disqualifying. In retrospect, I can see that I had made an excellent start in my work with them, but had not gone far enough in my efforts to bring forth healing coherences among both his and her experiences. Whether or not I could have provided more effective help remains speculative, but I find it useful to reflect and try to learn from my apparent failure, as well as from the initial success.

You Are What You Heat
or
Why Every Couple
Should Remodel a Home

Victor Nelson

My early training in family therapy helped me to understand how and why people change. Therapists help people change. I also learned early in my career that people change in a variety of ways and for a variety of reasons.

My idea of good training was to equip myself with a vast array of techniques. I also tried to learn as much as I could from my supervisors, since their wisdom and insight became my anchor. I figured I was at least approaching brilliance in the ways I could assist people in making the changes they wanted and needed to make. However, I finally learned that, in spite of my techniques, my supervision, and even my budding brilliance, change can take place anyway.

The following story illustrates that not all changes which happen in therapy are expected, planned, or the result of therapeutic acumen. I hope the reader can identify with my experience: if therapists are aware of what actually happens in therapy, they may also learn from and be changed along with the clients.

If every person's life is worth a novel, then every couple should have the chance to remodel a home in order to claim their own dramatic story line. Be it comedy or tragedy, a home remodeling project can be just what a couple needs in order to rebuild their own relationship.

This certainly was true for the couple who came to me in my early years of practice. Months of building frustration (pun intended) had finally reached a boiling point when the couple undertook the remodeling of their Victorian home. They came seeking the Bob Villa of marriage counseling. They got me instead.

Their story centered around their tragic logic. The husband had been downsized, and after some months of job hunting decided that, if he couldn't earn thirty thousand dollars a year, he could save thirty thousand dollars by remodeling the house himself. Initially, his wife agreed and actually supported this wayward notion.

Two events had occurred that culminated in her insistence on therapy. The first event alerted her that something was not going well. She had arrived home from work and found her husband sitting with a beer and mumbling that the book on plumbing had been checked out of the library. None of the plumbing in the home worked. They spent $30.00 on a motel that night. Needless to say, the evening did not approximate their honeymoon.

The second incident occurred shortly thereafter. He had actually jacked up the house in order to level the foundation walls and relevel the floors. In doing so, he had left the doors closed so that when he jacked up the house, the doors jammed tight. Unfortunately, she was the one who discovered this when she came home from work. She couldn't get in. He couldn't get out. (This was to become a central metaphor for their relationship, thanks to the house.) He finally climbed out a window and tried to coax her in the window. She went back to motel. Alone. $30.00.

When they came to the first session, it was clear that he did not want to be there and saw no reason for therapy. He thought he was being punished for a project that was moving slower than planned. When they related their story, I set the therapy fee at $30.00. It seemed like a strategic way to keep the husband involved—you can pay me now or your wife will spend the money on a motel room. I thanked my supervisors for teaching me about the illusion of choice and actually saw it working. The husband was hooked!

I must insert at this point that the house was blameless for this couple's struggle. It was not evil like the Lutzes' home in Amityville. It was not a money pit, which Shelley Long and Tom Hanks discovered to their dismay in the movie of the same title. It was without motive or intent. All the house did was reflect back to the couple on a daily basis the state of their own relationship. The canted floor reminded them of their imbalanced relationship. The stuck doors revealed a pattern in their relationship. The cracks in the walls had the appearance of dead-end roads that mirrored their communication attempts. The plastic tarps hanging in the doorway to the kitchen could no more keep the sawdust out of the kitchen than either of them could keep family-of-origin issues from contaminating their approach to their present difficulties.

Therapy progressed, albeit slowly. I identified a principle at work: progress in therapy proceeds at a rate directly proportional to that of the house remodeling. Therapists who work with couples who are remodeling a home cannot use a brief therapy approach. No home remodeling project was ever completed in six sessions or less.

Bowen theory served the purposes of therapy well. While working on their genogram, I evoked a strong reaction that I ended up discussing with my supervisor. The couple was childless. So here's how I asked about their plans for children: "If you ever decide to have children, do you think the house will be finished by the time your first child is born?" The husband glared at me. The wife began counting the cash in her purse.

The therapy led me to not only appreciate Bowen theory, but also speculate about Bowen's flashes of brilliance. I suspect it went something like this: Bowen had to have been remodeling his own home. He saw the advantages of improving on the roof design, so he began to work on pitch, angles, and slope. He no doubt turned out hundreds of drawings with detailed notes. He worked tirelessly to get it right. His wife just wanted him to get it done. He dug in his differentiated heels and insisted that he was proceeding at his own natural pace. His wife demonstrated that you can't live with a differentiated person without being one yourself, so she hired a roofing contractor. Murray came home from a coaching session and saw his wife on one side of the house looking up. He was in the driveway on the other side. He looked up. The roofer was at the peak, nailing the last of the cap shingles in place. Perfect new roof. Clean angles. His wife. Him. Roofer. Bowen Gothic. Triangle! She was happy. He relaxed. No more anxiety. (If my hypothesis is not true, it should be.)

I continued working with this couple for a period of months, during which time they made regular and sometimes impressive progress. They talked more, planned together, and occasionally worked on the house together. He studied for and passed his CPA exam. They recreated more. The house neared completion in December when they came to therapy with the first real crisis they'd had in months. They were anticipating the dreaded trip back home at Christmas and were immobilized. We went back to the genogram.

The couple has grown up in the same small Iowa farm town. Both sets of parents, as well as the grandparents, still lived there. Both parents celebrated Christmas Eve at a family gathering. The grandparents each hosted a Christmas Day gathering. The couple had always gone to all four Christmas gatherings, but could never please everyone. They'd have to leave one house early to get to the next one late. They were as stuck as their doors had been in their canted house.

I asked the obvious: "Have you ever considered doing just one Christmas Eve and one Christmas Day?" They had. "Have you thought about alternating Christmases between your families' homes?" They had. But they remained stuck because they couldn't decide which family to leave out first, because it would mean disappointing that family. I posed another question. "Which of your families would be the most difficult to live with if they were excluded the first year?" It was a toss-up. It seemed like Solomon's dilemma. The couple could get sliced and diced.

But then I earned my $30.00: I suggested that they present their dilemma to each of their parents and have the two sets of parents discuss it. The parents would decide which family would host the couple the first year and which family would host the couple the second year. As we talked about leaving the choice in the hands of the parents, the couple warmed to the idea. They saw the logic and the benefit of shifting the responsibility to their parents. They left with a strong resolve.

Our next appointment was not scheduled until January, so I was extremely curious to hear how the strategy had worked. They came into my office happier than I'd ever seen them. They looked healthy, energized, and suntanned. I asked what had happened.

They described how they had approached their parents in the two weeks before Christmas with their request. Both sets of parents were dumbfounded. But the couple stayed their course. They wanted to see everyone, but not have to do four Christmas gatherings in two days. They asked their parents to talk with each other and decide who would invite them for the first year. They explained that they would then plan to do Christmas at the other family's home the following year. With only four days left before Christmas, neither set of parents had spoken to the other. Since no agreement appeared likely, the couple quickly considered an alternate plan: they opted to celebrate Christmas at the Grand Canyon!

That decision proved to be the transformative event in therapy, not only for the couple, but also for me. I was amazed that the parents' stubbornness actually became the catalyst which freed the couple to make their own decision. At this early stage in my career, I had seen a creative array of methods that families used to influence the lives of clients. What I hadn't seen was differentiation in action. Getting my clients to claim autonomy and accept responsibility for their own actions meant going against their families' intentions for them. When they handed responsibility back to their parents, the couple was free to make choices based on their own interests. The parents' intractability was a force which the couple used to further their work.

The couple continued the session, reporting that the house was down to the finish work. The husband was doing serious job hunting. The couple had taken charge of their relationship. It was clear to me that therapy was over. Good timing. A few months later, I received pictures from the couple—a beautiful Victorian restoration with tricolored exterior, shiny hardwood floors, marble foyer, and beveled glass windows. There was a picture of the front door—opened. It was truly a stunning accomplishment. The last picture showed the two of them standing in bright sunlight with the Grand Canyon behind them. There was a small pile of snow at their feet, but instead of a snowman, they had built a snow house. More than a house, they had remodeled a relationship and built some memories along the way.

"Will Somebody Stop Me?"

Catherine E. Ford Sori

I'd like to share a tale about a couple who experienced more sexual dysfunction than many couples seen by the renowned sex therapist with whom I consulted. When I first saw them, they seemed to be heading toward disaster.

The story really began seventeen years earlier, when Buck and Alice first met in college. Buck was a seminary student; Alice studied art. They were drawn to each other because of their common religious beliefs and because both felt they had found a friend—the first real friend either of them had. Neither had received much nurturing or acceptance as children. Buck's family had been excessively critical and condemning. Alice's was extremely emotionally distant. Alice and Buck weren't a highly romantic couple. Their relationship was based not on passion, but more on casual friendship. They just sort of drifted into marriage because it seemed like the thing to do. Buck would become a pastor; Alice would stay home and raise the children, pursuing her dream of becoming an artist in her spare time.

Buck and Alice had a nice wedding, attended by their families and a few acquaintances, and set off on their honeymoon. That is when all the trouble began. Buck described the incident this way.

> We were riding in the car, and I started sharing an idea for a sermon with Alice. When I asked her what she thought of my idea, she said, "What? Oh, sorry, I wasn't listening. Could you repeat that?" At that moment, I became filled with rage. I knew she wasn't listening. I knew I had been tricked, and that this marriage was a huge mistake.

Special thanks to Fred P. Piercy, Jerome Bercik, and J. Mark Killmer.

At the time, however, Buck said nothing about this to Alice.

When they arrived at their honeymoon cottage, Buck's despair deepened. Both had saved themselves for marriage, and Buck tried to lay aside his sense of betrayal and anger so that he might enjoy their honeymoon night. When they tried to consummate their marriage, however, they were simply unable to have intercourse. Alice's vagina just clamped shut, and Buck was unable to penetrate her. She sensed her husband's acute disappointment, and was flooded with feelings of inadequacy. Later, they tried again . . . and failed again. Soon, Buck had difficulty maintaining an erection. Over and over, for the next seventeen years, the couple tried to have intercourse and failed. Every new attempt and failure fueled their disappointment, bitterness, frustration, and rage.

I didn't meet Buck and Alice until their last-ditch attempt to save their relationship. Buck was an assistant pastor in a small congregation, never having met his goal of being head pastor of a large church. Alice worked as a clerk in an art supply store. She had stopped painting years ago. Both were approaching forty, and the dream of having a family was fading, as was their dream of having a satisfying physical relationship.

For several months, we worked together, attempting to improve their relationship, but disaster loomed on the horizon. Buck had decided that this was his last chance to experience a satisfying sex life. Despite his strong fundamental religious beliefs, he had become sexually attracted to the church secretary. The secretary was not of their faith, and Buck had asked her out for coffee on several occasions, to "witness" to her. He even had people in the congregation, including Alice, praying for her. He had invited the secretary to come to the house for a little "talk" someday while Alice was at work. Painfully, honestly, he discussed his passion for this woman openly in sessions with Alice. Buck said that even if, by some miracle, he and Alice did manage to have intercourse, it wouldn't be enough. He needed to experience wild and passionate sex, and he would simply have to have an affair before he missed his chance. He became obsessed with the idea of an affair, and became progressively angrier at Alice, criticizing her for being passionless and frigid. Buck seemed determined to go through with an affair with his secretary, regardless of the fact that the church would find out, he would lose his position as a minister, be disciplined by the church, and thrown out of the ministry. He was also ignoring the fact that he had strong personal convictions that affairs were wrong and would ruin his relationship with God.

Because of Buck's high degree of criticism, contempt, and rage, and Alice's emotional withdrawal, I began by working to improve their relationship. Buck and Alice went through communication training, learned to take time outs, reduced their negative exchanges, and began to behave in more positive ways toward one another. Still, they were unable to have intercourse. Whenever they tried, she experienced severe vaginismus (which had no medical basis), and he experienced either impotence or premature ejaculation. When they tried to satisfy each other through touching, she was inorgasmic, which left her frustrated and him angry and hopeless.

We worked with emotions, and they delved extensively into the pain and rejection of their childhoods, sharing many intense emotional experiences with one another. On one occasion, Buck sculpted his family of origin and shared his sensitivity to rejection. Alice stayed with him, and for once, Buck felt understood and listened to by her. This was an exhilarating feeling for him. A glimmer of hope appeared on the horizon as a small seed of empathy and understanding took root and tentatively began to grow. That fragile plant was watered with a measure of forgiveness for past hurts and disappointments. It was fertilized, to some degree, by rethinking power and gender role issues in their relationship. Alice began to express how unhappy she was that Buck did so little housework. Buck began to appreciate the effort Alice put into running their home, and to share more in household tasks. They even, on occasion, had fun together! Once, after a snowstorm, they each made connecting snow forts. They took pictures of their dogs running through the connecting tunnel, and then knocked down the dividing wall. Buck tried not to obsess about having a wild affair with his secretary, and admitted that he would never forgive himself if he had an affair. He would "lose absolutely everything that has any meaning in life." Things improved in their relationship. Still, their sexual problems remained.

At this point, I suggested they stop trying to have sex, and we began the second phase of treatment: sex therapy. We spent a few weeks doing a more in-depth assessment of their sexual history and family attitudes about sex. Following that, we were ready to begin the first exercise: Sensate Focus. It was at this point that Buck resurrected the issue of the affair.

Buck and Alice came in that week looking sullen and edgy. When I asked them what had happened, Buck blurted out that he was tired of their no-sex relationship. He had decided that he would never be able to experience real passion with Alice, and his time was running out. After all, he was almost forty. He wanted it all: the heat, the passion, and the fireworks! When he looked at Alice, it was with disgust.

"I've decided I can't wait any longer! I have to find out what it's really like to find a 'soul mate.' Frankly, Alice makes me sick! She can't satisfy me, and she never will!"

At this point, I turned to Alice and asked her what she thought of Buck's tirade. She responded in a voice so soft and meek, it was barely audible. "Well, I understand Buck's disappointment. Lord knows, I've tried over the years, but it just isn't getting any better. I guess he has the right to have a real sexual relationship."

"Are you saying that this would be okay with you?" I asked her gently.

"Well, I wish things were different, but I do understand Buck's need," she replied.

"So let me see if I understand," I said. "You're saying that it's okay with you if Buck has an affair with this woman, even though you both say there will be a huge scandal, and he will be thrown out of the ministry. Because you understand his need? Is that what you're saying?"

"Yes, I guess so. I mean, I know what his needs are, that this is really important to him."

"And you would stay with him, not leave him? Not get a divorce if he has an affair?" I asked.

With head down while appearing emotionally resigned, she softly replied, "No, I would not leave Buck if he has an affair. He deserves to be happy."

As I turned to look at Buck, I noticed an interesting phenomenon. Although his wife had just given him her blessings to indulge his sexual needs outside their marriage, he looked at her, not with gratitude or relief, but with intense hostility and contempt. I asked Buck to wait in the waiting room so that I could talk to Alice alone.

When Buck was gone, I asked Alice to again clarify her position, just to be certain I had heard her correctly. I was silent for a moment, and then said softly, "So let me make sure I really understand you. You're saying that if you come home for lunch next week, and Buck is in your bedroom with another woman, that will be okay with you, and you won't leave him?"

She looked uncomfortable, and took a minute before replying, "No, I won't divorce Buck."

"Well," I continued, "what if you come home next week and find Buck in the bedroom with *two* women. Would that still be okay with you? Would you stay with him?"

Alice began to shift uncomfortably in her chair, and took longer to reply, "Well, yes . . . I guess I would still not leave him."

I waited a few minutes before continuing. "Okay, now what if you come home for lunch and find *three* women in bed with Buck? Is that still okay with you?" I asked.

Alice sat in silence, contemplating my question. After several moments, a spark began to flash in her eyes. She lifted her chin, drew in a deep breath, and announced, "No! That would not be okay! *I do not want Buck to have an affair, and I will leave him if he does!"* As we explored this decision, her voice grew stronger and her conviction intensified. A few minutes later, we asked Buck to return so Alice could tell him her decision.

I started by saying, "Buck, Alice has an important statement to make to you about the issue of you having an affair."

A new Alice, looking and sounding stronger and more confident (and somewhat defiant) told him, "Buck, I've decided that it is *not* okay with me for you to have an affair. I understand your needs, but if you do, *I will leave you.* It's up to you whether or not you have an affair, but I will not stay married to you if you do. It simply is not okay!"

Buck was struck by the conviction in Alice's voice, and there seemed to be little doubt in his mind that she was serious. He didn't have much to say the remainder of the session.

In the following week, I pondered what might be happening with them. Had Buck resumed seeing the secretary? Had Alice backed down from her new stance? Would they decide to give it one last-ditch effort and start sex therapy? Would they even show up for the next session?

A transformed couple walked into my office the following Wednesday evening. Buck looked joyous, almost rapturous, while Alice glowed with contentment and self-satisfaction. I could hardly contain my curiosity as I asked them what had happened.

As they pulled their chairs closer together, they looked at each other with laughter and delight in their eyes. Buck, never one to start subtly, blurted out, "Guess what? It's a miracle! We *did it!*"

Taken aback, I wanted to clarify his comment. "You mean, you did *it?* You had sexual intercourse—together—with each other [I added as an afterthought!]?"

Buck smiled at Alice, who lowered her eyes with a smile and a slight blush, and said, "Yup! I thought about what Alice said for a couple of days, and decided it was just plain wrong to have an affair. We prayed together about it, and I don't know what happened, but three days later, all of a sudden—*it* just happened! And it's been happening ever since! After almost eighteen years, we finally consummated our marriage! And we're *finally* on our honeymoon!"

Alice looked up coyly, smiled, and nodded enthusiastically.

While their names and identities have been changed to protect client confidentiality, Buck and Alice gave me permission to share their story with other couples who may feel that their relationship is hopeless. It has been almost two years since that last memorable session. I just spoke to Buck yesterday, and he said they were still doing quite well. He was calling to ask me to do a series of talks at his church. I've thought a lot about them, about Buck's close escape from disaster. I've thought about how everything changed when Alice quit trying to be so understanding, and about how Buck finally got his miracle!

When Lightning Strikes a Therapist

David C. Dollahite

Though they were attempting to whisper, I could not help but hear from the other end of the hall the terse, angry words Gail and Mark threw at each other. I walked down the hall to greet them for our marital therapy session, and as I came into their view, Mark gave me a look that seemed to say, "Go ahead, David, just try to get us to solve our problems tonight." As we walked down to the therapy room, they positioned themselves on either side of me. I could feel the sparks flying between them. It was obvious that this particular storm had been brewing for some time. I was in my second year of a master's degree program in marriage and family therapy. Having already endured a long day of classes, thesis writing, library research, and teaching, I was already tired and didn't know where the presence of mind would come from that I knew Gail and Mark needed. I also felt some apprehension from the fact that my clinical supervisor and several classmates planned to observe this session through a one-way mirror; past sessions had not brought great progress, and the observers were there to help me get unstuck.

Gail and Mark had been seeing me for about two months for a variety of marital and family problems. This was Gail's second marriage and Mark's first. They had the two children from Gail's first marriage living with them: a four-year-old who did her best to make life difficult for her stepfather, and a three-year-old who added contrast by being nearly perfect. Gail's elderly mother, who had Alzheimer's disease, also lived with them. Gail's role was that of homemaker and referee between her mother, Mark, and the children. Mark was a student and had been working two part-time jobs, but had just been fired from one; they were barely making it financially. On top of it all, Gail was pregnant.

Gail and Mark agreed that much of their marital strife resulted from their lack of contact and communication. They had little time to talk with each other; what talk they did manage usually flared into an argument. The rare times that the two actually faced each other and tried to discuss issues were in our sessions. We had practiced communication and problem-solving skills, but Gail and Mark usually did not do the homework we had agreed upon. Each openly laid the blame for their unhappiness on the other.

Gail and Mark seated themselves in nearly opposite corners of the room. They poised on the edge of their seats and began raining insults on each other, voices booming, arms and hands gesturing stiffly, eyes dark and cold, and necks taut with pent-up anger. The issue they were so heatedly arguing about was so trivial that I don't even remember what it was. However, the supercharged atmosphere in the room mirrored a thunderstorm just before lightning strikes. I made my first feeble attempt at an intervention by asking Gail and Mark to try some of the reflective listening we had been working on. Strike one. They were in no mood to listen to each other. They looked at me as though I was a stranger trying to cut in on their dance, and turned up the volume of their arguing.

I then plaintively asked them to go through the stages of problem solving that we had practiced in previous sessions. Strike two. In unison, they glared at me, as if to say, "You'll have to do a lot better than that." They continued flinging abuses at each other as only people who know each other's weaknesses intimately can do. I wondered why they had bothered to come to therapy that night.

By now, even I was beginning to feel tense and angry, as well as frustrated, confused, and embarrassed, knowing that my supervisor and peers were witness to my bumblings. It was as if two huge, dark storm clouds, looming just overhead, were rolling on a collision course and I was helpless to do anything about it. I had the sinking realization that the frustrations, fears, hurts, and harms welling up inside of Gail and Mark were about to pour down in a burst of emotional fury that would surely damage the fragile landscape of their relationship. I also had the oppressive feeling that nothing I could do or say would stop the torrents of rage. I really didn't know what to do next. All I could do was pray for the reprieve of one of those supervisory knocks on the door that often came to trainees wallowing in four feet of marital slosh and about to go under.

Then, in the midst of the tempest, a thunderbolt struck me. I heard myself telling Gail and Mark to please lie down on their backs on the floor next to each other. They stopped mid-insult, looked at me, at each other, and then at the floor. They looked back at me quizzically and lay on the floor. I asked them to close their eyes and mouths, relax, and imagine that they were lying on a soft beach with the warm sun bathing them and a cool breeze flowing over them. I led them through a period of deep muscle relaxation, having them tighten and then loosen all of their major muscle groups. This took about ten minutes.

After I sensed that they were both calm, I had them take one another's hand and think of a time when they were together and things were just right for them, a time when they remembered feeling calm, peaceful, and serene. I told them to imagine all of the details of that experience: the sights, sounds, tastes, smells, and feelings. I then asked them to share their memories with each other in as much detail as possible. It happened that they had thought of the same evening, one early in their marriage, in which they went for a long, tranquil drive in the mountains and shared feelings of love and appreciation for one another. As they spoke about their feelings that night, the tone in their voices radiated love and respect. They even revealed thoughts and feelings they had not shared with one another before. They smiled and squeezed hands.

I let Gail and Mark savor this feeling for a few moments. Then I requested that each share with the other the stresses they were currently experiencing. In the same quiet, respectful tone, Mark spoke of his feelings of inadequacy in providing enough for his family, his guilt over not being able to get along with Gail's oldest daughter, and his struggle to go back to school after many years. Gail calmly spoke of her pain in seeing her mother struggle with Alzheimer's disease, her concern for Mark and her older daughter's relationship, and her feelings of uncertainty about their financial stability.

I next asked them to offer what each would like to do for the other to relieve some of this stress. They each calmly mentioned things they would like to do and sincerely committed to do them. I let them relax and enjoy this calm after the storm. Finally, I asked Gail and Mark to return to their seats. They sat close to each other, smiling, and holding hands while I asked them to find time to have this kind of experience together about once a week. They gladly agreed.

The downpour had ended. The black clouds were breaking up and slowly moving away. Lightning still flashed in the distance, reminding us that the storm was not completely over; thunder rolled faintly, hinting that future storms would appear. But for now, a sense of renewal and hope shined through.

Over the next several weeks, we made good progress in strengthening their relationship. Gail and Mark did the things they committed to do to help each other. I gave them a deep muscle relaxation tape to use at home. They used the time after they relaxed to talk about their relationship and solve problems together. This did not eliminate all of their difficulties, but it did help them regain some of the freshness their relationship once had. Mark and Gail asked me what to call this activity that had made such a difference for them. I thought about it and suggested that, since it involves lying down (hopefully on a soft floor or bed), relaxing, imagining calming things, and sharing feelings of love and concern, we could call it a "CALM-DOWN" (Caring And Loving Messages-Down).

After our session, I felt intensely energized. I had participated in an exciting process where powerful opposing forces were diffused by a bolt of inspiration. My supervisor and fellow students asked me how I came up with the idea for the intervention I chose for Gail and Mark. I had to say that I really didn't know. I have often wondered how the idea for the CALM-DOWN experience came to me; the way I now think of it is that I functioned somewhat like a lightning rod.

To properly disperse the energy of a thunderbolt, a lightning rod must be grounded. I was grounded in that I had been trained to use deep muscle relaxation, guided imagery, and communication techniques. Without this training, I would not have been able to channel the energy into something constructive for Gail and Mark. To attract the bolt away from other things, a lightning rod must be made of electrically receptive material. By that point in my training, I had become more open and receptive to what was happening with my clients rather than being too narrowly focused on a clinical treatment a plan. (Of course, being wearied, confused, and completely at a loss for what to do added immeasurably to my receptivity.) Since a bolt usually strikes the highest point, a lightning rod is placed high in the air. Looking at it another way, the bolt strikes the closest thing it can come into contact with. I now understand why Gail and Mark came in that night. They somehow knew that they needed something to diffuse the tremendous energy they were experiencing. When the storm reached its peak, I was the closest thing around able to receive the flash of inspiration.

Before this, I thought the only way to obtain an effective therapeutic intervention was to carefully read all of the outcome literature, watch others and imitate them, or think enough about the problem to construct a logical, rational solution. The session that night helped me realize that the demands and the energy of a situation itself can sometimes elicit from a therapist a customized solution that may be created in no other way. Over the years, when facing an especially difficult therapeutic situation, I have felt some consolation in knowing the inaccuracy of the saying that lightning never strikes the same place twice.

The First Gift

Bruce P. Kuehl

I don't know how they ended up at the University Family Services Clinic. Perhaps it was because they were poor and didn't have anywhere else to go. I was a first-semester practicum student. This experience was as much for me as it was for them. My inexperience didn't seem to matter, however, because Mom, divorced and alone, wanted help for Tommy; she would take it where she could find it.

Tommy went straight to the toys in the corner of the room. He was five. I heard "grrrr" and "crsshhhhh" as one of the plastic people was run over by a toy truck. Mom untied her coat, but did not take it off. It was obvious that she had no intention of staying for the entire session. She thought Tommy's therapy would be just him and me. As a student, I had been told to expect this: parents wanting to drop their children off to be fixed while they run a few errands. We were only three minutes into the session and I was already squirming in my seat. "Cold outside?" I said. I was attempting to break the ice. Mother attempted a cordial response, replying, "Yes, it's kind of chilly."

It was early fall in the Midwest and the mutual assessment phase had begun. I had many questions in mind. What is the situation with Tommy? What kind of parent is this person? Did she do something to him? Where is Dad? Is he a resource? Did he do something? What did Mom want from therapy? What would she be able to do in order to get it? Would I know how to help? Would they approve of me? Would I be good enough?

Quick and to the point, skipping the social joining phase, I asked, "What brings you here today?" She twisted her gloves in her lap, "Tommy just came back from Los Angeles where he was visiting his father. I think he was abused." It was six minutes into the session and I was overwhelmed. I pressed on, asking, "Tell me, what makes you think that?" Shifting her gaze between her gloves and Tommy, she replied, "He has been real moody since he got back, but I didn't know why." Handing me a crumpled piece of paper from her purse, she continued, "He made this in school." It was a drawing of a horizontal child with a larger figure squatting above, and something falling. "He told the teacher it was Billy pooping on him." Billy was the eleven-year-old son of Dad's live-in male friend.

The teacher contacted social services who interviewed both Tommy and mother. According to Mom, Los Angeles authorities were now investigating the report. She described Dad as gay and having a history of drug use. Still coming to terms with my homophobia, I felt anger toward all gay men because of what might have happened to Tommy, but I knew enough not to express it. Many questions spun through my head. Did this event really happen? Can I trust Mom's opinion? If so, what else did Tommy experience in his father's house? Why did Mom let Tommy visit Dad if she knew he was unreliable? Where was she? To what degree is she reliable?

She went on, "I don't know how Tommy is dealing with all of this. He won't talk to me about it. I thought he might talk to you." Her eyes, worried and tired, revealed the dilemma. She loved Tommy very much. Knowing more of what happened would crush her. He couldn't tell his mother what had happened because she couldn't take it. That is where she hoped I could help. Since I didn't have a better plan, she waited in the lobby while Tommy and I played with the toys.

Later that week, in meeting with my supervisor, I expressed frustration over not knowing how to proceed with a child sex-abuse case. I apologetically admitted meeting alone with Tommy while mother waited, and wondered how I might correct this mistake and get her back into therapy. After recounting the process whereby I decided to meet one-on-one with Tommy, I was relieved and surprised to learn that meeting alone with Tommy was all right. However, I learned that with mother's permission, I could contact social services in order to get their perspective on the reported abuse. I agreed to get the release during our next session. (A note to the reader: It is important to be familiar with federal and state laws pertaining to mandated reporting of abuse by mental health workers.)

From consulting with my supervisor, I also learned that it was important to help the mother provide safety to Tommy and assure him that whatever might have happened in Los Angeles was not his fault. I was cautioned not to rush her, given her initial hesitation, however. This would be a lesson on timing and use of the therapeutic process. The strategy would be to consult with the mother for ten minutes of every session; the rest of the time would be spent with Tommy. The goals were to (1) provide Tommy with a safe place to express himself through play and drawing and (2) put mother at ease while continuing to afford her opportunities to focus upon herself. It seemed simple.

The mother and I had little interaction over the next two sessions. I was frightened by her vulnerability. She seemed more fragile than Tommy. Instead, Tommy and I expanded our relationship. We ran over more plastic people and drew on the chalkboard. He drew a face with an open mouth full of sharp teeth. A tiny person was in the mouth. Tommy was the little person; it was Dad's face. Then he resumed playing with the trucks. This was the first time Tommy indicated that something was wrong with his relationship to his father. I called social services, where a description of the drawing went "on record." During my second meeting with my supervisor, it was stated that "Tommy may be lucky." "Lucky?" I reflected incredulously, wondering if I had heard correctly. "Yup," came the confident response. "It sounds like his father may have been sexually abused when he was a kid. He didn't get help, though. Tommy is getting help. He opened up to you. I think this case has a good prognosis. Have you gotten anywhere with Mom?" I responded, "Not yet."

This case was weighing heavily on my emotions. Raised in a traditional male role, I was in foreign territory and wanted out.

During Session Four, I spent thirty minutes with Mom. Tommy was over with the toys. "How are you holding up under the strain?" I asked the mother. Down came a flood of tears. Tommy brought her a toy to play with. Tommy knew his mom was hurting, and she accepted his love as expressed through the simple offer of a toy. They hugged. I liked that. I felt effective for the first time. I liked that even more.

During Session Five, it was just Mom and myself. Tommy was at Grandma's house. There were lots of tears as she vacillated between anger at her ex-husband and her own guilt and shame. She asked the questions and she answered them herself. I just listened. Why had she married him? Because she wanted to get away from the farm and he seemed fun. Why did she have his child? Because maybe then he'd take their relationship seriously. "How dumb!" she said, reprimanding herself. Why did she take Tommy to visit him? Because he said he loved and missed Tommy and that he was off the drugs. What was she thinking? She heard these lies before! More shame, guilt, and anger. Would Tommy ever forgive her? Would she forgive herself? She didn't have answers to these questions. Neither did I. A dab with the Kleenex, a few sniffs, and she was ready to leave. I had hardly spoken, yet I was exhausted.

I had another meeting with my supervisor. "What is her relationship with her parents?" the supervisor asked. Not knowing, I dodged the question. "She lives in a trailer house on an acre of land her parents gave her. She says she grew up a lot since leaving home six years ago."

The supervisor moved on, asking, "Do they help her with Tommy?"

"Grandma watches him when Mom is working. Grandpa is busy farming, but says he likes having Tommy around," I replied, relieved that I knew the answer.

"Do they know about the alleged abuse?"

"Yes." More relief.

"Who are the primary parent figures to Tommy?"

"I get the impression Mom is."

"Let's find out. Ask her to bring her parents in and see how they all interact."

I called Mom to set it up. It took two weeks before everyone could come to the session. Grandpa and Grandma were framed as expert observers of Mom and Tommy. They sat next to each other on the sofa. Mom sat in the chair between them and myself. Tommy moved from person to person, but spent most of his time with Mom.

What were their impressions? They reported that Tommy was a good boy. He got along well with everyone on the farm. He especially loved the cats. They were happy that he and Mom were living close by. What might have happened in Los Angeles was unfortunate, but with the Lord's help Tommy would overcome that. Yes sir, their daughter shows more maturity than she did six years ago. A hard way to learn. She seems awfully sad. They worry about that.

During Session Seven, the first half hour was spent with Mom. As usual, Tommy seemed content to play, stopping occasionally to show us something. I asked Mom to comment on what her parents said during the last meeting. She agreed with their perceptions. Tommy was doing well. There have been no more alarming drawings in school or in therapy, and he was less moody at home. Child protection workers in Los Angeles were unable to support Tommy's allegations of abuse, but they did confirm the mother's description of father. He was uncooperative and his living conditions were described as questionable.

Mom seemed to be gaining strength from the feedback from social services, the school, therapy, and her parents. Indeed, she seemed more confident and composed than in previous sessions, and more at ease with Tommy. Tommy was the same as always. We played well together. He didn't have much to say and his play reflected it. We got along okay. We were playmates, nothing more.

That was the last session. Like so many of those early cases, the clients just didn't come back, and I wasn't secure enough to contact them to ask why. I used the rationale that it was the mother's responsibility to contact me. I thought they were probably doing well, but I didn't really know. Then, about two months later, I came out of a session to find Mom and Tommy in the lobby talking with another practicum student.

The mood was light. When they saw me, Mom smiled and said, "I'm glad you're here. Tommy has something for you." He handed me a small wrapped box. They seemed pleased. I opened it, and inside was a glass statuette of a little boy wearing bibs and a party cap. He was holding two balloons, one red and one blue. Next to him stood a little dog with a spot over one eye. The statuette, of course, was Tommy. He was all right.

Postscript

Although this case occurred twelve years ago, the statuette is still on my shelf. It has been broken as a result of moving, and glued back together, but a person has to look hard to notice the cracks. Perhaps it is the same with Tommy. Who knows?

Nonetheless, I continue to contemplate its significance. The lessons change as I gain experience. Initially, it was a thank you gift, nothing more. Today, because I teach and supervise marriage and family therapy students, the statuette reminds me that therapy is more basic than the complex web of theory and technique that we weave. For most clients, such as Tommy and his mother, therapy is about restoring love, trust, commitment, and forgiveness. Although it took some years to unwrap, I believe this understanding is the true gift they gave to me.

Yet, therapists seldom discuss love in the literature or with their clients. Perhaps it is because love does not lend itself to scientific inquiry. A more likely reason such discussions are slow to materialize is because like discussions on sex, death, violence, diversity, and a host of other topics, discussions of love require that we risk exposing our ignorance and failures. I believe love is something our profession can benefit by learning more about. I began this process in therapy with the help of Tommy and his mother. Wherever they are today, and whomever they are with, I hope they are secure in love.

I Gave at the Office

Lisa Aronson Fontes

It wasn't the incest that got to me so much, or the mothers without teeth whose children were much too skinny for their age, or even the pale, shaking child who pretended he was asleep and refused to go home at the end of sessions. Rather, it was the petty slights in the real world outside the office: the telephone solicitor who called me a "cheap bitch" when I refused to subscribe to a magazine, the chewing gum that stuck to the living room carpet, and the wood in the woodpile that refused to stack.

"I gave at the office," I'd think to myself. "I gave blood at the office!"

When I was working full-time as a child and family therapist with protective cases in a managed-care setting, it seemed to me that the stresses of the job should make me exempt from the nastiness of the world—as if straining to witness and alleviate people's suffering every day, day after day, should give me some special entitlement.

"The basil should grow, the sun should shine on my daughter's birthday party, and the oil filter should change itself—because I am working so hard." I knew how ridiculous and self-centered these thoughts were. The janitor, the nurse, and the receptionist were working at least as hard, and seemed to receive no special treatment from the cosmos. However, still, shouldn't good things happen to people who are trying to do good?

Sammie and my older daughter were both five, but Sammie was slighter and sunnier when I first met her. I thought that if the two were to stand side by side, my own plump and occasionally moody daughter would be more like the kid who was referred for therapy. Sammie could draw pictures of real people and objects, while my daughter seemed to be stuck on shapes and colors.

However, their hands said something different. My daughter's hands were strong, sometimes dirty under the fingernails from playing in the mud, but her skin was clear and smooth. Sammie could not stop chewing on her fingers and picking at her nails. Her hands were always dry, red, chapped, and bloody. It was hard to believe the two girls lived in the same climate.

"Draw me a picture of your family doing something," I asked her at our first session. Sammie's picture was of two aunts and a cousin. No Mommy, no Daddy, no Sammie, and no Nana, although Sammie was shuffled around each week between her grandmother's house, her father's apartment, and her mother's rented room.

After we'd met for a couple of months, Sammie began to reach out to me. The first time caught me by surprise. Sammie looked at me shyly, grabbed a puppet off the shelf, sat on my lap, and closed her eyes. After just a couple of seconds, she jumped up and banged the puppet hard into my shoulder, still smiling.

"I'm gonna go see my Nana," she said as she ran to the waiting room and hugged her grandmother. I followed, saying, "You just needed to check and make sure your grandmother was still there, right Sammie?" feeling a little foolish for saying the obvious. Sammie nodded and returned to the playroom.

In our private world again, I added, "In some ways, you feel like getting close to me." Sammie turned away and hummed to herself happily, as if she hadn't heard, as if she didn't have a care in the world.

*   *   *

My office was square and overheated, with two windows, a children's play table, and a big desk. I had decorated the office with my two daughters' paintings. "Who drew these?" the child clients would ask when they met with me for the first time, accompanied by their parents or social workers. I was vague. I wanted to break the news carefully that there were children who spent time with me every day and on weekends, and not just for fifty minutes a week.

"They're from a day care center," I would say, and that seemed to be enough.

Occasionally, a child would bring in a drawing for me, and I would dutifully hang it among my own children's pictures, sorry to upset the balance of colors and forms I had set up on the day I moved in. The pictures made by my own daughters seemed brighter, if not more artistic. I felt guilty about loving my own children more than the children who came my way professionally, who so often needed someone who could love them best of all.

I sometimes felt as though I was cheating on my daughters. I was constantly on the phone about my child clients—speaking with their parents, the schools, the courts, and protective services. I was getting paid for playing and talking with children for hours each week, and especially listening carefully to them. I rarely had this intense one-on-one time with my own children, uninterrupted by telephones ringing or dishes to wash. The few times my children had visited the office, they could not understand what I did there with a doll house, puppets, and a padded bat. They would ask, "Do you really just play with the kids?"

* * *

"The prognosis is bad, isn't it?" the pediatrician asked.

"I don't know. We thought Freddy had some strengths. He related to us well. He managed to complete many of the tests. We don't think it's too late."

"No, I mean, with home the way it is."

He was right. Freddy was probably headed for detention or suicide. At age ten, he was depressed, not eating, and striking out angrily at his schoolmates. I expected he'd turn to drugs or alcohol by junior high. My supervisor thought Freddy would probably end up in jail. His mother would have been happy to send him to residential care and start over again. She was pregnant for the first time in a decade, and was working hard to erase the past which Freddy embodied in his frail frame.

Along with the other members of the intervention team, I was determined to help Freddy rewrite his future. The pediatrician was committed to helping Freddy gain weight and wear his glasses. I planned to help Freddy's mother stand up to her husband when he struck his stepson. We hoped for a surprise. We kept reminding ourselves of those children who make it through, the resilient ones, and hoped Freddy would turn out to be stronger than he looked.

* * *

Although I am a weeper, I did not cry at work. The clients cried. I would set boxes of tissues and litter baskets close by before they arrived, so they would not think I was asking them to stop crying. Their tears usually did not bother me, and frequently seemed to provide relief.

I found myself turning away and wanting to "fix things" when seventy-year-old Mrs. Johnson shook with weeping. It was like seeing my mother or grandmother weep. After five decades of marriage, Mr. Johnson seemed to have no interest in comforting her. Mrs. Johnson blew her nose loudly when she sobbed, and I turned away to save her embarrassment. When she first came in, Mrs. Johnson reported that she had been inconsolably depressed for over a year about her daughter's sudden death. Her work with me had been largely successful. As Mrs. Johnson emerged from her depression, she resumed her baseline level of activities as one of the town "nuts," chaining herself to the doors of the abortion clinic and writing daily letters to the editor. When she asked me about my position on abortion, I avoided answering. I let Mrs. Johnson know that I was on her side personally, regardless of the issues.

*   *   *

Like many therapists, I live intimately with intense suffering, and yet rarely cry about my work directly. I do not believe I am denying the pain—I have just gotten used to it as someone living in a desert may get used to heat. It is always there, but with proper steps, I can keep it in the background of my life. However, I also expect to be crushed breathless from time to time, usually by my own feelings of impotence and the failure of the social net. I need to remind myself that incest, abuse, and abandonment are not the stuff of breakfast conversations or pillow talk.

I turn on the radio to clear my mind on the way home. Sometimes, I take long walks. For the first half hour of those walks, I think about Sammie, Freddie, and the Johnsons. By the end, I am thinking about my own children and anticipating curling up with them and a book at bedtime. This way, I keep the office at bay.

My daughter stood up suddenly in the shower when I was leaning over her. Her head slammed into my chin and I bit my tongue and cried out in pain. I was surprised at the depth of my cry. It came from well within my chest, like a cry during sex or childbirth, and I wondered if my daughter could tell. I was vaguely satisfied by hearing myself make a sound which came from within, although my tongue was sore and I hated the stale taste of blood that filled my mouth.

My own crying does not bother me. I cry like crazy at songs about love lost or found, or as I read stories to my children. I cry easily and fully at the poetic things in life.

Perdí Mi Perrito

Lucille Marmolejo Romeo

El Paso, "The Pass," has long been the corridor for migration into the United States from South and Central America and Mexico. Immigrants search for the "American dream" of equality, economic security, education, and freedom from social oppression. My family of origin migrated to El Paso, Texas from Parral, Chihuahua, Mexico during the Mexican Revolutionary War in 1912 searching for this "dream." As a child, my mother traveled by train to El Paso with her mother, grandparents, aunts, uncles, and cousins. They did not have to worry about passports or visas, as immigration laws such as those of today were not in effect. However, there was a fear of being apprehended by Pancho Villa, the Mexican revolutionary leader, and his soldiers, who frequently robbed train passengers of food and money. My mother informed me that her father had not traveled with them, as he had abandoned the family a year earlier. This was a family secret that was rarely ever addressed or discussed, and to this day, I do not know the details related to this incident.

Due to my family's migration into the United States, I was fortunate to be born in El Paso and be an American citizen. I am a product of that "American dream," as I have received my education and other opportunities for growth and development in the United States; however, it came with all the inherent stressors and difficulties related to acculturation and assimilation into the dominant culture. My family worked very hard at "Americanizing" me so that I could "fit" into the American culture. This was related to the anxiety and fear that immigrant families experienced during the Depression era in the 1930s, when repatriation and deportation to Mexico occurred. I have heard stories of an uncle and aunt who were deported because they did not have proof of legal residency. In reaction to this fear, I was taught to speak English well "without an accent" and to speak my native tongue, Spanish, only at home and with my family. This rule was also enforced at school, as children were harshly punished if they spoke Spanish in class or on the school grounds. Thus, I learned my lessons "too well," as my Mexican identity and culture began to fade and my assimilation into the American culture became stronger, especially after I relocated to Baltimore for my psychological training.

As the years passed and I matured emotionally, psychologically, and interpersonally, the need and desire for family and cultural reunification appeared. I returned to El Paso, border sister city to Ciudad Juárez, Chihuahua, Mexico with a voracious appetite to relearn and reexperience the language, culture, beliefs, and customs of the Mexican people. Unlike my mother and extended family who had migrated to the United States, I did not have to fear repatriation, deportation, or the loss of opportunity. Therefore, with deep gratitude and appreciation, I could once again nurture my roots and integrate my native culture into my existence as an individual, family member, and therapist.

My life experiences and work as a therapist in the El Paso/Juárez area have helped me to undergo this process and to understand the purpose of my return to *mi tierra* (my land). Perhaps this can be explained by an old Mexican wives' tale that states that the reason one returns to his or her homeland is because the person's birth placenta is buried close to where the person was born. This may also be a metaphor for understanding the strong pull to return to the motherland, roots, and nurturance.

Perhaps the same wives' tale applied to Cristina and Miguel, two Mexican-American children, ages seven and five, who were referred to me for evaluation and therapy by their school counselor. This referral was accepted through an agreement with the El Paso school system to provide pro bono therapy services to uninsured children and adolescents who may be at risk for future school drop out, gang involvement, or early pregnancy. During the first therapy session, Cristina and Miguel were accompanied to my office by their mother and their school counselor, who helped to explain the purpose of the referral and to offer support during this initial meeting. Both Cristina and Miguel were very shy and timid and spoke very little. They allowed their mother to speak for them and explain their present circumstances. The mother was very polite and respectful in her manner. In the Mexican family, children are taught to show *respeto* (respect) and deference to their parents by listening and not interrupting while their parents speak. The behavior of *respeto* is highly valued and is expected by parents and elders from their children. Thus, Cristina and Miguel were certainly behaving in a culturally acceptable manner. I, likewise, became aware that it was important to follow the mother's lead as she began to tell me her story and why she was asking for help for her children. I joined her in speaking Spanish and exhibiting *respeto* by listening carefully and valuing her decision to acquire assistance, especially in a setting which is nontraditional for an immigrant family.

The mother explained that she and her children had recently returned to El Paso after living in Houston for one year. She and her husband had separated due to marital problems and his increased drinking and violent behavior toward her and their children. She mentioned that this decision for separation had been an extremely traumatic one for her and her husband, as they had high hopes for *una buena vida* (a good life) in Houston. She and her husband had met in Juárez, where they were both born and reared. Their parents had migrated to Juárez from the interior of Mexico. During the early part of their marriage, they were generally content. However, after the children were born, the pressures of parenting and finances became increasingly stressful, especially in an underdeveloped country where unemployment and poverty are high.

Their dream to migrate to Houston, where the husband could work as a mechanic and earn good wages was a promising one, especially because his brother who had earlier migrated to Houston had written of his "good job and a weekly paycheck." However, the brother had not written of the difficulties and stressors related to the migration and acculturation process to a large American city that is highly competitive and in which the Mexican population is a minority. The mother mentioned that their excitement and high hopes of making a good life in the United States slowly began to deteriorate after her husband was laid off from his job after being employed for five months. His employer had not informed him that he was going to close his business in the next six months. Her husband was able to acquire a part-time job at a construction site as a helper, but the work was seasonal and the pay was poor. Even though the husband had a work visa, he felt fearful that he would be apprehended by the Immigration Service agents and detained for days. He had heard too many stories of this occurring to other immigrants, even those who had visas. He also did not know how to speak English well and was afraid that he would not be able to explain himself articulately if apprehended.

The mother reported that her husband gradually lost hope and began to drink more and more with his coworkers after work. She and her husband would fight when he returned to their small, one-bedroom apartment in an intoxicated state. She was not able to seek employment, as Miguel was not in school and he required parenting and medical care for frequent bronchitis and ear infections. The mother also felt inadequate, as she was not literate in English and was not able to fill out a work application. She had taken typing classes in a Juárez school and was literate in Spanish. Other than the brother-in-law in Houston, there were no extended family or friends that could provide help or support. Their situation seemed hopeless and unending. The mother explained that she finally asked her family in Juárez to send her money to return to El Paso after her husband lost his construction job and physically abused her and the children while in a drunken stupor. Even though it was extremely painful for her to leave her husband, she made this decision in order to protect her children.

Because the mother initially requested help for her children, treatment focused on Cristina and Miguel. To have focused on the mother's issues in the beginning may have not been culturally or socially acceptable due to the Mexican family rule of *marianismo*, i.e., that the mother be self-sacrificing and defer her needs to her children (Stevens, 1973). Thus, a play therapy session with Cristina and Miguel was held, and they were asked to draw a picture of whatever they wished. Cristina drew a picture of a puppy and herself. When asked to tell a story about this picture, she began to cry and stated, "Perdí mi perrito, Pepito" (I lost my puppy, Pepito). She explained that prior to relocating to El Paso, her eight-week-old puppy had been run over by a truck. She added that this puppy had become a friend and playmate to her. Miguel drew a picture of himself, his mother and father, and Cristina playing in a park together. He mentioned that he was happy when his family would go to the park and his father would push him on the swings. Cristina agreed, and both exclaimed that they missed their father very much. It was evident that the children were suffering from sadness, anxiety, and depression related to the separation from the father, the loss of their family unity, and relocation upheaval.

The presenting problem for this referral was that Cristina cried in the mornings prior to going to school, and while at school, would complain of stomachaches and headaches. Miguel's kindergarten teacher reported that he appeared sad, had difficulty in finishing his work, and would readily fight with the other children. Both were earning poor school grades and were having difficulty in socializing with their peers. The mother reported that her children often asked for their father and wanted to know when he was going to return home. The father would call the mother periodically and would ask her to return to Houston, promising that he would find another job. The mother was mistrustful and fearful of believing him, but she also did not want to return to a city where there were no extended family or friends. She mentioned that her first priority was to parent and care for her children well. After returning to El Paso, the mother and children lived with a maternal aunt and uncle who had agreed to help them and provide support. The children were also enrolled in bilingual education classes.

Throughout the therapy, I was immensely impressed with the mother's inner strength and fortitude to provide for her children and keep them in a school system where they would receive the type of education and opportunities that she and her husband had not received. The mother had completed eight years of education in Juárez, and her husband, six. In Mexico, only a sixth grade education is compulsory, and only the financially stable continue going to school. The mother reported that she was earning wages by taking in people's ironing and baking wedding cakes. Nevertheless, she appeared depressed, distraught, and fatigued. I recommended individual therapy for her, however, with the purpose of helping her children first. The mother also agreed, as we were building a positive and therapeutic relationship. Her individual therapy focused on providing support and empowering her to make changes in her life which would increase her chances for employment and financial security, e.g., enrolling in English classes, applying for U.S. citizenship, and acquiring Medicaid insurance and financial assistance for her children. Because the mother was suffering from a clinical depression, it was necessary to refer her for a medical evaluation. She agreed to see a family physician in Juárez whom she trusted, rather than going to a medical clinic in El Paso where she would have to fill out lengthy forms and answer intrusive questions. She also did not have medical insurance for treatment or medication. When she saw the family physician in Juárez, he prescribed an antidepressant which she was able to purchase for a nominal cost in Juárez.

In addition, family therapy for the mother and children was provided, helping them to undergo the grieving process concerning the separation from the father. Issues regarding the father's alcoholism were addressed, focusing on education and taking the blame away from the mother and children for his addiction. Cristina had blamed herself because she and Miguel had fought when the father was home. The mother had also blamed herself and believed that if she had been a better wife, her husband would have not drank. During the latter part of therapy, the mother and the children attended Al-Anon support groups which were facilitated in Spanish and by leaders who were also sensitive to the cultural norms.

During the therapy process, it was imperative to be aware of the impact of the family's cultural influence as related to their problem solving and decision making as separate from the family dysfunction. For example, the mother's decision to return to El Paso and to the support of her extended family would be considered appropriate due to the family interdependence and loyalty which are primary in the Mexican family as compared to the Anglo culture in which independence and individuation in the family are valued (Falicov, 1988). However, it is important to be aware that the mother's decision to return to the El Paso/Juárez area was also due to the deterioration of trust and attachment in her relationship with her husband. Other marital and family-of-origin issues and conflicts were factors in this problem as well.

Later, the husband returned to El Paso in an attempt to reconciliate with his family, but was not able to stop his compulsive drinking. With the support from Al-Anon, the mother was able to set limits on her husband's drinking and behavior. She decided not to attempt reconciliation until he acquired treatment. Treatment interventions for the husband were planned involving the parish priest and the husband's uncle, as per the mother's request. Unfortunately, the husband refused to enter a treatment program or attend AA meetings. This was a very difficult reality for the mother to accept, as marital separation and divorce in the Mexican family, as well as in the Catholic religion, are unacceptable.

Overall, therapy with this family was of a multimodal and systems approach which focused on the grieving process, relocation and adaptation to a new environment, and providing resources for economic security and family stability. The extended family's support proved to be crucial in helping the mother adapt to the El Paso area. The school counselor was effective in assisting the children to adapt in school by seeing them weekly for school-related counseling. Fortunately, the children were able to keep their native tongue and cultural identity while simultaneously learning English and the American culture and customs in school.

Eight months after therapy terminated, the mother, Cristina, and Miguel visited me at my office with a gift of *pan dulce* (Mexican sweet bread). Gratefully, I accepted and understood that it is common in the Mexican family for gifts and homemade items to be presented as a symbol of thanks and appreciation. The mother happily reported that both Cristina and Miguel had passed to the next grade and were not as fearful of being in school. Both were involved in a folklorico dance group, and Miguel was playing T-ball. The mother stated that she was taking English classes at a local community center and planned to take U.S. citizenship classes. She mentioned that she and her husband had attempted to reconciliate, but that this had failed. She added that she was not blaming herself for his alcoholism anymore, but that she hoped there would be a reconciliation in the future. The father visits the children sporadically. He was able to find a job in El Paso as a mechanic. The uncle with whom the family lives has taken an active role with Cristina and Miguel, and periodically takes them to the park or to the community swimming pool. Cristina and Miguel also visit their grandparents and other extended family in Juárez.

During their last visit, it was very heartwarming and rewarding to see Cristina and Miguel smiling, not depressed or traumatized as before. Before leaving, Cristina cheerfully stated, "Ya tengo otro perrito; lo llamé Pepito" (I have another dog; I named him Pepito). This seemed to be Cristina's way of metaphorically saying that she was healing from the separation and loss of her father and that others in her family, such as her aunt, uncle, and grandparents were helping to replace that loss and emptiness in her life.

In conclusion, it is my belief that clients and families who touch us the most are those who tap into our own family-of-origin experiences and issues. Family-of-origin theory such as that of Bowen emphasizes that in order to work effectively with families in therapy, it is important for the therapist to have identified and worked through his or her own family-of-origin issues and conflicts (Titelman, 1987). When this is not accomplished, there can be a danger of overinvolvement. Thus, it is necessary to allow family members to make their own choices and decisions without pressure from the therapist to behave in a certain manner. In working with this family, I was able to empathize and identify with their experience of separation, loss, and feelings of abandonment. This must have been akin to my mother's experience when her father abandoned the family before her family migrated to El Paso. Like my family, this family experienced trauma related to adaptation and acculturation into a new country and culture. Unlike my mother and myself, Cristina and Miguel were allowed to keep their native language in school without having to camouflage their identity, culture, and customs from those in authority. Like my family, they are proving to be survivors with a strong desire for equal opportunity, education, and growth in this country. I wish them well and God's blessings—Adiós!

BIBLIOGRAPHY

Falicov, C.J. (1982). Mexican families. In McGoldrick, M. Pearce, J.K., and Giordano, J. (Eds.), *Ethnicity and family therapy.* New York: Guilford.

Falicov, C.J. (1988). Learning to think culturally. In Liddle, H.A., Breunlin, D.C., and Schwartz, R.C. (Eds.), *Handbook of family therapy training and supervision.* New York: Guilford.

Jung, C.G. (1964). *Man and his symbols.* New York: Dell.

McGoldrick, M., Prieto N.G., Hines, P.M., and Lee, E. (1991). Ethnicity and family therapy. In Gurman, A.S. and Kniskern, D.P. (Eds.), *Handbook of family therapy,* Volume Two. New York: Brunner/Mazel.

Metz, L.C. (1989). *Border.* El Paso, Texas: Mangan Books.

Stevens, E. (1973). Marianismo: The other face of machismo. Cited in Falicov, C.J. (1982). Mexican families. In McGoldrick, M., Pearce, J.K., and Giordano, J. (Eds.), *Ethnicity and family therapy.* New York: Guilford.

Titelman, P. (1987). *The therapist's own family.* Northvale, New Jersey: Aronson.

Rules Will Be Made and Broken

James Morris

How could I have broken so many of my own rules about how therapy should be done? Everyone has a method, a manner in which they conduct therapy. In fact, teaching, writing, and talking about the rules of therapy constitutes the majority of our activities as therapists (except of course for the therapy itself). I fancied myself as one of those who took exception to the rules of the majority discourse. I included myself within the poststructuralist conversation that eschews rules. I didn't have rules! What I discovered from reflecting on my work with one family was that I did indeed have specific rules about therapy. Further, I realized that I had broken some of my own rules. Nonetheless, it was clear that my work with the family had proved successful. In an effort to figure it out, I wondered if there was something particularly different about the family?

Father and Mother had divorced some five years earlier after a marriage of about the same duration. They had one child, a son of eight years named Otto. Father and Mother were both originally from an eastern European country that is currently in the midst of a bloody civil war. Father, who was some twenty-five years older than Mother, had met her while on a visit to his homeland from the United States. They had married quickly and returned together to America. They lived on the west coast of the United States and enjoyed the first couple of years of their married life, culminating with the birth of Otto. Mother became homesick as well as a bit cramped under the control of her "fatherlike" husband. One thing led to another, which led to a separation and then divorce.

Mother had taken up with, and eventually married, a man she had met on a visit back to her homeland. Father had primary care of Otto, as Mother's resources were insufficient. Mother and her husband failed to return Otto to Father after a visit and it was several months before Otto and Father were reunited. Thus began an ongoing distrust between Mother and Father. Father and Otto subsequently moved to another state, and not long after, came to our agency requesting therapy. My therapeutic work with Father and Otto also included long-distance phone conversations and conference calls with Mother. Both parents had basically stopped speaking to each other except through attorneys, and expected me to mediate and relay messages. We worked together to orchestrate visits by Mother, which eventually proved to be the turning point toward a successful therapeutic outcome. Though this family certainly was interesting, they didn't seem that different from other families I had worked with. So I decided to examine these rules (which I had assumed I didn't have) and how I broke them.

First, there was the fact that I had met with the family for nearly two years. One of my rules about therapy is that it should be brief, lasting no more than three to six months. If I'm focused, adept, inviting, etc., then the family and I should be able to create solutions in a relatively short amount of time. In fact, this particular rule is widely held across disparate groups of therapists. In some circles, the briefness of therapy is assured by following clearly outlined and specific steps. I had experienced exasperation while working with the family because we were "late"—we should have been done already! I kept pressing on with the family even though I sometimes thought it was more like maintenance.

Next, I broke my rule that I should not meet with children alone. That is, I believed that the best possibility for change was when I worked with the family as a whole. I knew this rule was one not widely held in the field. There are a variety of opinions about who is required in order for therapy to work well. Nonetheless, I was particularly committed to this rule, especially when parents came in asking me to "fix" their kid(s), assuming they would not have to be part of the therapy. Father had asked me to meet with his son alone because of the trauma his son had experienced. (The son had been "kidnapped" by his biological mother and her husband against the biological father's wishes, and kept from his father for a period of months.) Dad said he was there to support his son, and it was clear from Dad that his son was to be the object of therapy. There were a couple of occasions when the son and I met alone together that eventually proved important for the overall therapeutic work. At the time, though, I didn't believe it amounted to much more than friendly chit-chat.

I have a rule that I should always think, speak, and act "possibility" with a family. That is, it is imperative that I take a stand for what is possible since there are so many negative voices the family endures, including their own voices. Yet, there I was, finding myself feeling like giving up with the family, feeling like the work was impossible. I would sometimes trance out during the session as I experienced a hopelessness of possibility. I had come to the point where I couldn't imagine that Mom and Dad, as divorced parents, could ever cooperate for the sake of their son. I kept this sense of impossibility to myself, though it must have been somewhat apparent to my colleagues.

I broke another rule I have about how therapy should be done when I agreed to act as a communication conduit between Mother and Father. This rule states clearly that family members, especially parents, should speak to each other directly. Mother lived in a distant city and requested that she be able to send letters for her son to me, and that I would then forward them to the son at therapy sessions. This arrangement was necessitated by the fact that Father would not reveal his mailing address to Mother. There had been a "kidnap" of the son by Mother and her husband some years earlier, and Father believed Mother might still try it again. So, when Mother asked me to act as a go-between, I discarded my rule and agreed to her request. I exacerbated my mistake when I agreed to, at Father's request, return one of Mother's letters that Father took exception to. It took several months before Mother called me again and accepted my apology. The breaking of this rule was particularly costly in terms of time and trust.

Finally, I believe it is best that I work in a nondirective manner with families. It is not that change will not occur when directed by the therapist, but such change will less likely include and honor the creative abilities of the family. I realize, of course, that this topic continues to be hotly debated in the field. In fact, a colleague, who is a skilled directive therapist, and I have done some work on the connections between directive and nondirective therapy. Nonetheless, I adhered to my nondirective stand with the family. It came as a surprise to me when I could take my frustration no longer and blasted Father with a good dose of "this is what you should do or things will stay the same." I believed I was justified in speaking this way to Dad. I had tried my nondirective best, and he was just not listening! Father stopped to listen to me, and then proceeded right on with what he had been saying all along. I sank back in my chair wondering if there was anything I could do to make a difference.

Against all odds, and with my broken rules, the outcome of our work together was quite successful. Mother and Father decided to once again speak to each other directly—in contrast to communicating with each other only through their attorneys (or through me). Thankfully, when I tried my hand as a go-between a second time, it was in the role of setting up conference calls with Mother and Father. It was during these calls that Mother and Father took their first tentative steps toward being reasonable with each other. Father apologized to his son for being overbearing. Mother gave up her attacks against Father. Son improved his schoolwork, experienced less anxiety about his folks, and stopped wetting the bed. The parents continue to cooperate for the well-being of their son, and have even been able to compliment each other about being good parents.

I'm left with how to explain such progress in the face of all the rules I've broken. One possibility is to simply admit I don't have very useful rules! Of course, that would necessarily imply there are better rules I might adopt. Another possibility is that the family did what it was going to do in spite of my rules—broken or kept. Who knows? I do know that the family was quite grateful for the work I had done with them. They said they couldn't imagine things turning out the way they had without me. It could be that all this talk about rules is yet another story I've created to explain how therapy works—or doesn't work!

I have a sense that there is a mystery in this work of therapy. However, since we have continued to persist in our belief that therapy is a science, conversations about mystery have been rarely entertained. Political and financial considerations demand that we know how and why therapy is successful. Rules are generated as a by-product of acting on the basis of knowledge. But what if we're really up against mystery? What sort of knowing would be possible in mystery? What sort of rules would be possible? Somehow, we are able to speak together with families in such ways that possibilities are created where none seem to exist. Maybe we don't even need all this talk about rules and explanations. Yet, I suppose we're hopelessly destined to keep trying!

Open Mouth, Insert Foot:
Two Tales of Dumb Mistakes
by Experienced (?) Family Therapists

Joseph L. Wetchler
Jerome Bercik

We have a confession to make. No matter how long we practice, we continue to make dumb mistakes. I suppose this would not be so bad, except that we are experienced family therapists. We have between us over forty years of practicing family therapy and over thirty-five years as supervisors. Each of us used to think we were alone in our ability to occasionally say really embarrassing things in therapy until one day, over coffee, we got up the courage to share our gaffes. What a relief to find that someone else could screw up just as badly!

With our newfound sense of relief, we decided to write an article about dumb things that family therapists have said in therapy. Perhaps this was a way of further ameliorating our sense of personal embarrassment, as misery does love company. Boy, was this a bad idea! After interviewing several experienced family therapists, we found that none of them had ever said a stupid thing in therapy in their whole lives! Our worst fears had been realized: we were the only two therapists to ever make these types of mistakes! (Of course, there is the possibility that all of our colleagues lied to us.)

We have found that there is usefulness in experiencing complete embarrassment as a therapist. When our students and trainees experience failures in therapy, we have just the stories to pick them up. It is amazing how sharing our mistakes helps our trainees place their situations in perspective. Needless to say, we have a good laugh and go back to our business. We offer these two tales in hopes that those supervisors who have never said a foolish thing in therapy can use our mistakes to help their trainees feel better about their own work.

JOE'S DUMB TALE

I once worked with a family in which two brothers in their early twenties had repeatedly engaged in sexual activity with their thirteen-year-old sister. This had gone on for several years until the girl shared this with her school counselor. Even though the family was mandated to therapy by child protective services, they were committed to resolving this problem. They had numerous strengths and were willing to work. Therapy had proceeded smoothly, with the parents being able to ensure the safety of the daughter and set limits on their sons' behavior; the sons had accepted responsibility for their actions and apologized to their sister; and the daughter realized that she had done nothing to deserve her abuse.

Midway through the therapy, the sons reported their father had pulled them aside to have a discussion about sex. This was the first time he had ever done so. While the boys felt they were a bit old for this discussion, they greatly appreciated what their father had done, and found it to be a good example of "better late than never." In a subsequent session, the father expressed remorse that had he not had this talk earlier. Using a sports analogy, he stated that he could not call this a victory, but perhaps it was a tie. In an attempt to put a more positive spin on the situation, and without thinking, I responded, "They say a tie is like kissing your sister, but I think you have a victory!!!"

After thinking, "Oh my God, did I really say that?" and eventually crawling out from under my desk, I apologized for my mistake and we completed the session. Guess what happened? Nobody died from my comment! In fact, the family continued to come for therapy, and we eventually had an extremely positive outcome. I dodged a bullet, and would like to say I am somewhat wiser, but I am sure I will say something equally ridiculous in the future.

JERRY'S DUMBER TALE

I once worked with a veteran who was experiencing severe depression after losing his legs in war. He lived with his mother, who had made the request for therapy. She claimed that her son would not come to see me, yet begged me to help him. A subsequent phone call proved her correct, as the son refused my help. Because the mother was desperate, I agreed to make a home visit.

I was nervous when I arrived at the family's home. While my office felt safe, I was not used to doing therapy in my clients' homes. The mother answered the door and led me to the son's room, where he was asleep. It certainly was a gloomy place. The lights were dim, the shades were drawn, and a wheelchair with a prosthesis in it sat near his bed. As I entered the room, the mother again begged me to help her son. She then left the room.

With much trepidation, I approached the son's bed and tapped him on the shoulder. As he awoke, he angrily told me to get lost. With my heart racing, I said, "Hello, I am Jerry Bercik. I have come to talk with you and help you get back on your feet!"

I couldn't believe what I had just said. I immediately apologized for my mistake. I was grateful that the room was so dark that he could not see how embarrassed I was. While my opening comments would never be seen in an introductory chapter on joining, a most amazing thing happened: the man chuckled and told me everything was okay. We had a relatively smooth first session and a very productive therapy. We eventually moved our sessions from his home to my office. On the last day of therapy, he showed up with a war buddy. As he introduced us, he told his friend that he wanted him to meet the guy who said he could help him get back on his feet!

DISCUSSION

How did these cases end up being successful? With the severity of our mistakes, we had assumed our clients would never want to see us again. Yet, in both situations, our clients returned and had successful therapies. Perhaps we should claim that we have developed an amazing new family therapy technique called the "Open Mouth, Insert Foot Maneuver." Maybe we are on the verge of developing a new theory of family therapy. Stranger things have happened . . . but we doubt it.

It is interesting to us what a tortuous path therapy can take. At one moment, we are master therapists, and the next, we fall on our faces. What must our clients think as they wrestle with their own demons? How can they trust their therapist if he/she messes up in the same way as they do? If there is a positive spin on all of this, perhaps it is that in these situations our clients get to see us as complete people, with both our strengths and weaknesses. We have learned through experience (?) that masterful technique and theoretical knowledge cannot compensate for the lack of a caring relationship. While we are not encouraging family therapists to purposefully say stupid things, we are aware that no person or situation is perfect, and the best we can hope for is to overcome adversity. This reminds us of the old saying, "While the worst part of therapy is that it is conducted by human beings . . . it is also the best."

Some Things You Just Can't Ignore

Frank N. Thomas
Kent Slayton

I (Kent) came into the observation room on a typical "team" night at my agency. The shock was immediate: all of my team members behind the one-way mirror were laying on the floor, doubled over in laughter and unable to speak. One team member, who was holding his stomach and shedding tears, pointed at the mirror and continued his fetal-position hysterics. So, unable to get a word out of anyone else, I simply walked over to the mirror and began to observe the session that was in progress.

In the therapy room, a young female therapist was casually conversing with a rather large elderly female client. There was nothing funny or disturbing about my first minute of observation—two people were simply talking comfortably with one another about personal concerns. All of a sudden, the left side of the client's blouse began to wriggle and gyrate! I was taken aback with the movement, not knowing what to make of it until, a few seconds later, a *Chihuahua* popped its head out of the top of the client's blouse and began to pant! The funniest part of the scenario was that this inexperienced therapist, who was learning to "join" with clients and "convey appropriate empathy and support," *did not respond in any way to the dog's sudden appearance!* As I hit the floor in hysterics, all I could see in my mind's eye was this therapist's pose of concern with a facial expression that exuded quiet understanding, undaunted by blouse wiggling or the sudden appearance of a canine client!

Needless to say, we had wonderful discussions about teams, appropriate responses, and selective blindness for the rest of the year!

Kent's story emerged during a luncheon that I (FNT) hosted at the Texas Association for Marriage and Family Therapy (TAMFT) Annual Conference a few years ago. The topic of discussion was "Humor in Therapy," and I don't think I've laughed as hard with a table full of strangers before or since . . . absurdity is a part of every person's life, and learning to laugh at ourselves is good for the soul.

A New Approach to Suicidal Patients

Edward J. Weiner

About fiifteen years ago, I encountered my first suicidal patient, a man I'll call John. I was called by John's partner, who said John was suicidal and had left a suicide note. I called John on the phone and told him that I knew about the note and needed him in my office immediately. I also told him that if he did not arrive in thirty minutes, I was sending the police out to get him. He arrived at my office within the half hour. When he arrived, I locked the doors to my office and apologized, saying, "John, I'm sorry, but I'm going to have to drive you to the hospital for your own safety." He agreed to accompany me to the hospital, which was a mere quarter of a mile away . . . thus begins the interesting part!

I am 5'7"; and John was 6'3". I put him in my red Alpha Romeo and drove him across the street at fifty miles per hour, through an S-turn, over some railroad tracks, and through a red light. In that quarter-mile trip, John bumped his head on the roof several times. When we arrived at the emergency room, John's pupils were dilated and he was visibly shaking.

John was in the hospital's psychiatric unit for one week. He later told his therapy group that the hospitalization was really redundant—when I took the S-turn at fifty miles per hour over the railroad tracks, he knew then how badly he wanted to live and said that he was probably cured of suicidal tendencies at that point!

First Impressions:
Doctor, You Are Human

Donald K. Granvold

I opened the door to the waiting room and greeted my client. She appeared visibly anxious to meet me for the first time. I invited Joey, a twenty-two-year-old English teacher, into my office, and on the way down the hall, asked if she would like some coffee or water. Observing the Coke machine in the coffee room, she said, "Thanks, I'll just buy a Coke." While Joey fed the Coke machine her change, I put my coffee cup under the spout of the coffee urn located adjacent to the Coke machine. Joey had trouble getting the Coke machine to take her change. I turned to offer assistance, thinking the coffee spout switch was on "automatic shut off." After a minute or so, I managed to get Joey's Coke and turned to find my coffee cup overflowing—the spout switch had been on lock, and did not automatically shut off! The countertop was covered with coffee and a puddle stood in front of the cabinet. I said with a smile, "Joey, my cup literally runneth over! I'll bet you are wondering how I can possibly be of any help to you; I can't even pour coffee!"

Joey grabbed my shoulder and said, "I'm so glad you did that. I've been so scared to come see you!" A gentle smile came over her face and I could feel her sense of relief.

First impressions are as important in counseling as they are in other areas of life. Showing one's human flaws, foibles, and fallibility may actually make us as therapists more accessible to our clients. The readiness to laugh at oneself when one experiences human folly and self-created calamity is an important quality to be modeled by therapists. While apparently paradoxical, displays of imperfection may be far more effective in engaging the client than a well-rehearsed, flawlessly presented introduction to counseling. Or perhaps all of the above is merely a rationalization for my momentary lapse of *savoir faire*!

Help Me Rock the Boat

Thorana S. Nelson

My client grew up in a very dysfunctional household. Not only did she not know how to set boundaries for herself, she was often very unsure about what boundaries were or when they were appropriate, especially for herself. This was so in nearly every one of her relationships: family of origin, her husband and his family, and work. She had very few friends, and was beginning to recognize that her inability to understand others' boundaries had something to do with that. She was very afraid of men and of anyone she perceived as being in authority or "better" than she, which was nearly everyone.

We had been working on how to recognize boundaries; setting them was just beginning to be a glimmer in her therapeutic imagination. She especially wanted to become more assertive at work. She was the only clerical person in her office, under three staff workers and a boss, but was unable to recognize that this put her in a position of power, given how much knowledge she had by virtue of her position. She was being sexually harassed by a male member of the staff, but was unwilling to approach the boss or anyone else about this. I had framed this situation as an opportunity for her to practice her assertiveness skills, and even to use some humor to get the man to back off, since she was afraid that more formal steps would backfire on her. We had used reason to help her calm down in other situations ("when your mother-in-law asks if you think you have put enough salt in the stew, pretend it's a straightforward question rather than a criticism") and, on occasion, fantasy ("think about what it would be like if you 'accidentally' spilled salt into the stew"). We had some success with these ideas. She had trouble calming down enough to think of these things, however. So, she had begun to put little toys on her desk as metaphorical reminders of what we talked about. I had given her a small wooden egg as a reminder that she was the one to decide when and how she was going to peck her way out of her shell.

We talked about how she was afraid of "rocking the boat" at work, that saying or doing anything might make the others or her boss angry and, perhaps, get her fired. She knew in her head that this was highly unlikely; the boss was clearly fond of her and had even made covert comments about the male staff worker. My client couldn't seem to talk with her boss about what was happening, however. I sympathized: I think we all have had such situations in our lives. I asked her what would help her remember that she was really in charge of the boat most of the time, since the other staff depended upon her for her knowledge. She bought a little toy boat and put it on her desk to help remind her of her strategies for remaining calm and using her head.

One day, she called me. "Ooh, I think I'm getting seasick," she said. "Have you tried Dramamine?" I asked. She laughed and said, "No, but that gives me an idea." I didn't hear from her again until the next session, which I had eagerly anticipated. When she arrived, I couldn't contain myself. "What did you do?!?" I asked. The thought of her doing anything was amazing to me, but perhaps she really had grown.

"Well," she began, "the first thing I did was get some Tylenol out of my purse and put it on my desk to remind me what a pain in the neck he is. Then, I realized that he was more of a pain in the butt than neck, so I fantasized about getting some Preparation H for him as a gift. I started to laugh so hard, the boss came out to see what was going on. I got real flustered, because I just couldn't tell her what was going on. So, I got up to make some coffee instead and fantasized about 'spilling' it on the jerk. This idea struck me as funny and one that I could tell my boss about because I think she knew I was mad at him. She agreed (emphasize agreed) [my client was absolutely amazed that her boss could talk to her this way—as an equal] and we had a great time joking about this guy. About that time, he came in and wanted to know what was going on and we both burst out laughing.

"The really funny thing, though, is that the next day, when he asked me to fix his coffee, I really did spill it on him!"

Behind and Beyond a Locked Door

Marjorie Roberts

A number of experiences in my work as a therapist have paved the way for me to embrace a more collaborative approach to clinical work than was suggested by my earlier training. This collaborative approach was evolving in my work long before I had a theoretical orientation on which to hang it. For me, collaboration in clinical work includes shared expertise with clients, as well as shared leadership and followership and a great deal of the use of serendipity.

Some years ago, I was working with a middle-aged couple who had been married for twenty years. My initial contact had been with the husband, who addressed several issues of concern, including his dissatisfaction with both his career and his relationship with his wife. After several meetings, we both agreed that it would be useful to include his wife in future meetings. He had conveyed his perception that the relationship was stuck and limiting, but that he was resigned to stay.

While the couple had lived for most of their marriage in Northeastern United States, they came from very diverse cultural backgrounds. Mary, the wife, had been born in Ireland, but had moved to the United States to work for an airline during her young adult years, while her family remained in Ireland. Martin, her husband, had been born in Mexico and moved to the United States to pursue an advanced degree in physics; he was now working in the defense industry, literally as a rocket scientist. For all of their differences, their issues and struggles were somewhat familiar. Mary complained that Martin was absorbed in his work, left piles of papers around the house, and was not very helpful or handy at home. Martin complained that Mary was not romantic, purchased more clothes than were necessary, and was raising their nineteen-year-old daughter to be "too American." He worried that their daughter was not serious enough about her education, and like her mother, purchased too many clothes.

I remember being very aware of the complexity of their issues, to include culture, context, and life-cycle issues. While they seemed engaged in our work, our movement was very slow, and possibly stuck. One morning at the conclusion of our meeting, as they were leaving, we discovered that the deadbolt lock on the metal door of my office had jammed. The office was on the second floor of an old Salem, Massachusetts building which was over one hundred years old. The view outside of my window had always delighted me since it overlooked a swimming pool in a neighbor's yard. On warm summer days, I had fantasized that I could simply dive into the pool from my window. However, on this March morning, not even this fantasy offered comfort.

After each of the three of us tried in succession to open the door, we all agreed that we were locked in. I phoned the receptionist in the building, who immediately notified the four agency directors, who assembled outside of my door. They included two psychologists, one CEO, and the Director of the Emergency Services Team. After each in turn pushed and attempted to twist the doorknob, they agreed that the door was in fact locked. As discretely as possible, with probing questions shouted through the door, they attempted to assess an appropriate intervention in terms of concerns about psychological or physical risk to the three of us, as we were confined together. The level of intervention that was determined to be appropriate was quite ordinary—a locksmith was phoned, but alas, he would not be available for four hours. The directors dispersed and offered to check back with us periodically.

I decided to think of the day in smaller increments rather than the emerging bigger picture. I phoned my next scheduled appointment and matter-of-factly said, "I am sorry that I cannot meet with you today because I am locked in my office." I have a long-lasting gratitude for the client who simply accepted my explanation without inference, interpretation, or questioning. Each time that I remember this phone call, I laugh quite hardily at myself. What seemed like a reasonable description of my reality must have seemed strange, indeed, to the client on the other end of the phone.

In the meantime, my rocket scientist client asked me if I had any tools in the office. A quick survey of my inventory unearthed the following "high tech" equipment: tinker toys, a flat metal hinge from a child's easel, paper clips, and a small paper hole puncher. Mary checked the contents of her purse and found more paper clips, keys, and a nail file. There were no hacksaws, blowtorches, or crowbars to be found.

In retrospect, I remember how easily we shifted our focus from therapy, in which it was agreed upon that I would provide some structure, to a new focus of freeing ourselves from the office. Martin took the lead in trying to unjam the lock while Mary and I looked for more "tools," offered words of support, and looked on with curiosity and hope.

In fact, the rocket scientist did unjam the lock with a tool that many therapists may possess without knowing of its power: the flat metal hinge from the easel. We would later learn that he simultaneously freed us from my office and from the stuckness in our therapeutic work. The couple returned (courageously and empowered by the knowledge that they would find a way out if we became locked in again) for one or two meetings following this eventful morning. They reported placing much less significance to Martin's leadership and to our shared collaboration in freeing ourselves than did I. However, both described increased satisfaction with their relationship. Mary also casually mentioned that she appreciated Martin's handiness and helpful behavior at home.

My morning of confinement with Martin and Mary provided a wonderful lesson to me in shared expertise as well as in serendipity. Allowing myself to be a follower at times and to be open to learn from and with my clients continues to be formative to my clinical work. An absolute insistence on the leadership role might have led to longer term stuckness both behind the dead-bolt door and in our clinical work.

THERAPY WITH MEDICAL ISSUES, DEATH, AND DYING

Standing on Her Own Two Feet: Relying on Our Clients Rather Than Our Theories

Michael Durrant

Rebecca came to my office with her mother for support—literally. This eleven-year-old girl half-staggered and was half-carried through the front door and flopped onto a waiting room chair. A few minutes later, Mrs. Harrison said to her daughter, "Come on, up you go. He's ready for us now." There began a process of Rebecca struggling to her feet, groaning quietly as she grabbed for her mother's arm, and barely putting her weight on the floor as they moved slowly toward the office door. I had never thought of the journey from waiting room to office as particularly long; however, on this day, the twenty or so feet seemed a vast distance. Mrs. Harrison had obviously become used to assisting her daughter in this way and offered gentle encouragement as they navigated the short corridor. Rebecca braced herself against the walls of the narrow passageway, taking a little weight off her mother for a few steps, and eventually they were both seated, looking exhausted.

Once the physical difficulty of getting to the room was over, Rebecca and her mother were both eager to proceed and talked willingly and cooperatively. At this point, I had no information about why this mother and daughter were consulting me, and I gave only a cursory glance to the physician's letter Mrs. Harrison handed me as we began. Rebecca was, I learned, one of three children, all girls and reasonably close to each other in age. Mother was not in paid employment, but was involved in various school, community, and church activities; and father had a management position within an engineering industry. Rebecca was happy to tell me about school, where she performed well academically, about her love of books and dance, and about the family's two goldfish (named Gordon and Fang). My impression was of a polite but gregarious girl—apparently with some physical disability—and a supportive mother. I was wondering what could possibly have brought them to see me.

"What do you think would be helpful for me to know about what brings you here?" I asked to neither of them in particular. "'Cause I get dizzy," Rebecca replied quickly. When I enquired further, she told me that she feels dizzy all the time, gets headaches and blurred vision, and cannot walk without falling over. At this point, mother handed me an impressive-looking collection of papers, saying, "Here are the reports; it's been going on for a year and a half now and we've been to see lots of people. Would you like a copy of these?" I noted that there were two reports, one from a prominent pediatric neurologist and one from the child psychiatry department of a large hospital; however, I put these aside as mother was still talking.

"It sort of comes and goes; you know, it might be a few hours or a week or two, then it might go away for a few weeks, but this is the longest it's been. She hasn't been able to walk for six weeks now, and it seems to be getting worse. The frustrating thing is not really knowing what it is. Dr. Richardson said she couldn't find anything, so it must be an emotional problem, but I don't know what."

I commented to Rebecca, "I saw how hard it was for you to walk in here. Is that pretty much how it is most of the time? It must be a real nuisance for you—and for Mum—if that's what it's like."

"I hate it; it's a big, big nuisance. I can't play netball and I can't do my ballet, 'cause I just get dizzy and fall over," said Rebecca.

Mother added, "It doesn't seem to have affected her at school too much—that is, she still gets on with her work and still has her friends, but they are getting tired of having Rebecca lean on them any time she has to walk from one room to another."

In my mind I had been wondering if some well-placed questions about exceptions might reveal that the dizziness and walking difficulty were less when Rebecca was at school and this might provide the way in to constructing a solution. I mentally crossed off that possibility, realizing that the problem was apparently fairly pervasive, and "tuned in" again as mother was saying, ". . . seventeen months now, since just after her sister died, and it has been fairly constant, you know, coming and going ever since then."

Since her sister died!

It was interesting that neither Rebecca nor her mother had mentioned a deceased sibling, either whilst I was asking general information about the family or since we had been discussing the dizziness and falling over problem. Thus, I thought, it was important that I not suddenly seize on this lest I be attributing greater importance to it than they perceived it to have.

Matter-of-factly, I asked, "Oh, so you had another child?" Equally matter-of-factly, mother replied, "Yes, Julie would have been ten— she was only a year or so younger than Rebecca—she died just over a year and a half ago from cancer." She went on to explain that Rebecca's first bout of dizziness was two months after her sister's death, and that it had recurred every few weeks ever since. Each time, she was fairly constantly dizzy and usually unable to walk without assistance.

I noted that when Julie's death had been mentioned, both Rebecca and her mother had become a little quieter. The atmosphere in the room was, appropriately I thought, a little subdued. At the same time, the discussion moved on to their current concerns fairly easily, and I decided it was important that I follow their lead rather than imposing some view of what was significant.

Following a fairly standard solution-focused therapy plan, I proceeded to pose the miracle question* and Rebecca was quite forthcoming about her "miracle picture." Not only did she mention the

---

*"Suppose that one night, while you were asleep, there was a miracle, and this problem was solved. How would you know? What would be different?" (de Shazer, 1988, p. 5).

obvious differences (walking easily, not holding on to people, etc.), but she was able to broaden this to include such things as being happier, cooperating more at home, and not fighting with her younger sister. Her mother was less forthcoming, but seemed to be able to begin to imagine the day after the miracle. Given that we had developed a fairly complete picture of the miracle, and that Rebecca had seemed quite enthusiastic about it, I decided that a "pick two days and pretend the miracle has happened" task followed naturally from our discussion.

Later that day, I finally read through the physician's letter and the reports. All mentioned the sister's death prominently and saw it as *the* reason for Rebecca's problem. The physician's letter said, simply, "The problem relates to the loss of her sister." The neurologist's report concluded, "there is no organic basis for her symptoms, and they are probably psychosomatic in origin, most likely related to her sister's death." The psychiatry report concluded, "Rebecca's symptoms are conversion-like symptoms and her ataxia is functional ataxia . . . The family has not been able to adequately mourn Julie's death and Rebecca's symptoms are a manifestation of the intense anxiety that all family members feel about confronting the sad and angry feelings related to the loss of Julie."

I was struck by the presumptuousness of these conclusions and the automatic assumption that, if there had been a significant traumatic event in the family's recent past, it must be the cause of whatever symptoms now presented. This represented, to me, the worst of the "expert diagnosis syndrome," wherein professionals believe they know better than clients. The psychiatry report's recommendations continued in this vein: "I recommend family therapy so that the loss of Julie can be worked through in a family context. All family members need help in being able to express their feelings." I found myself beginning to feel angry at the prescriptiveness of this recommendation. What if they don't *want* to express their feelings in this way? Who are we to decide that they have not "worked through" this loss? After all, in our first interview, they had not seemed to afford great significance to Julie's death and did not seem to see it as related. For me to decide that this should be the agenda would be imposing my prescription. Thus, my righteous indignation at the oppressive nature of so-called "traditional" approaches led to my determination that I would pursue this one in a "pure" solution-focused brief therapy manner. This would be much more respectful of my clients.

When Rebecca and her mother returned a week later, I was sure that she moved just a little more easily as she shuffled into my office—however, it might have been wishful thinking on my part! To my question of "What's better?" both Rebecca and her mother recounted some improvements. Rebecca said she had felt less dizzy overall, had not had any "really bad days," and she had walked further without holding on to things. They both agreed that these were improvements, but Rebecca and her mother were a little vague and I found it hard to get them to elaborate on them.

Remembering that Rebecca had seemed enthusiastic about the pretending task, I wondered how successful mother had been at noticing Rebecca's pretend days. Rebecca seemed to delight in pronouncing her mother wrong and proceeded to explain that on her miracle days, she had run down the stairs, not held on when walking in the house, and had been able to prepare her breakfast without holding on to anything. These seemed major steps forward to me— particularly running down the stairs. Mother agreed that these had been noticeable and encouraging improvements and tried to brush off the fact that she must have forgotten which days they were, although she went on to say that it had been hard to identify specific days because her daughter had been noticeably happier throughout the week and had been generally moving more easily.

I smiled to myself, feeling vindicated in my decision to reject the complications of the more traditional approach. Sticking with the problem as presented and focusing on how the clients wanted it to be different was quickly achieving results.

We talked more about the week and the many ways in which things had been better and, when Rebecca and her mother left with my suggestion that they "keep doing whatever it is you have been doing," they seemed enthusiastic and I was excited.

Two weeks later, my asking "What's better?" yielded a vague description of "some days there has been less hanging onto things." That was it. Both agreed that things had been okay, and even that some of the improvements from the last session had continued, but they could not elaborate on the changes. The mood of the session was flat and frustrating as I reiterated the changes they had reported previously and sought to find out more detail about when they had seen similar things in this past week. The frustrating thing was that they were *not* saying that things were worse; they were just not saying much at all.

I asked about small signs that would show that the changes were continuing. Rebecca was able to talk about walking a little further without holding onto something. We were able to describe how far she could now walk unaided and how much further such a small sign of progress would be. She was cooperative and seemed to be able to envisage further change without too much difficulty; she still seemed to be able to describe how further change would make things better for herself; she just didn't seem very interested in it!

My response to this session was a mixture of puzzlement and frustration. I was sure we were on the right track, and the changes between the first and second session had seemed to confirm this, yet this last session had me feeling terribly stuck. I decided it must be an aberration and awaited the fourth session, two weeks later.

If the third session had been hard work, the fourth was downright torpid. Again, the improvements had "kind of continued"; however, neither mother nor daughter could detail anything about these improvements, nor had either showed the slightest enthusiasm or pleasure. Was it my imagination, or had Rebecca seemed to be relying even more on her mother when she came into my room?

I was aware of the importance of my not becoming more enthusiastic about the changes than they, and of not trying to convince them that things were better, so I patiently and persistently asked gentle questions about various activities and the possibility that there had been some improvement in these. I even began to regret my previous public statements about no longer believing in the concept of "resistance," as Rebecca seemed grudgingly to admit small changes and her mother seemed to get more and more into a "yes, but" mode.

It seemed that I could not ignore the frustration in the room that was almost palpable; I had to make some comment. Worried that our seeming impasse might be interpreted by some as evidence that I had ignored the "real problem," I suggested the following:

I guess it must be frustrating for both of you that things don't seem to be changing very quickly, particularly after the major achievements you had between our first and second sessions. I can see how much you want things to be different and I remember how proud of yourself you were, Rebecca, when you were able to tell me about running down the stairs. You knew that you had done it. You had done it by trying, not by anything complex that a psychologist did.

So how do we make sense of things feeling stuck again? It seems to me that there are two possibilities, and I'll need you to tell me which you think is the right one. One possibility is that we just got a bit carried away after our second meeting. You know, we all got excited by the changes you had made and we kind of expected that they would continue at that same rate. I got carried away and forgot to warn you that changing has its ups and downs, so when things slowed down it was easy for all of us to be disappointed. Now, if this is right, I guess it's a matter of just persevering, of figuring out small steps you can take to keep moving forward.

Now, some people would say that that possibility is too easy. Even though you managed those huge changes after our first session, some people would say that it is much more serious than that. These people would say that this problem has something to do with your sister's death and that the only way for us to get things moving is to talk about that. Now, I know that this might seem unnecessarily complicated, but that's what some people would say. They might even suggest that you are telling us that the family has not properly dealt with Julie's death and that what we need to do is have everyone here and talk about it.

Looking back on this now, perhaps my wording of the options was just a little weighted. However, there had been no indication that Rebecca or her mother saw any link between Julie's death and the current problem, so giving them this choice would hopefully serve to get us back on our solution-focused track.

Before I even finished my last sentence, "So, maybe you need to think about . . . " Rebecca sat up and said, "Get them all in."

"Huh?" I asked.

"Yep, get them all in here and talk about Julie," she said.

"That's what you think we need to do?" I asked.

"Yep!" Rebecca responded.

"And that's what you think might be the most helpful thing, right now?" I continued, not quite knowing what had gone wrong with the script I'd thought we were following.

"Uh huh!" Rebecca replied, sounding increasingly certain.

"Oh, okay. So do you think that's something we need to do at this point, or should we wait until we've got this walking problem figured out?" I wondered.

"No, at the next appointment," Rebecca stated with certainty.

We made an appointment for a week later. Mrs. Harrison explained that her husband had only recently started a new job and would find it difficult to take time off but that, if Rebecca wanted him to, Mrs. Harrison was sure her husband would find a way. They left, with Rebecca having obvious difficulty negotiating the walk, leaving me somewhat dumbfounded. This wasn't the way I had envisaged things would proceed. I certainly had not intended to find myself involved in a therapy session that was designed to "work through" and "come to terms with" the feelings of the various family members about Julie's death. I was not looking forward to the next session; I wasn't even sure if I knew what to do.

The following Wednesday was one of those days that drags. Each time I looked in my appointment book, I was reminded that the Harrison family was coming at 4 p.m. and I began to dread this more and more. At five minutes to four o'clock, the door burst open. With a broad grin on her face, Rebecca said, "Hi!" as she half-walked and half-waltzed through the door. Her parents and sisters followed a short distance behind, a fact which just made even more clear that Rebecca was walking unassisted. As she walked around my waiting room, it struck me that Rebecca had raced ahead of her family and hurried into my office not to show off that she was now walking (for she seemed hardly to give this a thought) but because she was looking forward to the session.

After we were all seated, it struck me that I was sitting amongst five people who appeared happy, seemed to be getting on well, and seemed to be a "normal family." Somehow, it did not seem appropriate to suddenly encourage them to express their feelings of grief, upset, or whatever. So I began by asking all, on a scale of zero to ten, how well they thought they had dealt with Julie's death as a family. All rated the family's success at around eight—except Rebecca, who rated it at nine-and-a-half. The obvious question to them seemed to be, "How did you manage to do it so well?" We had a pleasant, active, if still fairly general discussion about how the family had been able to support one another, had got on with life, still talked about Julie from time to time, and still missed her. It was hardly catharsis; the discussion was still light and, in some places, perhaps superficial. They did not "work through" their grief, or "come to terms with their loss" there in my office, so much as pleasantly agree with one another that, as a family, they were doing okay.

After only thirty-five minutes or so, it seemed that we had naturally exhausted the subject and Rebecca was anxious to leave. We shook hands as Mr. and Mrs. Harrison assured me that they and Rebecca did not feel the need for a further appointment.

So, in the end, we did not embark on a process whereby "the loss of Julie can be worked through in a family context [and] all family members [can get] help in being able to express their feelings." Yet, somehow, the anticipation that we were going to do something like that was sufficient to enable Rebecca literally to stride forward. Even when we did not do that, her gains continued. I really have no idea what it was that brought about the change, except perhaps that I listened to my client.

A few months later, I sat in the audience as one of my children sang in a concert performed by children from a number of different schools in the area. A few items later, I could not help but be struck by a dance item from another school. As the curtain opened, at the front of the stage was a familiar eleven-year-old girl, perfectly balanced on one foot—not holding onto anything for support.

BIBLIOGRAPHY

de Shazer, S. (1988). *Clues: Investigating Solutions in Brief Therapy.* New York: Norton.

Living with Dying:
Stories of Working with Dying Patients
and Their Families

Kristin A. Wright

I live continually with death. I myself am not actively dying—at least no more so than anyone moving toward an eventual but yet undetermined rendezvous with death. However, I am in the middle of a dissertation on death and dying, and I have experienced the recent deaths of several friends and family members. I also see many clients (and their families) who are facing an imminent end. Still, I do not consider myself an expert—the only experts in dying are those who are actively involved in the process.

Through both my personal and professional experiences, I understand the time approaching death as very special: it is painful for the dying person and his or her family members, but with minimal involvement by someone who can attune to them, it can also be meaningful and healing. Previously, I asked myself, "What could I possibly offer to clients who were terminally ill?" I was not an expert on dying. Through my conversations with these patients and their families, however, I was surprised to learn that being an "expert" was not what was necessary or even useful. By not assuming I know best, I am able to sit with patients, hear their struggles, and possibly offer an alternative perspective which may be healing or helpful. Although many therapists believe it is necessary to manhandle dying patients such that they progress through stages of coping, I find this viewpoint both inaccurate and disrespectful.

The author gratefully acknowledges Douglas Flemons, PhD, for his helpful suggestions and comments. Names of clients have been changed to protect confidentiality.

115

Instead, as the following stories reflect, I follow a minimalist approach in which families teach me how I can be helpful to them.

I was asked to meet with the O'Hara family, who were described as having difficulty adjusting to Mr. O'Hara's terminal diagnosis. Mr. Michael O'Hara was a seventy-eight-year-old man who was diagnosed with metastatic melanoma and had a life expectancy of only months. During an interdisciplinary staff meeting, several hospice staff members expressed their feelings of frustration regarding Mrs. O'Hara's desire to place her husband in a nursing home. The staff members believed that since Mr. O'Hara's wife was relatively young (she was fifty) and only worked part-time, she could appropriately handle Mr. O'Hara's care in their home with occasional supportive services.

The nursing staff "prepared" me for my meeting with Mr. O'Hara, describing him as "hateful" and verbally abusive toward his family. At the same time, they were saddened by Mrs. O'Hara's desire to place her husband in a nursing home, as they believed she was abandoning him in his time of need. The staff members were hopeful that I would be able to convince Mrs. O'Hara to keep her husband at home. As much as I hated the stereotypical picture we all have in our heads of someone wasting away alone in a nursing home, I knew that trying to "convince" Mrs. O'Hara of anything was not going to be useful. I recall reminding myself before I went to the O'Hara home, "A nursing home may be what is best for this family."

Upon my initial visit to the O'Hara home, I clearly heard the loud voice of Mr. O'Hara yelling for his wife's assistance as I approached the family's front door. I introduced myself to Mr. O'Hara, who immediately questioned me regarding my Irish heritage and was pleased when I confirmed his guess that I, too, was of Irish descent.

Michael sat in a living room recliner, the one place which seemed to offer some relief from his pain. His cancer had metastasized to various organs and was slowly whittling away at a man who, at one time, was strong and independent. During this visit, I talked with Mr. O'Hara and his wife, who wept off and on as she attempted to cook dinner. As Mrs. O'Hara prepared the meal, I sat at the kitchen table with Mr. O'Hara and listened to them both reminisce about happier times. Mr. O'Hara recalled how he and his wife had met years ago, and he reminded her that she had been attracted to his military uniform and his wonderful sense of humor. Expressing apparent appreciation and love, Mrs. O'Hara recalled many stories of their courtship and subsequent marriage. Most notably, she reflected upon how Mr. O'Hara had become a father to her two daughters from a previous marriage, treating them "as if they were his own."

The O'Haras had recently moved to Florida and were, therefore, separated from the support system of many friends and family members who remained "up north." Mr. and Mrs. O'Hara shared two children from their marriage, Michael Jr., who was sixteen years of age and Anna who was twelve. As Mr. O'Hara's condition deteriorated, his wife became more concerned about their children witnessing their father's impending death. She worried that if Mr. O'Hara were to die in the family home, the children would feel uncomfortable remaining in the home. Compounding these multiple concerns, Mrs. O'Hara was also feeling overwhelmed with the pragmatics of Michael's care. Worrying that she was not able to make him comfortable, she contemplated placing her husband in a nursing home. Understandably, Mr. O'Hara did not want to go to a nursing home and became teary-eyed at the mere mention of leaving his family and his home. He was likewise worried about the children's reactions to his impending death, yet wanted to remain with his family. Mr. O'Hara expressed his desire to live for as long as he could, but also expressed his desire to die soon so that he would be released from his pain. As we discussed the various struggles facing this family, Michael admitted that he was feeling lonely—that his wife and children were "going on" with life and leaving him behind.

I listened to both Mr. and Mrs. O'Hara's stories and attempted to "make sense" of their concerns and fears. My goal was to simply listen without immediately attempting to make things different for them. The reality was that I could not make Michael O'Hara better, something that crosses my mind every time I work with a terminally ill patient and his or her family. I reminded myself that I could, however, help make whatever time this family had left together more meaningful.

That evening, I left the O'Hara home feeling sad about Michael's impending death and the overwhelming concerns facing the O'Hara family. I understood that nursing home placement was a viable option for this family, but also hated to think about Michael being separated from his family.

Later the following week, I received a phone call from Mrs. O'Hara, who stated that things at their home were very tenuous. She explained that Michael had become "very difficult" and "hateful" toward her and the children. She wept throughout our phone conversation, indicating that she thought the time had arrived to place Michael in a nursing home, as she could no longer handle the stress.

The following evening, I arrived at the O'Hara's home to find Mr. O'Hara sitting alone watching television, Mrs. O'Hara cooking dinner, and the children at opposite ends of the house. We all gathered in the living room, and Mrs. O'Hara immediately expressed her feelings of frustration. Financially, the family was near ruin, and Michael was "constantly barking" at her and the children. Mr. O'Hara was, likewise, frustrated by his inability to assist his family financially. He was also saddened by what he perceived as his family distancing themselves from him. Michael Jr. was negotiating the struggle of being a "carefree" highschool senior while also witnessing his father die. To help ease the family's financial burdens, Michael Jr. was also working after school. Anna tearfully recalled the recent changes in the family: her mother's frequent crying and her father's frequent yelling. She worried about her father's impending death and wondered what life without him would be like for the rest of the family.

Again, I attempted to simply make sense of each family member's story, describing feelings in such a way that normalized each person's experience. I shared with the family that it made sense that Mr. O'Hara had become so "loud" in the family since physically, he was literally fading before their eyes. I suggested that no one in the family could ignore him if he yelled loud enough. His loudness, however, presented a dilemma for both he and his family: If he continued to be loud, his family would surely continue to "notice" him; however, most probably, his family would avoid him more and more. Thus, Mr. O'Hara would feel increasingly more alienated. If, however, he decreased his yelling, he risked going to his death feeling lonely and unnoticed. I empathized with the O'Hara family regarding the difficulty in "watching" someone they love die. I suggested that although seeing their father/husband suffer might make them want to distance themselves from him, they might later regret being robbed of that precious time together. These ideas seemed to resonate with the O'Haras, who nodded with affirmation.

I questioned the family about how things used to be before Mr. O'Hara's illness and subsequent terminal diagnosis. Immediately, they all smiled and began reflecting upon happier times. Mr. O'Hara was the first to offer a glimpse of their "previous" life: "We laughed a lot" and "Pat (Mrs. O'Hara) talked to me more instead of avoiding me." Mrs. O'Hara followed by noting how her husband had previously smiled at her more often. Anna said, "We use to all sit down to dinner together." Given these vivid descriptions of happier times, I suspected that the O'Haras might similarly give concrete examples of behaviors that would signify that things were improving. I simply questioned each family member asking, "What would be a sign to you that things were improving?" Again, each family member promptly responded and described specific behaviors. As we concluded the session, Mr. O'Hara jokingly reflected upon his bachelor days of dating redheaded women and stated, "I'll know things are better when a redheaded woman walks through my front door."

I met with the O'Haras again the following week and was told things were going very well. The family reported that there had been a lot of joking and laughter in the home, something which they had all missed. Mrs. O'Hara noticed that Mr. O'Hara smiled when she returned home from work, and Mr. O'Hara noticed that his wife was spending more time with him. The family also reported that they had shared two dinners together in spite of the hectic schedules which accompanies having teenagers. I left the O'Hara home that night in awe of this family's ability to make things better for each other and for themselves.

I continued to follow the O'Haras throughout Mr. O'Hara's illness; however, my visits simply consisted of supportive talks. Mrs. O'Hara no longer felt the need to place her husband in a nursing home, as the urgency seemed to be removed once we contemplated the possibility openly. Mr. O'Hara became less "hateful" with his family, although his "loudness" stayed with him until his death. The most shocking aspect for me happened when I went to the funeral of

Mr. O'Hara. As I approached Mrs. O'Hara to express my condolences, I was surprised to see that she had colored her hair bright red. Later that evening, I recalled Mr. O'Hara's words that he would know that things had improved when a "redheaded woman" walked through his door.

Things had gotten better for the O'Haras, and I asked myself, "How was this family (or any other family) able to come together and make things better in what was probably the most difficult time of their lives?" I am consistently surprised by families, such as the O'Haras, who struggle through tragic times and bring their families to a better place. From a therapeutic perspective, I think the most useful thing I offered was to listen to the O'Haras and maintain a nonjudgmental stance. I wondered if anyone could have coped better, given the circumstances. I did not pretend that I had the answers for this family, but always presupposed that they were the experts and would find the necessary answers.

*   *   *

The following stories reflect my experiences at a free-standing hospice unit which serves terminally ill patients and their family members. This unit assists those patients who have symptoms which are periodically out of control (pain, nausea, agitation, confusion, etc.). A number of patients also come to the care center to die, as family members are unable to manage the patient's care at home. I worked as a therapist at this fifteen-bed unit, floating among the rooms talking with patients and their family members as needed. Unlike the above story, my involvement with the following families typically involved meeting with them only once, as the patients were actively dying and there was not the time or the need for multiple sessions.

I was asked by one of the RNs to assist her with a patient's husband who was insisting that his wife continue to be fed through a G-tube, as she was no longer able to take food orally. The nurse was frustrated since every time she attempted to put formula into the tube, the fluid simply rushed back out, and the patient, although minimally responsive, jerked with apparent discomfort. The nurse had explained to the patient's husband that the tube feedings were not helping his wife and in fact, were possibly causing discomfort and pain since her body was unable to absorb the forced feedings. With or without the feedings, the patient was actively dying. The feedings appeared to be making her dying more of a struggle, as she was literally "drowning in fluids."

The nurse and I entered the patient's room, where I saw a rather small man sitting next to his wife's bed, stroking her hand as she lay unresponsive to his touch. I introduced myself to the patient's husband, Sam, and sat in the chair next to him. Immediately, he began talking about his wife, Millie, recalling how he had cared for her throughout her rather extended illness. He took great pride in caring for Millie, and I immediately joined Sam by sharing with him staff comments concerning the apparent loving care Millie had received while at home.

I questioned Sam about his life with Millie, at which time he removed a photograph from his wallet and shared it with the nurse and myself. Sam relayed stories of how he and Millie loved to dance together, recalling that their favorite dance was the tango. After Sam reminisced for some time, he shifted the conversation to his desire for his wife to be comfortable and "at peace." At this time, I talked with him about the nurse's concern that Millie was not receiving nourishment from the feedings, as her body was presently so full of fluid that she could no longer absorb any formula. From Sam's perspective, the thought of discontinuing the forced feedings was the equivalent of giving up. He admitted that feeding Millie in the past had become the way in which he showed her that he was committed to keeping her alive. For Sam, "a good and loving husband fed his wife."

I talked with Sam regarding what I perceived to be a dilemma: he wanted to show his love and support to his wife by keeping her alive with forced feedings, and yet, these feedings were possibly creating more of a struggle for his wife. I suggested that while in the past Millie needed Sam to insist upon her eating (to help nourish her and, therefore, fight against the disease process), this may no longer be what Millie needed (as fighting was no longer an option). Sam nodded and recalled Millie's wish to die when she could no longer have "quality" of life. He began to weep as he admitted he simply was not ready to "let go." The nurse and I sat with Sam, empathizing with his pain. I did not push Sam to make a decision regarding the forced feedings, but simply talked with him regarding his pain. Later, Sam decided to stop the tube feedings. Millie appeared to be more comfortable and died peacefully later that evening.

This story reflects one of the many difficult struggles that sometimes face families when a loved one is dying. Unfortunately, there are no easy answers, and what is "right" for one family may not be "right" for another. Sam was being asked to "give up" on the woman he had loved and danced with for over forty years. He was faced with being alone when she died. By talking about Millie and his life with her, Sam was able to reflect upon her wishes and allow her to die more comfortably.

Many times, by sitting with and listening to families, they feel heard and are able to find some meaning in what is notably the most painful time of their lives. I offer an alternative viewpoint which sometimes is very different or, as in the next story, similar to what family members are thinking, but unable to say overtly.

*   *   *

Eric, a twenty-seven-year-old HIV-positive patient, lay dying of several AIDS-related opportunistic diseases. He and his family had flown to Florida from the Northwest for vacation when Eric's health suddenly deteriorated. Only a week prior, Eric had left his home following the death of his partner. Now, Eric's three brothers and their respective spouses sat around his bed talking to him, caressing him as he lay minimally responsive, but noticeably struggling.

Eric's parents had divorced many years prior, and he had been estranged from his father, who had disapproved of his homosexuality. Recently, however, Eric and his father had reestablished a relationship, and Eric's mother shared that her son had been "living life to the fullest." Regardless of past conflicts, the entire family came together at the care center and took turns being with Eric. His mother admitted that her relationship with her ex-husband was rather strained, as she was resentful of old wounds. As she and I talked in the hallway, Eric's father paced back and forth nearby. As he paced, and she and I chatted, I was struck by the eeriness of the situation. I was bothered by the thought that not so many years ago, Eric's parents had waited for him in a similar manner, but at that time, they waited for his entrance to life. Now, they were waiting for him to die. I contemplated this idea for sometime before I decided to share my thoughts with Eric's parents. Upon uttering my thoughts, Eric's father stopped abruptly, looked at me, and for the first time, began to talk with his ex-wife. Eric's mother began to cry recalling, "Yes, he came into this world fighting and now he is going out fighting." Together, they remembered Eric's breech birth and his struggle to enter this world. It seemed to make sense to them that he, likewise, was now struggling to die.

My intervention with Eric's family reminded his parents of a time when they had been together and happy: the birth of their son. It was a commonality which they shared, and it became a bridge for them to begin talking about his impending death.

Previously, I asked myself, "Is this therapy?" This question no longer seems relevant. As long as I am helpful to patients and/or their families, I accept that my work is "therapeutic," which is good enough for me. The following story illustrates this notion.

* * *

Eighty-nine-year-old Sophie was at the care center because her family was unable to manage her pain at home. Previously, she had breast cancer. Recently, the cancer had returned with a vengeance. Sophie was a lovely woman who delighted the entire staff with her wonderful sense of humor and cheery personality. As I sat chatting with Sophie one afternoon, she shared with me her concern that she was sleeping too much and experiencing vivid dreams. She complained that she could no longer differentiate between her dreams and what was "real." Concerned that Sophie was possibly having "nightmares" instead of "dreams," I asked if her dreams were unpleasant. Sophie quickly clarified that the dreams were reassuring, and giggled as she recalled seeing her brother and father who had died many years prior. What was distressing for Sophie, she reported, was that eventually she was distracted from her dreams only to find that she was still alive. Sophie was ready to die and was frustrated that it was taking "too long."

Sophie then brought up the subject of "heaven," at which time I asked her if she thought she was experiencing "a little piece of heaven" when she dreamed. She looked at me very surprised and responded, "That's exactly what I was thinking." Sophie and I chatted about what heaven might be like, fantasizing how wonderful it might be. I asked if she thought that God was possibly giving her "little snippets of heaven" to help prepare her for her eventual death. Sophie nodded while tears welled up in her eyes. This suggestion seemed to offer her a more comfortable way of looking at her dreams, and took away the pressure for her to distinguish between what was real and what was only a dream. A few days later she became unresponsive and died shortly thereafter.

I am not suggesting that through my involvement with any of these patients or their family members that any huge changes occurred in their lives. I was available to patients and their family members, empathized with their suffering, and possibly offered a more useful way for them to think about their situations. I gave the gift of my attention. They gave me the gift of taking part in their struggle to find meaning in dying. I am greatly indebted to them for that gift.

The Strength to Swallow Death

Douglas G. Flemons

Alec had heard of my hypnosis practice through a mutual friend. He called one morning to ask whether I could help make his father eat again. His dad, Mac, was seventy-four and dying of cancer. Following an operation three months earlier to remove a tumor from the base of his spine, Mac had all but stopped eating, complaining that he couldn't swallow without a great deal of discomfort. He had contracted thrush while in the hospital, but it had cleared up, and an endoscopy and other tests had revealed no physical cause for the pain in his throat or his inability to eat. Although the doctors had found no tumors in this part of his body, Mac couldn't help but wonder whether the cancer had spread.

X rays had revealed lesions on Mac's ribs, and chemotherapy had been ordered. However, Mac hated the side effects of the chemo, and he didn't wish to prolong his dying, so he decided to discontinue treatment. He also had decided to quit taking medication for his dangerously low blood pressure, as well as the antidepressants and appetite stimulants that had been prescribed. He continued to take a pain killer every four hours for the "hot spots" on his spine and ribs; unfortunately, it made him sleepy all of the time. His oncologist gave him six months to two years.

Each day Mac managed to sip one-half of a cup of coffee and a glass of root beer, and he could get down an eight-ounce cup of blueberry yogurt, but that was his limit. The doctors were concerned about dehydration and the physical complications resulting from Mac's diet—he had lost thirty-five pounds since the operation. Every day, Mac's wife, Hanna, cooked him tantalizing meals and chided him to at least taste what she had made, but his throat refused to cooperate; Mac had no choice but to decline.

I told Alec when he called that I couldn't and wouldn't try to make Mac eat, but I would certainly meet with the family and see what, if anything, could be done. Mac was too weak to come into my office, so I went out to his and Hanna's home. Laura, their daughter, happened to be in town visiting, and Alec and his brother Jack were also available. I stayed two and one-half hours that first visit; Mac joined the conversation for about an hour, after which he got fatigued and needed to lie down. He believed his wife and children were making too much of a fuss about his not eating. They accused him of giving up, of not trying, but he said such was not the case. He would eat if he could, but he couldn't. For whatever reason, his throat wouldn't open up, and he found it too upsetting to try to force anything down, so why didn't they all just back off?

Everyone agreed that Mac had always been the head of the household. All of them had a stubborn streak, but Dad, as Jack put it, was "Chief Billy Goat." He was a fiercely independent man who had encouraged the same in his children. In fact, he was irritated that Laura was flying in too often to see him.

"There's no reason for it," he grumbled, "I'm not about to croak yet. When I get close, okay, why not? But it's stupid for her to be spending all this money now."

Laura, of course, stubbornly refused to stay away, and she and her brother Jack lent their voices to Hanna's effort to convince Mac to be more reasonable about taking care of himself. Since he couldn't swallow, his health was deteriorating quickly, so they wanted him to agree to intravenous feeding or a feeding tube. He thought their suggestion was ridiculous.

Mac pressed his point stating, "This isn't a life anymore. What's the point? I feel like a nothing—why should I prolong this? For what? I've had a good life and now I'm ready to die. End of story."

Tears filled Laura's eyes as she angrily denounced Mac as a quitter. "All my life you've pushed me to try. If I came to you for comfort, you told me not to be weak, to get back on my feet and keep fighting. So now its your turn, and you just want to quit."

Hanna joined in. "The doctors say you could have two more years. But you're starving yourself to death. They say you've stopped eating because you're depressed. But you won't take the pills they gave you. They say there is nothing wrong with your throat. If you would just *try* to eat. Why can't you *try*?"

"I have tried, goddamn it! If I could eat, I would, but I can't. My throat doesn't work, okay? After the first swallow, forget about it—it closes up. And anyway, I'm not hungry."

Alec seemed to be the only person who wasn't battling with Mac. He wanted his dad to enjoy his last days, but he wasn't pushing him. I wondered what would happen if others took the same approach. I asked the family many questions, but I think the most relevant one for them, the one that turned the discussion in a new direction, had to do with whether any of them could tell the difference between quitting and acceptance. I wondered how long before death arrived they would deem it appropriate for Mac to stop fighting. "If the doctors had said to you that Mac had only weeks, rather than months or a few years to live, would you consider his stopping the chemo and the medications a sign of depression and giving up hope, or evidence of his strength, his ability to stare death in the eye without flinching?"

Most of the family members agreed that if he had only a few months left, not fighting would be a sign of strength and acceptance. But what if, they asked, he still had a couple of years? Only then could his not eating and not fighting be seen as the actions of a quitter. So what was he, strong or weak? It all depended on how much time he had left. "What if," I asked, "Mac's body knows something that the doctors don't? What if it is telling him that it is time to start preparing for death?"

Mac had to go lie down at this point. He was exhausted, and he wanted a cigarette. I continued the conversation with his children and, when she returned from settling Mac into bed, with Hanna. They told me that Mac had the disturbing habit of not calling for help when he needed to go to the bathroom. He would pull himself out of bed and wobble across his bedroom by himself, despite the fact that with his blood pressure so low, he could easily faint and, given how frail he was, fall and break a hip. This didn't sound, I suggested, like the action of a broken, depressed man, but rather that of a proud and stubbornly independent one. If he had given up, why was he able to keep all of them at bay so effectively? None of them had been able to convince him to budge an inch on any of the decisions he had made. I wondered aloud if the frustration and anger they all felt was a measure of just how strong and stubborn Mac still was.

I asked if this self-reliant man had ever compromised on anything that mattered to him. All concurred: the answer was a definitive "No!" They all, at various times in their lives, had gone head to head with him, and he always stood his ground. Chief Billy Goat. Not that he wasn't sensitive and caring, they assured me—his and Hanna's marriage had been one of equals, and he often had made changes in response to her suggestions. But if push came to shove, no one was a match for him. It was ironic, I suggested, that if they *were* successful at convincing him to eat, it would be because he had lost the strength to fight back. It thus made sense, given Mac's signature stubbornness, that the only way he was likely to begin eating again—if he ever did—would be if it were *his* idea. The family agreed.

I reflected with them on how difficult it would be for each of them not to cajole Mac to eat. They loved him dearly, and if they were to stop fighting with him over food, it could very well feel, at least at first, that *they* were giving up, that *they* were contributing to his early death. This was a very real risk. What if, when they stopped pushing, Mac simply relaxed into the decision he had already made? Would they then feel like collaborators? However, it seemed to me, I said, that Mac would only begin fighting for his life, if he did so at all, when he was given the freedom to do it for himself. If his wife and children wanted to find out whether or not he could begin eating again, they would have to let it be his discovery. This would also help him to save face: Would it not be easier for a proud man to begin eating again because he had discovered his throat had somehow mysteriously figured out how to work again, rather than because he had been forced into it by his family?

Hanna agreed to continue cooking tantalizing foods, but not to directly encourage Mac to try them. She would let the aromas do their own convincing, and she would ensure that, if Mac felt the urge to sample something, it would be available. The children, too, would provide their father with the opportunity to discover on his own whether or not food would be something he could enjoy again before he died. I reassured them that I would show the same respect for Mac as they, and thus would do nothing to "make" him eat. I would be willing, however, to explore with him whether it was possible for his throat to find a different way of working.

When I returned a week later, Laura had flown back home, and Alec and Jack were at work. Hanna met me at the door. Before ushering me into Mac's room, she told me that she had been making food for him, but with the attitude that "if he eats it, fine, and if he doesn't, fine." She realized that she had been angry much of the time, and that their arguments over food had gotten them both upset. This past week they had both been much happier.

I then met alone with Mac. We talked about cancer and death. I told him about my run-in with cancer a couple of years earlier: It was so strange to realize that my tumor had been growing for a long time without my having had any clue what was going on. In response, he told me a story about touring an army hospital ward during World War II. The colonel who had shown him around told him, "Mac, you can never tell how sick someone is by looking at him. That first guy you saw looked good, but he isn't going to last long; and the one who looked like he was on his last leg isn't nearly as sick as he thinks he is."

"Right," I said, "and you don't know if the new pains you are feeling are from new tumors, or from the healing process following your operation." Pain from healing can be a lot more tolerable than pain from something that is slowly killing you. I went on to tell him stories about how some people are able to feel sensations that aren't attached to anything physical (such as phantom limb pain), while others (such as mothers who manage to have pain-free childbirths) are able to do the reverse. In so doing, I was indirectly introducing the idea that the sensations he was experiencing could be unhooked from their physical source. This laid the foundation for the hypnotic diminishment of his pain and the freeing up of his throat to work again.

Mac reiterated that he wasn't afraid of death but *was* afraid of dying too slowly. We talked about whether not eating would hasten the process. He told me that he really wouldn't mind eating if his throat allowed it. We agreed that he would talk to his oncologist about whether he would recommend hypnosis—if he did, we would meet for a subsequent appointment. I then walked him through the various ways he might find himself able to eat again, if that were to become possible. I didn't formally invite him into trance, but I offered my ideas in a way that appealed not only to his understanding, but to his body's experience:

> Your body has been on a long fast, and I'm not sure, if a reawakening of your ability to eat becomes possible, how it will come about. Hypnosis might be helpful, but you may notice changes in your eating and drinking even before we meet to do that, or even if we never get around to you going into a trance. If your ability to swallow changes, and whether that happens before hypnosis, after hypnosis, or without hypnosis, it could come about in a whole variety of different ways. There is no predicting just how such a thing might occur, just how a person's fast is brought to a satisfactory completion. I don't have any idea how your ability to take in and enjoy food and drink would be reawakened. . . .
>
> It could be that you start finding the aromas wafting out of the kitchen becoming interesting again. Your appetite may not change, you may still not, at this point, be able to swallow anything other than root beer and yogurt, but your sense of smell may become sharpened, your appreciation of smells heightened. . . .
>
> Or you may hear your stomach gurgling and suddenly realize you smell bacon frying. Or you may first notice the sizzling and only then notice the complementary gurgling. . . .
>
> Then again, the first sign may well not be a heightened sensitivity to the smells of bread baking or steak grilling. And you may continue not to be interested in the sounds associated with cooking—with the sound of a spoon stirring batter in a glass bowl, or of the clanging of a frying pan, or of popcorn popping. Ever been in a movie and eaten the popcorn without quite knowing that you were doing it? It may be that you are sitting at the table talking with Hanna and, without realizing it, you start munching on something on the table. You might not even know you've been eating until you see an odd look, a look of surprise in Hanna's eyes. . . .
>
> So too, you might simply find yourself *thinking* about food—thinking about it at odd times, or about odd foods at

meal times, or odd foods at odd times, like when pregnant
women get it in their heads that pickles and chocolate ice
cream are a perfect combination. . . .

It could be that you don't start thinking about food, or start
eating it with that automatic enjoyment of someone watching a
movie, or get intrigued with the sounds or aromas of cooking,
but you just start feeling hungry. Maybe you'll be lying in here
and you'll just, out of the blue, remember some special meal
from your past. Perhaps it will be a romantic meal with Hanna,
a birthday party when you were little, your first hot dog at a
baseball game, the first good meal you had when you got out
of the army. . . .

Or maybe you will just notice some subtle change that
happens when you swallow your saliva, some small, almost
imperceptible shift in how it feels to swallow, something that
suggests to you that swallowing something other that blueberry yogurt is now possible. Perhaps you'll just decide, out of
the blue, that you are interested in peach yogurt, or vanilla, or
some other flavor. Your appetite may not change, but your
interest in some sort of variation of flavor may be the first sign
of something different. . . .

I don't know what will be the first sign that your body is
ready to swallow something different, nor how it will come
about, but if you decide to have another appointment, I'll be
interested in what happens. It will be important for you to take
care, though, because breaking a fast takes time and patience.
You won't want to overburden your digestive system. . . .

Hanna called me a few days later and told me that Mac wanted to
schedule another appointment. His doctor had told him that he
could have anywhere from six months to two years to live, so Mac
figured hypnosis was worth a shot. When I arrived at the house,
Hanna told me that soon after I had left the last time, Mac suggested
that she wheel him around the neighborhood in his wheelchair. He
hadn't been outside, except to go to doctor's appointments, since
his operation, and he had consistently refused to go for strolls with
her when she had suggested it. They had gone out a number of
times since. She also mentioned that Alec's wife, who hadn't seen

Mac for a few weeks, had been over to visit and couldn't believe how upbeat her father-in-law had become.

I went into the bedroom. Mac told me he had been surprised the night before when he found himself enjoying a cup of chicken noodle soup and some crackers. A few days earlier he had tried, unsuccessfully, to eat a sweet potato, but he did pretty well with the brisket and gravy. He didn't understand how his throat had managed, the last three nights, to swallow something as dry and hard as pretzels, but he had enjoyed eating them, along with some ice cream.

I invited Mac into a trance at this point, and told him a number of stories that related to eating, swallowing, relaxing, body learning, changes in body sensation (for pain management), ending fasts, and so on. One of them had to do with how a friend of mine, a plumber, had managed, in a way that I didn't understand, to unplug a clogged drain in my house. Now I could put anything down it. Once he had finished clearing the pipe, my friend broke the news that he was moving soon, and he invited me out for breakfast the following week. We met and ate and reminisced about the times we had shared and what we had learned from one another. My friend's way of saying good bye—the sharing of a meal and memories—had meant a lot to me. He told me he had been having many such breakfasts, saying good-bye to each of us who mattered to him.

When we finished hypnosis, Mac said, "That was soft." His family didn't call for another appointment. I learned through our mutual friend that over the next six weeks, Mac was able to enjoy eating once again with Hanna, and that the family was warmed by his turnaround. Despite Mac's progress, he then began to decline; a month later he died, after a short stay in hospice.

Alec told me a year or two after his dad's death that he and Mac had some meaningful talks during those last weeks. Mac, a man whose rough-hewn exterior had sometimes kept the people he loved at a distance, found the time and strength to "get a grip on things," to rethink and reevaluate his life and his choices, and to say what he felt to those who could listen. When death came, Mac took his time chewing, and then swallowed it whole. He held on until the day *after* Hanna's birthday—a last testament, in Alec's view, to his love for his wife.

John: Lessons in Caring

Jenny Speice
Steven L. Barnett

We work in the fields of medical and mental health care. We work at the Family Medicine Center of a hospital whose slogan is "Where Caring Comes First." We routinely provide collaborative health care to our patients and their families. But, like many other therapists and physicians, we do not often stop to think about the *care* that we provide or even ask ourselves, "Do we *care* for our patients and their families?" or "How do we show our *caring*?"

Fortunately, opportunities abound to learn about real *care* from our patients. One lesson in *caring* came from a bright and energetic man named John.

John was born in a small New England community. He was raised learning how painful being a child of an interracial marriage in a small town could be. He learned as a child to be sensitive, kind, and gentle with others. He spent a lot of time alone or with his mom. Of all her children, John was the closest to her. She died when he was eighteen years old, leaving John deeply grieving her death. John's father had died just a year earlier. The closeness John had hoped for with his younger brother and older siblings never developed. Instead, after their mother's death, the siblings parted ways and John was left generally to fend for himself.

He was quite resourceful. He worked episodically as a waiter. He was an artist and designed his own clothing. He collected and refurbished old furniture; he filled his apartment with treasured pieces from his mother and others. His apartment was full of chairs, more than necessary to seat all the people that would fit into his apartment—so many chairs, that most hung on the walls. He had many dreams. He hoped to travel, then settle down, and maybe have children of his own someday. Or, he would sell some of his clothing designs and move to New York City, where he would find a "home." Or, something else, even better, that he was not sure of yet. He just knew that it would be very special; he was sure he would leave a legacy.

At twenty-six, John was full of hopes and dreams. He also was dying. His first visit to the Family Medicine Center was in December. He had thrush, a fungal mouth and throat infection that is sometimes associated with immunosuppression. He met Steve (a family physician) and they discussed HIV risk factors and other health concerns. John knew he was HIV-infected since he was eighteen years old; he was diagnosed just before his mother died. He had not had any medical care related to his HIV. John was still not ready for tests or medicines associated with HIV treatment. He agreed that a "complete physical" would be a good idea, and he left with a prescription for thrush medication and an appointment for a physical in January.

In January, he had a longer appointment at which he and Steve spent more time talking. John talked about plans and dreams. He spoke as if he was immortal. He had survived this long with HIV without medical intervention. He had no complications, except for the episode of thrush, which had been resolved with the medication. John and Steve negotiated medical interventions. A blood test for CD4 count (a measure of immune function) was out of the question—John did not want a "report card" on his progress. He agreed that a skin test for tuberculosis was a good idea because of the time he spent in New York City. Medication three times a week to prevent opportunistic infections was not acceptable, because John did not want "foreign substances" in his body. He would, however, consider some vaccinations to prevent the flu and other infections. John did not want to meet with the social worker about his lack of health insurance—he did not want the government to know about his HIV or his other health needs. John was not ready to discuss his family in terms of his HIV, or to meet with counselors or join an HIV support group. The two men agreed that John would consider his treatment options and let Steve know which interventions he was ready for and when.

In March, John had his first seizure. It occurred at 3 a.m., while he was out on his bicycle. He was looking for a new apartment, and was scouting for "apartment for rent" signs to help focus his search during the day. He was evaluated at a hospital emergency room, where doctors recommended that he be admitted for further evaluation. He requested a transfer to Highland Hospital, because that was where Steve worked. During that admission, a family physician with a special interest in HIV was informally consulted. The results of the hospital evaluation were reviewed. With John laying in his hospital bed, Steve and their consultant discussed HIV and AIDS. The consultant delivered a prognosis: six to twenty-four months to live.

John was angry and scared. His doctors thought he would die because of his AIDS, very soon. However, John had a lot of work to do yet and he needed help. Although HIV support groups were still out of the question, John was willing to meet with the hospital social worker and with a counselor. He met Jenny (a family therapist) prior to his hospital discharge. He felt that he still had to reconnect with his siblings. And we still had lessons to learn in *caring*.

We had our first lesson in March. We met together with him as we routinely do when we work collaboratively in providing bio-psychosocial care for our patients. We sat in the exam room together—family physician, family therapist, and patient. After a review of his recent hospitalization and follow-up treatment plan, John seemed quite unaffected by it all. When asked how often he thought that he'd come to the clinic for medical care, he replied, "Probably every six months for checkups until I'm one hundred." Steve told him that he would need to come much more often—probably even weekly—for blood work to monitor his new seizure medications and other care. We searched for a "hook" to get him connected to routine medical care. Jenny asked him that if he were to come in more often, what would he want from his providers that would keep him coming in? Well, John had a way of telling stories, so he proceeded to tell us some stories about his images of medical care. In his elaborate and rather dramatic way, John wove threads of stories to describe what he needed. He said very clearly, "I want you to touch me, I want you to listen to me, and I want you to be hopeful."

Here was a man, dying of AIDS, who longed to be touched. He needed to feel that he was not going to be cast off, that he still was worthy of the basic human need to be touched in gentle and caring ways. He knew what was ahead. He wanted to be reassured that he would not be going there alone. He needed to hear that we would listen to him, especially when he felt most powerless and weak. He wanted to know that he had a voice in decisions about his medical care; he wanted to know that he could tell stories about his life, both painful and full of joy, and that we would listen to him. Beyond all else, he needed a sense of hope. He hoped for a cure, he hoped for time to pursue his dreams, and he held onto this hope despite all odds. He needed us, as his doctor and therapist, to never lose that hope either. We entered into this contract with him without knowing how much more he had to teach us.

As family therapists (and family physicians), we often ride the wave of exhilaration and frustration when working with our patients and their loved ones. Our work with John was no exception. He challenged medical decisions and treatment plans. He developed his own plan for complying (or not) with his medications, and he kept to his own schedule for medical and therapy appointments. He would miss his routine visits and then ask to be taken to the emergency room after explicitly agreeing not to use the emergency room. He would want to be admitted to the hospital when he knew it was more dangerous for him there due to the risk of acquiring an infection. Then, at a point of utter frustration for us, he would demonstrate some remarkable new insight about his living and dying. He openly shared his fears of being alone and losing control to a terminal illness. He poignantly described his anxiety about what was to come. Again, we would feel the satisfaction of working with him. Even in the most challenging of times, he would teach us something about living while dying. He trusted us to meet our contract of caring and in return, he gave us his insider's view of fighting against dying alone.

In August, he finally agreed to a family meeting. Steve had met his older brother during a previous hospitalization. His older sister was coming from the West Coast to visit. We learned that his younger brother, also HIV positive, had been missing for years and was presumed dead. John was very anxious about this meeting. He wanted desperately for his siblings to be there with him in his dying, but was afraid of being disappointed again. His siblings wanted medical certainty. They wanted to know how long John would live and what they could expect while he was dying. His sister-in-law wanted to know if it was OK for her young child to kiss Uncle John on the lips. We wanted to know if the family could experience some healing from years of pain and could they pull together for each other during yet another death. The meeting was a start, but no one got the answers they were hoping for.

The end was beginning. John's health detiorated more. He had seizures more frequently, was nauseous most of the time, became weaker, and was losing more cognitive functioning. He got more scared and felt more alone. It was harder for him to maintain hope for a cure or for time to pursue his dreams. He needed a new hope. We all did.

September and October brought more emergency room visits and more crisis calls to the office. His brother and sister-in-law got involved in some caregiving at his home, but were being stretched to their limits. John wanted more; his brother and sister-in-law were getting more and more frustrated. They were fighting over daily living tasks, but the years of resentment went unaddressed. John still felt he would die alone. He became more depressed. He wanted to kill himself. He asked for help to die.

The race was on. We were working against the clock to encourage the family's forgiveness and healing while trying to keep John alive so he didn't die "alone." We often remarked to each other how we felt like parents during this time. We made joint home visits and had family meetings with John, his brother, and sister-in-law, while his sister was on the speaker phone long distance. We worked hard to bring the siblings together and reflected together about our own family-of-origin images of sibling relationships and a "good death."

In November, John's sister came to visit from from the West Coast again. She was ready to grieve the loss of their youngest brother, whom she felt she abandoned when he needed her. She wanted to do something different this time with John. Together with her brother and sister-in-law, they started a caregiving marathon. The physical touch John had been longing for had not come too late. They listened to his stories and shared some of their own. They laughed together about a silly song John had loved and they played it over and over again. They were hopeful about finally coming together as family. We were hopeful too—and relieved.

John made a remarkable recovery in time for Thanksgiving dinner at his brother's family's home. His sister and her family were there. John was able to sit up, play with his nieces and nephew, and eat. He wore sunglasses, and his sister commented that he looked like a jazz musician. He had such a good time, he asked if he could be invited back for Christmas dinner.

That was John's last meal. He died over Thanksgiving weekend, in his own apartment, amongst his treasured family heirlooms and furniture. He was surrounded by his brother and sister and their families. We had been relieved of our previous roles in their family and could admire their caring. We were each privileged to say good-bye and to thank him for being a great teacher. We each went to be with our own families to share Thanksgiving.

It has been over a year since John died. We sometimes reflect about the months of work with John and his family. We learned a lot about *caring.*

Primarily, we acknowledge that we do learn from our patients. John provided a model of caring for all of our patients: "Touch me, listen to me, and be hopeful." It is hard to imagine a person who does not want to be respectfully cared for in that way.

We also learned that it is possible, sometimes, for years of pain to be healed in families, that family members can overcome great obstacles to provide that type of caring themselves.

We relearned that caring for patients and their families is difficult, but rewarding work. Despite the challenges, we honor the experience of sharing John's dying with him and his loved ones. There are few privileges as great.

We especially learned that we need to care for each other as collaborators too. Working together provided opportunities to share information, to coordinate treatment, and to balance our perspectives. We also provided considerable emotional support to each other. We vented our frustrations, expressed our concerns, and often laughed together. During John's dying and death, we grieved together. We held our own private memorial service by going to a restaurant where John used to work and by visiting his hometown.

We each cared for John and his family very deeply. Grieving together made it easier to say good-bye.

We also learned that we need the care of our colleagues. They listened intently and supportively to our frustrations and joys of working with John and his family. They provided welcome suggestions for clinical care. They encouraged and explored with us the family-of-origin issues that arose when addressing death, sibling relationships, and missing parents. They witnessed our grieving.

We experienced one model of collaborative family health *care*. We are honored and we thank John and his family for their lessons in *caring*.

When You Are Searching for a Miracle, Always Get a Second Opinion

Linda Metcalf

To a parent whose child's life is at stake, there is nothing more difficult. Such was the case on a spring morning three years ago, when Anna, the mother of a very ill little boy, entered my office. As my office manager handed me the intake sheet, I noticed a young woman sobbing in the waiting room. Hurriedly, I went out to meet her and gently walked her back to my office. On the way, I glanced down at the intake sheet where she had noted the reason for seeking counseling: "My twenty-month-old little boy has to have a heart transplant."

Although her child was not of school age, the situation could have occurred at any age. It must have been the transference which caused me to cry along with Anna that morning. Through her tears, she explained what seemed to be a parent's nightmare of the worst kind. Having three children of my own, her tears and exclamations of "It's not fair; he's just a baby!" tugged at my own maternal feelings, practically crippling any ideas that I was trying to put together. I struggled mentally while she relayed the chain of events which led her son to this point. Her son, Ben, had already experienced two open-heart surgeries by the time has was twenty months old. Doctors were now telling Anna and her husband that Ben's heart was found to be enmeshed with a tumor so large that neither tumor nor heart could be seen as separate. Ben was one of less than one hundred children (all of whom died) since the 1800s to be diagnosed with that particular tumor. According to the pediatric cardiologist, if her son did not have the heart transplant, he would die. If he did have the transplant, it would only give him a life expectancy of ten to fifteen years. In other words, it would not solve the problem, it would only exchange it for another problem.

For several moments, I did not know what to say to her. I empathized with her pain, and tried to comfort her as much as I could. It seemed like a hopeless situation. Then I thought about the information she had given me when we first met:

- She was currently an engineer with a local manufacturing plant.
- In spite of the current crisis, she was still working at her job.
- She was obviously a determined woman, seeking help from me so she could be more helpful to her son.
- She was already coping, although sadly, and not allowing her sadness to keep her from searching for more answers.

I slowly began thinking of some solution-focused questions which might assist her in her plight:

LM: With all of these concerns about Ben, what can we do here, in our time together, that might assist you just slightly?

Anna: I want to learn to cope with knowing he has to have a heart transplant. It's so hard every day. I'm an electrical engineer and I have debated about quitting my job and spending every second with him, but my husband and I didn't think that would be good either. We're also concerned about the medical bills and whether the insurance will cover the heart transplant. I've decided to keep on working.

LM: I know this is a very difficult situation for you, but I wonder how, in the past, you coped with tough times . . . . In other words, what works to help you cope with difficulties?

Anna: Well, I do research on my job when things get tough. I'm a very logical thinker, and when I get into the computer at work and research projects, it makes me think I've got some control.

LM: What else helps?

Anna: My husband helps . . . we do a lot with Ben. I also talk a lot with my neighbor. She knows quite a few physicians and is always giving me names to contact. I often get stuck there, trying to find out where the specialists are located. There seems to be such a dead end with this situation. Everyone I know is looking for answers. It helps to look for answers . . . I've read everything I can find on the tumor.

LM: Since you're a logical thinker, and enjoy the computer at work, feel more in control and get comfort from reading and searching, I wonder how you might use that even more during the next few weeks as you await the donor heart . . . I wonder . . . are you on many databases at work?

Anna: Yes.

LM: We have two medical schools in our area [she was from the Northeast], two nursing schools, and a large university. It might be interesting for you and I to check into which databases they might suggest for you to consult with to learn as much as you can, since you said that works.

Anna: I like that idea. I haven't thought about checking medical databases. The more I know, the more I feel prepared. That always helps me with the stress.

That morning, she and I called the two local medical schools, two nursing schools, and the university in our city to inquire about medical databases which might give her information. She made another appointment and went back to her job that afternoon. I continued to search on my own to assist her with more information, calling her sporadically to let her know what I had found. She appreciated the information, and said that she at least felt productive now. Her intentions were to use the databases to try to locate the physicians that her neighbor had heard were specialists in pediatric cardiology in the Northeast.

A week later I received a call from Anna, canceling her appointment. She told me she had searched the databases and had located the surgeon who recently separated Siamese twins. He requested information which she faxed to him. He then referred her to a physician at UCLA who, upon receiving the X rays, requested the complete medical file on Ben. Shortly after receiving it, he called to tell Anna that she needed to call his office right away and schedule surgery. Frantic with worry, yet elated that a miracle might be happening, the family was on their way to Anaheim a week later. Their first stop: Disneyland. Their second stop: a physician who would make a difference in Ben's life.

Ben underwent surgery in Los Angeles, and the surgeon removed the tumor that was intruding on Ben's normal life. The operation was a complete success.

Ben is fine today, and is expected to have a normal life. He will visit the surgeon in Anaheim every two years for a while, but the physician who made a difference expects no complications.

For a time, Anna and I exchanged letters and phone calls, updating me on Ben's condition. After she returned home, Anna wrote me a long letter describing the ordeal of the surgery. After Ben mended and was enrolled again in day care, Anna returned to work, this time, describing a much happier scene:

> This time I looked forward to returning, . . . last time was so depressing. I only had bad news when people asked how Ben was doing. This time I can tell them about the miracle that happened. . . .After going through all of this, I have three more things to say:
>
> 1. Believe in miracles. They do happen.
> 2. Always get a second opinion.
> 3. Don't sweat the small stuff!

My experience is that it helps when people believe in their competencies, strengths, and abilities, *especially* at times when the pain of a difficult situation seems insurmountable. Anna taught me many things when I had the opportunity to work with her, the foremost being that I should believe in miracles. She's right.

Every day that we see clients and are invited into their lives, we witness the miracle of people coming together as humans in search of a higher meaning for the moment. The problems our clients bring to us can turn into gifts for our own lives if we allow for it. After my time with Anna, I must admit, I treasured the time with my own children even more. I have told this story to many workshops in order to enlist the belief of others that the complicated often only needs a simple solution, and that our clients have the simple tools. Solutions can indeed happen when the context is such that people are able to see who they are and how they are capable. An instrument of change lies within each of us . . . and that is a miracle.

If I were absolutely certain about all things, I would spend my life in anxious misery, fearful of losing my way. But since everything and anything are always possible, the miraculous is always nearby and wonders shall never, ever cease.

I believe that human freedom may be stated in one term, which serves as a little brick propping open the door of existence: Maybe.

Robert Fulghum (1993)
Maybe (Maybe Not), p. 5. Villard Books

REMARKABLE CLIENTS

Three Hundred Pennies

Jamie Raser

I'm not sure why this case sticks in my mind so much. I'll tell you about it, and then maybe we'll try to figure it out.

Early in my training at the Galveston Family Institute (now known as the Houston • Galveston Institute), I was assigned a client who was typical of the kinds of clients we saw then, but she was different from clients I had been used to. Before going back for my MSW, I had been working as a therapist at a private clinic where many of the clients were more "middle class." I saw many cases of troubled children and parents, but the families usually had average or above average intellectual and financial resources. This client was different.

"Sarah" came in because she was terribly depressed. She had been sexually abused by several family members for a long period in her childhood. She was married and had two children. She felt that her children were totally out of control. Her husband was frequently out of work, and was very insensitive to her trauma over the sexual abuse, her continued mistrust of men, and her dislike of sex. She was often suicidal, frequently called the Crisis Hotline, and wound up in the hospital for depression and suicidal ideation on several occasions. She was never admitted. She was seen by a physician, who gave her medication and sent her home.

She was one of those clients one might call "needy." She called often between sessions, and always wanted to know what she should do. I, frankly, had no idea. I felt pretty helpless with her, and never felt I could really help her. Yet, she came regularly. She was always on time, even though she had to take the bus, for which she sometimes had to borrow the fare from friends or family. I saw her twice a week because she begged me to.

I knew that just to be there to listen to her was maybe more than she had elsewhere, but it didn't feel very useful for me. I felt compassion for her and her plight especially since she seemed to feel compassion for *my* plight. My plight was that I couldn't help her by changing the world and her history. She seemed to understand this and began to feel bad about my feeling helpless. She was a very compassionate person herself: not selfish, not a victim, but a person in a realistically difficult situation. I knew that I would not have been able to handle the things she had put up with. In many ways, she was much stronger than I. We talked about that some, but of course, she could not accept that.

She was an expert dollmaker. This was around the time when Cabbage Patch dolls were popular, and while her dolls were similar, they were better and much cheaper. She would make them in the evenings after all of her chores were finished and she had put everyone to bed. She worked on them between 10 p.m. and 2 or 3 a.m. No one helped her with these projects, even though selling the dolls was often the only income the family had.

Because she was making this little bit of income, she decided to express her gratitude to me for seeing her by paying me. I, of course, said that wasn't necessary. Her income level made her able to be seen for free. She would not accept this. I wanted to be nice and charitable. She wanted to pay. We argued about it for a few sessions, until I finally asked her how much she felt she should pay. She wanted to pay the full amount but was very apologetic that she could only afford $3.00 a week, or about $1.50 per session. I continued to try to convince her that it was not necessary for her to pay; she continued to insist that she would pay until finally I gave up. If it was that important to her, I should respect that. From then on, at the end of each session I asked her for the money.

I'm not very good about finances. I often forget to collect money from a client, but in Sarah's case, I made a point to remember to ask for the money. I somehow felt it was important to her.

All of that leads to the situation that sticks in my mind the most. One week she had not been able to pay me at the first session, so at the end of the second session, she took out a small bag. She said that she didn't have any money but that she had brought pennies that she had been saving. Now I really felt bad. I wondered if my asking her for the money each time had caused her undue hardship. I reverted to trying to convince her that she didn't need to pay. I didn't want to take the last of her money and suggested that maybe she should save it for food for the family. She insisted that she pay for my services. The bag had three hundred pennies that she said she had counted out at home, and she wanted me to have them.

I experienced a dilemma. Do I take the bag gratefully? I decided that doing so was too easy. I took the bag and dumped the pennies out on a table and proceeded to count every one.

Me: ". . . 298, 299, 300. They're all here."

I looked at Sarah and she was beaming. "You bet they are," she said. She seemed so proud that she was able to pay and that I took her effort seriously.

Now, why does that incident stay with me after twelve years? I think I learned a lot about respecting people because of my work with Sarah. I realized the strength it takes for people to make it in this world. We often think of the people who are handling their lives "well" as being psychologically and emotionally healthy and strong. However, anyone can handle a good life and easy circumstances. The really strong ones are the people who handle terrible circumstances—people such as Sarah.

Sarah was proud to pay for my services. For me to take away an opportunity for her to show me her appreciation, to take it away by my being charitable, would have been, I think, a great show of disrespect. Back then I was learning that things are not always as they seem. Kindness isn't always kind. Charity and compassion can sometimes be disrespectful.

I'll never forget the proud and appreciative look on her face when I verified and accepted her three hundred pennies.

The Courage to Fly

Debra W. Smith

Your children are not your children . . .
You may house their bodies but not their souls,
For their souls dwell in the house of tomorrow,
which you cannot visit, not even in your dreams . . .

—(From *The Prophet,* by Khalil Gibran)

Successful parenting includes the ability to give one's children roots and wings: roots to be connected to home, and wings to be able to separate and fly alone into uncharted skies.

Mary Quinn, a spirited and engaging nineteen-year-old, had been initially unsuccessful when she attempted to attend an out-of-town college after graduating from high school. Having been unable to successfully leave home, Mary completed her freshman year at a local community college and was now preparing to begin her sophomore year at a small New England college about four hours from her home.

I found myself able to relate to Mary because her struggle to leave home paralleled my own struggle with the same issue when I graduated from high school. After a very brief and unsuccessful attempt to attend an out-of-town school as a freshman, I returned home and completed my college education as a commuter student, a decision I regret and have carried with me throughout my life. Knowing how important it was for me to successfully complete this life-cycle challenge made me all the more determined to help Mary and her family succeed.

Mary, the older of two siblings, had always been a "difficult child," unwilling to accept help (even as a toddler), and possessing a "strong will and independent nature." By the time I first met Mary

151

and her parents—about four months prior to her departure for college—the level of tension and amount of conflict in her home had become so intense that her parents, Jan and Tom, were considering asking Mary to move in with her maternal grandparents. Mary and her parents disagreed on just about everything, from Mary's choice of clothing to her choice of friends, boyfriends, and personal values. These points of conflict had escalated over the years, now reaching a point where a third party needed to step in to aid the family and try to establish some sense of peace. Yet, despite the intense level of conflict and her parents' disapproval of Mary's choices in life, there were many positive feelings and a lot of love and caring between them. In fact, one could almost say that in some respects, the Quinns were *too* close.

Jan was quite intrusive, voicing strong opinions about Mary's friends, manner of dress, career choice, and course of study. She repeatedly said that when she was Mary's age, her life "had been set" and she had already been married and had a child. Mary was infuriated that her physical and emotional boundaries were not being respected by her mom, who would regularly intrude on her daughter's space, entering her room in Mary's absence and reading her opened mail and her diary, searching through her drawers, and listening to the messages on her answering machine. Tom, a man of few words, assumed more of an outsider's role in the family. Though he agreed with Jan, he had settled into a comfortable, backseat role in terms of confronting Mary about her unacceptable behaviors, letting Jan be the more vocal one, as well as insisting that Jan be the one to dole out the disciplinary consequences to Mary.

The Quinn family dance seemed to be a two-step, alternating between Mary and her mom being overly close to being too distant. When the two women danced too close, the sparks of conflict would fly. As they backed off, that, too, was painful and they ultimately were drawn together once again. The tricky part of the dance was to add that third step, the one that would bring Tom into the dance and allow Jan and Mary to create a more comfortable space between them.

I noticed that the more Jan criticized Mary's behaviors, the more Mary retaliated by acting inappropriately. She became emotionally and sexually involved with someone younger than she who used drugs habitually and recently had been arrested for selling drugs. Behind her parents' backs, Mary sneaked out of the house at night to see Joe, loaned him money, and skipped work to go and meet him.

In one particularly violent verbal exchange between Mary and Jan about Mary's involvement with Joe, Mary struck Jan in the face, breaking her nose. After a subsequent argument, equally as explosive, Mary took an overdose of pills, ended up in the local hospital emergency room, and had to have her stomach pumped.

I tried to help each of the Quinns establish more appropriate boundaries. Additionally, I worked with each of them on communicating with one another in a more open way. Mary and I discussed her ambivalence about leaving home and also talked about the fear she felt about having to rely on her own judgment. Jan discovered, through my coaching, how to be less intrusive with her young adult daughter and began to understand that much of Mary's "rebellious" behavior was age appropriate. I discussed with Tom his involvement in the family and about taking a more active disciplinary role with Mary. All three of the Quinns put a lot of effort into becoming more comfortable in acknowledging and expressing feelings related to loss or sadness. This seemed to be the most difficult emotion for all of them to deal with, since both Jan and Tom came from families that rarely expressed their feelings, especially those of sadness or loss.

An assignment completed by the Quinns which turned out to be particularly important in their struggle was one involving letter writing. Each family member, including Mary's grandparents, wrote a letter to Mary about her special place in the family and which family values they hoped would connect her to the family as she ventured out on her own. In fact, the family ended up putting all these letters together in a scrapbook, complete with special photographs, for Mary to take with her to college.

The letters to Mary that touched me the most were the ones from Tom and those from Mary's maternal grandmother, Jean. Grandma Jean wrote:

> My dearest Mary, You are my oldest grandchild and I love you with a special love . . . You join a family of women who

have struggled with flying on their own: my mother, when she came from Ireland with her older sister and brothers to live in a new world; me, when I left my family and traveled East to marry Grandpa and start a family; and your mother and Aunt Susan, who struggled with leaving home and starting a family of her own in a new state. It's scary to be on your own . . . to make those decisions and know that they are the right ones, but the growing up is in the trying . . . in the errors you'll surely make sometimes . . . and in knowing you can go forward. Most important, Mary, is knowing you can always come home and rest up before you try again.

In contrast to Grandma Jean's more flowery style, Tom wrote sparingly yet powerfully:

I was so young and unsure of what to do when you were little. You were so fragile yet so determined as you tried to walk on your own, always pushing away my outstretched hand. Now I am once again unsure how to help you as you struggle to fly on your own. I know that it's all a part of growing up . . . but it pains me to see you hurting all alone with us all around you . . . I want to tell you how much I love you and that I will try to reach out more if you will just try to let me into your world. How can I help?

Jan's contribution to Mary's scrapbook consisted of two photographs: one of a very young Jan holding her arms open to a teetering ten-month-old Mary, who was trying to walk toward her, keeping her balance by holding onto a nearby chair. The other photograph, probably taken shortly after, showed Jan chasing after Mary as she ran off. Jan wrote:

My arms and our home will always be open, and so will my heart. Maybe one day you'll feel safer about sharing your feelings and I won't have to chase after you as hard to be part of your life. Then we can meet in the middle and hold one another's hands . . . and be friends. I know you will be successful in your struggle . . . I love you.

In the same vein, I encouraged Mary to write each family member a short note telling them why and how they were important to her and what family legacies they had passed on to her that she would cherish. Unexpectedly, I received a call from Grandma Jean who shared the contents of the note she had received from Mary:

> Your home has always been my safe place. . . . Whenever it gets too hard to be home, I know I can count on you and Pop-Pop to take me in and ask no questions. . . . Mom is so much like you, except she pushes too much where you just are there without prying . . . I need that space, Gran, and they have invaded it. . . . They shouldn't go through my stuff, that's wrong! . . . I have learned from you how to give space to others and how to accept others with no strings attached. I will try to do the same. . . . I've always loved your stories about your family. I keep them in my head and in my heart and they give me courage that I can make it too. I want to succeed so badly . . . but I'm so afraid to leave.

This assignment was pivotal in opening up the lines of communication between Mary and her entire family. Jan and Tom made a point of telling me later on how personally fulfilling they had found it. As a result of writing and sharing the letters, the generations began talking amongst themselves about the subject of leaving home and became more open about expressing their feelings to one another. Without too much actual discussion, the boundaries in the Quinn household began to shift, particularly between Jan and Mary, as Jan started to step back and became less intrusive. Mary's rebellious behavior lessened considerably within a short period of time, and the family was free to confront and experience the very real spectrum of feelings associated with launching a young adult.

Mary's adjustment to college was not a smooth one. During the first semester, she called home in tears quite frequently, sometimes several times in a day, expressing a desire to come home, asking her parents to come and visit her, or needing to talk about various social and academic concerns. She needed the contact as well as the support from Jan and Tom in order to have the courage to try out her wings and fly. Those few months were equally as hard for the Jan and Tom. They admitted to me in several sessions that took place during Mary's first semester that it was so difficult to just maintain that support and encouragement at a loving distance, while not rushing off to bring Mary home or to visit her every weekend.

Mary has been back to see me periodically during her various school breaks. She is engrossed in her studies and loves the snowy wonderland of New England and her new friends. She has shared many wonderful stories of college life with me, as well as her scrapbook. Turning the pages of that scrapbook started by Mary's family during our time together, I was touched by the progression of old memories and family legacies to her new life: the three generation picture of Mary, her mom, and Grandma Jean; the photo of Jan, Aunt Susan, Jean, and Jean's mom share pages with shots of Mary with her roommate, her college friends, and her dorm.

Helping the Quinns struggle with and successfully resolve their problem with separation and launching a young adult out into the world was both a rewarding and timely experience for me. I was able to get a retrospective (and painful) look the difficulties my family and I experienced when I was unsuccessful in my attempt to leave home for college. I, like Mary, was afraid, unable to separate, and even became physically ill by the thought of leaving home. However, our family did not look beyond its borders for help. In fact, my inability to negotiate a very critical life passage was never acknowledged aloud in our family. Consequently, as a young mother, years later, I was forced to confront this challenge and enter therapy in order to move one state away from home when my husband switched places of employment. Thus, Mary's victory has remained a particularly rewarding and bittersweet one for me.

At this juncture, I am preparing, with mixed emotions, to send my first child off to college. Working so intimately with the Quinns has given me insight into the details of so many issues that my daughter could potentially be experiencing as she prepares to leave the security of our home. While my husband and I worry about the concrete details of finances, safety, alcohol, drugs, sex, and grades, I know that she will be concerned about peer and academic pressures, being accepted, making her own decisions and trusting in those decisions, as well as with being homesick. Knowing my own difficulties with leaving home, I have attempted to pave the way for my daughter by providing her with numerous opportunities to experience separation throughout the past years. We talk periodically, sometimes jokingly and sometimes very seriously, about what it will be like for each of us when she goes to college. On occasion, we have even cried, as we've realized how our relationships will change as we enter this new stage in our family's evolution.

Knowing the Quinns has given me strength, resolve, and hope: strength to acknowledge and share the gamut of emotions I am feeling about the changes my family will be experiencing; resolve to encourage my child to test her wings and fly; and finally, hope and confidence that her own personal flight into the land of tomorrow will be a successful and rewarding one.

"I'm Exercising as Fast as I Can!" Driving Missy Crazy

Frank N. Thomas

"Missy" sat across from me wringing her hands, a train wreck in slow motion. Each time we met, I felt more helpless. Her life seemed so out of control. Her husband had done everything to tear down her life prior to their separation, and now he continued to dominate both her view of life and her view of herself as the couple slogged toward divorce. He was relentless: calling her over one hundred times a day to harass her, letting himself into the house against the court order whenever he felt like it, even bribing the maid to look for tapes Missy might have been made of his telephone threats. There's paranoia . . . and then there's appropriate fear. Missy was appropriately afraid; I felt pretty helpless myself.

"Whip," her husband of thirteen years, had used physical intimidation and continuous emotional abuse to keep Missy and her two kids in line. Somewhere along the line, perhaps even in her first year of marriage, Missy began her daily use of laxatives to control her weight. After all, if she wasn't thin, she was of no use to Whip. Needless to say, Missy was very thin, and her physician hospitalized her when she couldn't maintain a safe weight.

She started drinking in their third year of marriage, thinking that a bottle of wine prior to five o'clock would help her deal with Whip's tirades. When alcohol didn't do it, Valium was added to the daily ritual. Later, Missy revealed a penchant for cutting herself to "relieve stress." All of this came out little by little, and I, a "brief" therapist, got an education in pacing, trust, and change.

One of the things I learned in my relationship with Missy was that since I'm going to make mistakes, they may as well be obvious so we can see them and not make the same mistakes twice. Here is an example of a BIG one:

Missy was feeling both in control and out of control when she stopped using alcohol, Valium, and laxatives over a four-week period. She'd given up some of her "stress relievers," and she now felt like she would *explode* without some relief. She had avoided the cutting behavior but felt that she needed a potent stress reliever or she'd slip back into old patterns.

Frank: OK, let's try something old . . . long, LONG ago, you didn't drink, right?

Missy: Right.

Frank: OK . . . you must've had stress back then?

Missy: It's been so long . . .

Frank: What did you do to relieve your stress back then, before you were married?

Missy: [pause] I exercised . . . I was a champion racquetball player.

Frank: Really?

Missy: Oh, yeah—I felt great then . . . but that was before I was married . . .

Frank: So, playing racquetball . . . that helped your stress?

Missy: I think so.

Frank: Do you think that might work for you again?

Missy: Well, not racquetball . . . but exercise does seem to help me feel better . . .

Reluctantly, Missy began to talk about other exercise programs she had been on during the last ten years, all of which made her feel better both physically and mentally. She then told me that she did "some exercising" on a "regular" basis now. Since her weight was up to about one hundred pounds (the highest it had been in years), I proposed that she "do a little more of what works" to see if it helped relieve her stress. Only now do I recall her cautious agreement to this . . .

When she returned two weeks later, she said her stress level was even *more* elevated, a statement that surprised me . . . until I recalled our usual pattern of "I'll tell you a little now and a little more later." So, I asked what happened.

Missy: I just ran out of energy and time to do any more exercising than normal.

Frank: Normal?

Missy: I mean, I have to work and get some sleep . . .

Frank: [sheepishly] Missy . . . what is "normal"?

Missy: Well . . . I was doing five hundred push-ups and one thousand sit-ups . . . [pause] and running eight miles on the treadmill in the garage . . . [pause] and riding my stationary bike for one hour . . .

At that point, she began to laugh . . . and I started to chuckle . . . and it deteriorated into guffawing and tears of laughter very, very quickly!

This redefined our counseling relationship in several ways, as we discussed it in future meetings. First, it was clear to Missy after this snafu that I needed her help to make our therapy work. As simple as that seems, this idea wasn't clear to her until after I had suggested she do more of "what works." Through all the other revelations of her abuse of alcohol, laxatives, and Valium, Missy held tightly to the belief that I had some ability (either God-given or professional) to know her needs better than she did. Near the end of therapy, we laughed about her standard answer to every question I asked—"I don't know"—because it was the only predictable phase of our relationship! It's such a fine line . . . I often feel I'm discounting my abilities as a therapist to get the point across to clients that I'm not withholding "the answers" from them, that I need them to inform me in order to be helpful. Sometimes I feel I say this too often, promoting my ignorance almost to the point that clients don't believe I have what it takes to help them. As Steve de Shazer has said: If it doesn't work . . . don't do more of it! With Missy, I came to the point where I didn't feel I could do more without risking more errors. When I stopped trying to be helpful, change happened.

Second, both Missy and I learned to laugh at my limitations. Throughout my career, I've led from the front. As supervisor and professor, I've learned how to motivate and initiate change from the lead-dog position. With Missy . . . well, I learned that collaboration is more important than leading or following. When I moved too quickly or tried to force change, she would move to her "I don't know" position until we kept the same pace. Somewhere along the way, we hit on the idea that Frank isn't omniscient, and we worked on that until we were both convinced that I had very few answers to offer at all . . . at that point, we were successful.

I also rediscovered my need for client feedback. Years ago, I was involved in research that centered on clients' views of the therapeutic process with Tracy Todd, a valued colleague.[1] I now realized that I had been neglecting this area of my learning. Six months after our last session, I asked Missy to meet with me and review her case for my benefit. Although my intent was to gain a more encompassing understanding of our therapy together, Missy stated that she too had found the "review" helpful.[2] I gave her a tape of our conversation, which she reviews now and again to remind herself of the changes she has made. In our "research interview," I learned that my views on what made a difference were not necessarily the most valid or important views to hold.[3] Beauty may be in the eye of the beholder, but truth is a shared reality.

At this writing, Missy handles life quite well. She doesn't cut herself anymore, nor does she use laxatives. She holds a responsible position in a prominent company and is involved in a relationship that she describes as kind and healthy. She and her kids had to make an enormous lifestyle change after the divorce, but they've managed quite well. Missy also maintains her weight without *too* much exercise(!) and has been substance-free for over two years.

I learned something important that day: when I ask someone to "do a little more of what works," I always ask them to describe what "a little more" would look like! The limits of my knowledge never cease to amaze me, especially when I assume that "a little more" couldn't hurt!

No client comes with an instruction manual. So, Missy and I wrote one together. It's a first draft, filled with miscues. I wouldn't be the same therapist without it.

NOTES

1. See Todd et al., (1990).

2. For an example of such an interview, see Thomas, (1994).

3. This has led to other research, including that of Metcalf and Thomas (1994) and of Metcalf et al. (1996).

BIBLIOGRAPHY

Metcalf, L. and Thomas, F.N. (1994). Client and therapist perceptions of solution-focused brief therapy: A qualitative analysis. *Journal of Family Psychotherapy, 5*(4), 49-66.

Metcalf, L., Thomas, F.N., Miller, S.D., Hubble, M.A., and Duncan, B. (1996). Client and therapist perceptions of solution-focused brief therapy: A qualitative analysis. In S.D. Miller, M.A. Hubble, and Duncan, B. (Eds.), *Handbook of solution-focused brief therapy: Foundations, applications, and research* (pp. 335-349). San Francisco: Jossey-Bass.

Thomas, F.N. (1994). The experience of solution-oriented therapy: Post-therapy client interviewing. *Case Studies in Brief and Family Therapy, 8*(1), 47-58.

Todd, T.A., Joanning, H., Enders, L., Mutchler, L., and Thomas, F.N. (1990). Using ethnographic interviews to create a more cooperative client-therapist relationship. *Journal of Family Psychotherapy, 1*(3), 51-64.

The Lesson of Courage

Tina M. Timm

It is courageous for someone who has been sexually abused to be sitting in my office. I honor the courage it takes for people to tell their stories. The most important lesson I have learned from my clients is to be courageous, to be willing to say the unspeakable and to move into the fear instead of away from it. This is not easy. Both therapists and clients need models of how to be courageous. I have been blessed to work with clients who have shown me the true meaning of courage. These experiences have enabled me to respect and nurture courage in myself and my clients.

I started learning this important lesson when I was fresh out of graduate school. I am currently a therapist in a program treating adult survivors of sexual trauma. Nothing in any textbook could have prepared me for this clinical experience. I started learning about courage from Judy. She and I were the same age, but she had lived far beyond my years. As she started telling her story I asked myself, "Could I do what I am asking her to do?" I was not sure, but I quickly learned that I needed to be able to match her courage or she would have felt the need to protect me from the truth. If I was horrified at the things she considered "minor," how would she have the courage to tell me the rest?

Judy had experienced more terror than I could imagine. She grew up in a home filled with ritualistic sexual, physical, and verbal abuse. For her, there was no one, no time, and no place that was ever safe. She had lived in a world where hope had been destroyed over and over. And yet, here she was in my office, telling her story. There was no reason for her to trust me—I didn't expect her to as I listened to her story.

Her stories created images in my head. I pictured her mother putting her in a bathtub of scalding water and scrubbing her skin

165

with brushes until she bled. I saw Judy chained in the backyard during a hailstorm, curled in a little ball to try to stay warm. I saw her little face filled with terror as she watched animals being killed and being told that it would happen to her if she told of the abuse. I saw her in the bathroom as a teenager cutting on her body in order to be the one in control—how much, how deep. These images will stay with me for the rest of my life. At times I wish I could forget. However, instead of forgetting, I remember these images to honor her courage.

My images are only a fraction of the memories that Judy lived with every day. I could not know her terror. Her memories were like a nightmare from which she could never wake. It was her courage that pulled her through. She had courage as a little girl to not let the abuse break her spirit. She had courage as an adult to now tell the story. I hold the images with respect because, if she had the courage to tell them, surely I have the courage to hold them.

I like to pretend that evil people do not exist in the world. But they do. Judy helped me realize that sometimes they come disguised as mothers who torture little girls before they can even walk. I learned that some of the worst forms of abuse come from people whose job it is to protect.

I am still Judy's therapist. I wonder almost every day, "How can I be helpful to her? What can I do for someone who has suffered so much?" As is often the case, the most important part of therapy is not a miracle intervention or a creative insight. In sitting with Judy session after session, week after week, I learn that belief in her story becomes one of the most therapeutic things I can give her.

My reason for writing this story is not to say how I helped Judy, but rather, how she helped me. I grow by being confronted by the unspeakable and, like Judy, moving into the fear instead of away from it. To not believe Judy's story would be comfortable. I could go on pretending that these things really do not happen to little girls. To believe means I have to move out of a safe world and enter a place where evil exists and little girls are forced to have sex with animals. To enter this place takes courage.

I sometimes ask myself, "Who learns more from therapy, the client or the therapist?" I believe that in most cases, both client and therapist learn equally from each other. With Judy, I think I must have learned more. I saw courage at its finest. I learned that it takes courage to speak and to listen. It takes courage to enter a place where evil exists. The lesson is powerful. It came at a time when I sometimes thought I wasn't ready. It has changed the way I do therapy.

I respect the courage it takes to talk of pain and trauma. I respect that clients must be in a lot of pain or they wouldn't be in my office. I thank Judy for teaching me the lesson of courage. I will be more courageous because of her example. I will be a better therapist because I have the courage to hear evil and move into the fear.

Act III: A Continuing Story

Monica Scamardo
Carol Williams

While sitting in a supervision meeting, preparing to begin our day of home and school therapy visits, we listened intensely as the facility's case manager began describing our newest client. "Marsha is a sixteen-year-old, retarded student who has been in 'the system' for years and years. She is dumpy, goofy, lacks social skills, and has severe hygiene problems. She has many issues related to her mother, and has been sexually abused." The more Marsha was described, the more the possibilities for seeing her as being different from the case manager's description were diminished. "The teachers do not like Marsha," she continued. "In fact, her primary teacher has been trying to get her to change the way she dresses, change her hairstyle, and convince her to wear makeup. The teacher was even nice enough to arrange for Marsha to get a permanent for a discounted fee at a nearby beauty salon. However, Marsha was not excited about this and she didn't seem to appreciate it. She has few friends and is barely making it in her classes."

Out of desperation for discovering something positive about Marsha, we asked about her family. The case manager said, "Oh, the family is really bad. She lives with an aunt who has been on welfare forever. Their roof is leaking and they have holes in the floor too. The previous therapists refused to go back out to the house after reporting that there was some sort of problem with cats. That's why you will be seeing her in the school environment." With that, we were off to meet Marsha.

We were pondering many questions as we made our way to Marsha's school. Will she want to talk to us? Does she know why we are coming to see her? What are the expectations of Marsha, her teachers and the school? How, if at all, can we be helpful? What will it be like working with someone who has so many other people involved at different levels with her problems?

It seemed appropriate to develop a working relationship with Marsha's primary teacher for several reasons. First, since the teacher was attempting to change Marsha, she may have some ideas about what had or had not worked from past experiences. There would be no need to repeat those attempts. Second, we were interested in talking with the teacher on a regular basis about the changes she noticed in Marsha between our meetings with Marsha. Finally, we were hopeful that the teacher would be able to provide us with more information regarding Marsha's family history.

We went to Marsha's classroom anticipating that the teacher would welcome our help. Wrong. She wanted to know who we were, why we were there, if we were really qualified, how we thought we could help Marsha, and the amount of time that Marsha would be missing classes because "her grades [were] already bad enough." While attempting to develop a "working relationship" with the teacher, we explained our credentials and openly answered other questions and concerns that were important to her. We were warned that Marsha would be impossible to change since the teacher herself had been trying to do so for the past three years, without any success. It was at this point that we began to understand the situation more—changing Marsha was everyone's agenda but our own.

We decided to try something different. After asking the teacher how we could be most helpful and how she would know that things were changing, she answered, "If Marsha would wear clothes that match and do her work on time, I would be happy." Again, we were advised that Marsha would probably not be "socially appropriate" and that she may not even speak to us.

We finally had the privilege of meeting Marsha. As we introduced ourselves, she extended a hand to shake ours and all of the previous descriptions of her began to fade away. Marsha invited us to go to a place that was comfortable for the three of us to talk and get to know each other. This place, and the meetings within it, would later become the stage for Marsha to create and choreograph a new life story. Act I was underway.

Marsha talked about her concerns with our set appointment times because they were often scheduled during the end of one of her favorite classes—drama. Marsha loved to act. She liked to perform. Her band class was another one of her favorites. Her choir class was also exciting because she was preparing for the duet of her life—her dream—singing with Daryl Hall (whom she was intrigued with, in spite of the fact that her classmates preferred more modern music). After exploring our options for meeting times, Marsha suggested that we attend the end of her class on those days and observe her performance before our sessions. We accepted this invitation after her performing arts teachers welcomed the idea of having an audience.

During our weekly sessions, Marsha talked with us about her past experiences with her family, her present experiences in school, and her future aspirations (some hopeful, of course, which included Daryl Hall). Marsha described her past as being a "sad" time, intertwined with confusion related to her father also being her maternal uncle. Furthermore, she felt alienated and unwanted by her mother, who gave up her parental rights since the father was unwilling to acknowledge Marsha's existence. Since this time, Marsha resided with her aunt and received infrequent visits from her mother. She desired a close relationship with her mother, but circumstances prevented this from occurring due to her mother's substance abuse, incarceration, and restricted visitation because of inappropriate sexual interactions with Marsha in the past. Marsha's present school experiences centered around her interest in boys, music and acting pursuits, and her difficulties in completing school assignments.

As we continued to meet with Marsha, her story continued to unfold, a story that was quite different from what had initially been described to us. Sometimes it was difficult for her to remember some of the ideas that she had during the week and wanted to share with us. This difficulty was resolved by Marsha, who independently began keeping a notebook of these ideas. Our weekly meetings began with the readings of the phrase entries and elaborating on them during our conversations. As we continued talking together, we discussed how she would like her problems to be different and how her current situation would change her if her problems were altered. Over time, these entries evolved into Marsha rewriting her life story in the notebook. Act II was underway.

Although the past was discussed, it was now the future that Marsha was most interested in. She had many questions about life and many ideas about her future. Although the notebook had been useful, it was time to move on to bigger and better things. Her talents in the performing arts paved the way to her next accomplishment—writing a play about her future. It was here that Marsha was able to incorporate her successes into a project that would provide her and others with a different view of her future. Act III was just beginning.

Actors and actresses, both real and fictitious, were "cast" and their personalities were developed. She was careful in deciding who would play her mother and father, for in this play, their influences would be quite different than they had been in her past. She decided that she would play the lead role of Marsha. The leading male role went to Daryl Hall. Some of the music and songs that she had learned in choir would be influential in the play, and her drama skills would be creatively utilized as well. We were privileged to have begun this process with her, but it was Marsha who would follow it through after our time together was completed.

Throughout the school year we collaborated with the teacher about changes that she had noticed in Marsha. "Oh yes," she would say, "she is changing in dramatic ways. I don't know where it is coming from, but she is finally growing up." We guessed that could be true, while we hoped that our time together was helpful. We also believed that by allowing Marsha the space to grow and change in her own unique way, she would be provided with some fulfillment and freedom that had been taken from her in the past. The issue of Marsha's "fashion and beauty sense" had become unimportant to the teacher who was most impressed with Marsha's "new ways," which included the completion of most of her daily assignments.

It was difficult for Marsha, as it is for most of us, to identify specific changes that have occurred until time has passed by. We did notice, however, some smiles and laughter that had been absent before. It is through these small changes that we knew that larger changes had occurred. Looking back on our time with Marsha, we see her growth, as well as our own. And so, Act III continues.

Defining specific interventions that we used with Marsha is a difficult task, since we see the process of therapy—the conversation—as the focus of the intervention. During our work with Marsha, ideas were offered which related to her difficulties. Ultimately, however, Marsha had the responsibility to choose the ideas that suited her best. Another difficulty in describing our way of intervening with our clients in a step-by-step manner comes with the word "intervention." Our intention is not to discredit the techniques that therapists successfully use, but to refrain from using prescriptive measures in our work with clients. Because our clients are unique, the ways we work with them must be unique as well.

One way we consider ourselves to have intervened in Marsha's system is by our initial contact with her primary teacher. The teacher developed new understandings of Marsha, viewing her in a different, more helpful light. It is remarkable what can happen when we help change the "lenses" through which people view the world. Similarly, we expanded Marsha's vision of herself to help and allow her to see something other than the negative labels that had been ascribed to her.

Another identified intervention was the way in which we engaged in conversation with Marsha. Marsha had been in therapy before. She was accustomed to recounting the difficulties and dysfunctions in her life as she taught each new therapist about her situation, particularly her past. We were interested in learning something different about Marsha. We were aware of some of the difficulties in her life. We were more interested, however, in the positive aspects of her life: what kind of music she liked (and boy, did she like this subject), who her love interests were, what her favorite television shows were, what her hobbies and interests were, what she did when she was not in school, and how all of this would influence her future. This direction of inquiry opened up an entirely new world for Marsha and for us. This conversational style was an intervention of sorts. It was a conversation different from any conversation that Marsha had ever had with anyone else.

We worked to expand Marsha's world within a context that was familiar and comfortable for her. Since she loved music and theater arts, we created with her a way to utilize her interests and enthusiasm in these areas. Journal writing was a skill that she already possessed, so we capitalized on this asset. We wondered what it would be like for Marsha to write a play and what that play might be about. It was Marsha's idea to write about her life. The three of us exchanged ideas about how the play might develop, and this became the basis for our work together. As therapists, we did not brainstorm ways that we could strategically intervene to change Marsha's perceptions about her past or ways that we could make her see a more hopeful future. This, paradoxically, we see as being the crux of our intervention. By not having a specific intervention in mind, we were free to be open to more possibilities which emerged out of conversation. This is why we see the conversation as the intervention—an intervention that continues to guide us in our work.

Although challenging (and dependent upon the systems that therapists work in), one of the most important lessons from our work with Marsha which continues to guide our work today is that of attempting to keep the pejorative information received about our clients separate from the clients themselves. Perhaps such information could be useful; however, in this experience, it was discouraging. Such information often leads to more of the same therapy that was not effective in the past instead of improving the opportunity for other, more helpful possibilities to evolve. We believe that separating the pejorative information from our clients has enabled us to be more effective therapists.

Our work with Marsha was also fulfilling, for it was she who substantiated our belief that the client is the expert on her/his life. Therefore, the client has the resources to make the necessary changes. This experience has further taught us that our lot as therapists is to facilitate the search and the implementation of the clients' resources in order to institute change. Through this process, Marsha taught us, herself, and others within the system that she had the resources. Marsha provided us a means to facilitate the unfolding of her new life through her interest in drama and music. Once she was able to see a new future for herself, she was able to change the present. Through the art of theater, Marsha taught us about art in the process of therapy.

Understanding the Sandwich Man

Scott D. Miller

Ed was a forty-something veteran who had been struggling with his war experiences ever since his return from Vietnam. His medical records read a bit like a W.E.B. Griffin novel, except that Ed seemed only to have experienced the pain and little of the glory of military service. He had made a number of suicide attempts, been in and out of the psychiatric wing of the local V.A. hospital, and treated on several occasions on an outpatient basis for what in current clinical parlance might be called "post-traumatic stress disorder." In fact, at the time of our first outpatient session, Ed had recently been discharged from the hospital following another suicide attempt. As the student-intern who happened to be next in line to receive a client, I was assigned to Ed. Needless to say, I was frightened.

At our first meeting, Ed talked about his various experiences in treatment. In a matter-of-fact way, he told me that there was little hope of my being able to help him. Not because I was a student, he insisted, but rather because no one—whatever the training or experience—could possibly understand what he had gone through as a soldier. "If they did," I remember his telling me at that first visit, "they wouldn't wait for me to off myself; they'd do it for me."

Partly out of fear and partly because I desperately wanted Ed to believe I was trying to understand him, I spent most of our first hour that we were together simply listening as he talked. At the conclusion of the session, I asked Ed if he would be willing to return for another visit. He agreed and we walked out to the front desk to set up a time for the following week. As Ed walked down the hall toward the elevator on his way out of the building, I noticed myself feeling somewhat encouraged about the prospects of helping him. For whatever reason, we seemed to have connected and that was certainly something to feel hopeful about.

Ed showed up on time for his session the next week. In contrast to what I expected (and had hoped), however, he seemed much more despondent at this meeting. With little effort on my part, he freely confessed that he had been thinking about suicide again. I listened—once again, mostly out of fear—and then, recalling his statements from the previous session about not being understood, asked Ed to help me understand why he felt so compelled to end his life. Even though his medical record had contained considerable detail about his experiences in Vietnam, I wasn't prepared for what Ed told me next. The story was unlike anything I had ever heard of or could have imagined. Indeed, as shocking as it may sound, by the conclusion of the session, I caught myself thinking that it might be best if Ed *were* dead. He had a been a party to some horrible, horrible acts.

In spite of these thoughts, I ended the meeting by establishing a suicide contract. Needless to say, he was familiar with the questions. In fact, as soon as I initiated the sequence, he asked and answered the remaining questions himself, "No, I don't have a plan," "No, I haven't written a note," "No, I don't have a means," "Yes, I will call you if I am going to do it." I couldn't help feeling that Ed was disappointed with me for asking the questions. The look on his face, the resignation with which he answered, all seemed to say, "I hope *you* feel better now, Scott."

As the weeks progressed, Ed's suicidal ideation continued to worsen. My supervisor worked to allay my mounting anxiety by reassuring me that Ed's behavior was part of a predictable pattern. He would, I was told, eventually end up in the hospital again. This was simply a fact about which there was little or nothing I could do. Sensitive to my feelings, the supervisor talked with me about not taking the failure of the case personally. This pattern of behavior, he reassured me, had been going on for a lot longer than I had been around, and the best I could do was provide supportive care to Ed and monitor him until he required rehospitalization.

Discouraged by the rather bleak prognosis, I picked up the phone and called an old supervisor—now a friend—to ask his advice. As luck would have it, he was between clients and had a few minutes to talk. Quickly, I recounted the history of my client and his recent treatment with me. When I finished, there was a short pause on the other end of the line and then my friend simply asked, "So, what does this client want?"

Surprised by the seeming naivete of his question, I responded, "Why, to be dead, of course."

"Hmm," he said.

"What other reason could there be?" I asked rhetorically.

"Scott," my friend then said, "I think your fear is getting in the way of listening to what this guy *really* wants."

"My fear?" I responded with mounting frustration, "I can't let him kill himself."

"Killing himself is just a means to an end," he said and then added, "and your fear keeps you and everybody else he interacts with from hearing what that end is."

"Tell me, what is it? What does he want? I don't have any idea."

"I think to be forgiven. Think of your own reaction to him, to what he told you he had done. You found his story revolting, enough so to think that it might be better if he *were* dead. I think this man is trying to pay for what he did, and you and everybody else keep getting in his way." There was a another short pause and then I heard some muffled conversation on the other end of the line. "My client just walked in so I've got to go," my friend said, "Give me a call at home tonight if you want." I did and, before that second conversation was over, I finally understood what my old supervisor was trying to say. We then worked together to develop some ideas for my next session with Ed.

As usual, Ed showed up on time for his scheduled appointment. This time, however, he was looking and sounding worse than ever before. He talked about the emotional pain he was experiencing and his near overwhelming desire to commit suicide. In spite of the anxiety it caused me, I ignored the ideation and the threats and attempted to explore what Ed was trying to accomplish by committing suicide.

In other words, I focused the conversation on the ends—the personal meaning, the latent content—rather than on the means—the symptoms or the manifest content. As my old friend and supervisor had somehow intuited, Ed talked about his death as a way to make restitution for what he had done in Vietnam. "It is," he concluded, "the only way for me to give back some of what I took."

"You feel a great debt is owed," I reflected.

"Mmm huh," Ed said, bowing his head growing quiet.

Relying on my new understanding, as well as the ideas generated together with my friend in our two short telephone consultations, I responded, "Ed, I don't believe that one fell swoop death or repayment is going to be enough to pay off the debt you owe."

Ed looked up, began to cry, and said softly, "I know, I know."

At some point, I suggested that we work together to rethink his *method* of repayment. He agreed and, in the time that remained in our session, we discussed several alternatives. As we made our way to the front office to schedule another appointment, Ed told me that he needed some extra time to "think things over" and asked if it would be alright to meet in two weeks rather than one. When I looked over at him, he said, "I really need to think things over." Nervously, I watched as Ed made his way to the elevator, appointment card in hand. "Would he return?" I wondered to myself as I walked the now familiar corridor back to my intern office, "and what am I going to tell my real supervisor?"

Two weeks later, however, Ed did return. I had, on recommendation (read: heat) from my supervisor, made a call to Ed a day or so after our session and offered to see him earlier. Not surprising to me, he declined, citing once again his need to "think things over." Unlike our previous meetings, Ed rose to greet me when I met him in the waiting room. Once in my office, however, he resumed what had been his usual posture in our sessions—head bowed, hands folded in his lap. At that, I began preparing myself for another challenging hour.

"I thought a lot about our last session," he said in a soft tone of voice.

"Uh huh," I responded, feigning composure.

"And I don't think I'll ever be able to repay the debt I owe," he continued. It was not exactly what I had hoped to hear him say after spending two weeks thinking.

"But I have to try," he said, "I have to do something."

In contrast to what I expected to hear, Ed then went on to explain what he had been doing the last week to begin repaying the debt he owed. Without suggestion or encouragement from me—or anyone else that I ever became aware of in my short contact with him—he had been spending each evening making sandwiches and then personally distributing them along with something warm to drink to the homeless (including fellow Vietnam veterans) who lived under the viaducts.

While there is much more that could be said about this session, and the case in general, it is sufficient to say that Ed and I met only a handful of times after that visit. I do know that he was still handing out sandwiches and coffee when I completed my internship and graduate work and moved out of the state nearly a year later. As far as I know, he still may be working to pay off his debt. It was a large debt, indeed. And Ed wanted to repay it.

Voices of Wisdom:
The Reality of Delusions
and the Usefulness of Hallucinations

J. Scott Fraser

Don't speak! Stop! Think! Your thoughts are leaking. You
must protect others. You're a psychological genius. They are
going to fire you from the bank. They are saying you are
paranoid. Mr. Taylor is a playboy. Ms. Johnson is a witch who
practices voodoo and burns candles. The Thompsons belong
to the Ku Klux Klan. Don't eat those greens! The neighbors
are talking about you. Don't go out!

This is the running dialogue of the voices which were being
heard by a woman who consulted with our team* in the Crisis/Brief
Therapy Center a number of years ago. Although her complaints
presented clear signs of paranoid delusions and psychotic hallucinations, we rejected these labels and pursued another path with her
and her husband. This path honored her own constructed reality.
Not only did it lead her and her husband to a better life, but it led us
as therapists toward even more respectful and effective approaches
to brief therapy. This case was one of a number of pivotal delusional
cases that helped to shape my thinking about constructivism and
effective approaches to paranoia and brief therapy.

A number of years ago, I published an article titled "Paranoia:
Interactional Views on Evolution and Intervention" (Fraser, 1983).
It began with the quote, "Just because you're paranoid, it doesn't

---

*Our team with this case included Melissa Lowe, Bill Hanlin, Gary Goetz, and
Tina Grismer. I am grateful for their sensitivity and respect for our clients, their skill
and creativity as therapists, and for their continuing friendship.

181

mean that everyone isn't out to get you . . . . Author Unknown." The basis for the article was that we all co-construct our realities. Even though some realities may be more unique, constraining, or problematic than others, the experience and potential validity of each should be honored and worked within between clients and therapists. Hallmarks of paranoia are said to be delusions. The psychotic end of the spectrum may also involve hallucinations. A delusion may be simply described as a misinterpretation of reality, whereas a hallucination is a misperception of reality. The question remains as to whose reality we are using as a base. Most traditional approaches to therapy with paranoia are based upon a loose definition of the problem as a false belief which is resistant to logical counterargument. Such logical counterargument is most often based upon the therapist's version of reality. The problem is that these traditional approaches have often fed into and exacerbated the very delusional cycle which therapists hope to interrupt. In simple terms, asking a suspicious client to trust you when he or she has no reason to do so is not only unempathic, but also breeds mistrust. Presenting evidence counter to a client's strongly felt belief about an elaborate and dangerous plot to harm him or her will probably be counterproductive. It is most likely to draw the client into stronger arguments to offer further evidence of its existence. This sets up a vicious cycle in therapy where the more the client protests, the more he or she fits the therapist's definition of being delusional. The theoretical foundation of my alternative position was based upon the classic work of the sociologist, Lemert (1962), and in Watzlawick's early discussions of constructivism (Watzlawick, 1976, 1984). The practical bases for our interventions were drawn from the brief therapy approaches of the MRI group (Watzlawick, Weakland, and Fisch, 1974; Fisch, Weakland, and Segal, 1982) and from my own work in strategic rapid intervention (Fraser, 1989, 1995). The validity of our approach for my colleagues and I, however, came through our experience with our clients.

Our position was to accept, respect, and to work within the reality which our clients brought to us. In doing so, we joined with their view of their history, and helped them achieve their goals within their own points of view and through their own means. We came to view the dilemmas of "delusional" clients, similar to those of others, as having been trapped within vicious cycles. Through joining with their reality, we found ourselves not only understanding it, but also helping them along the path out of their problem cycle. Our position was to accept their reality and build new action within it

THE VOICES OF WISDOM

Pam came to us after having seen several psychiatrists. She had been hospitalized once, and she was on a considerable dose of Stelazine to help with her delusions and hallucinations. Nevertheless, she was still being harassed by voices which kept her mainly secluded in her home. Her main requests to us were to find out why she had started hearing these voices and what she could do get her life back on track.

We worked with Pam and her husband as a team. In response to our typical question as to what she had been doing to deal with the voices, she said that they frightened her and that she tried to ignore them as much as she could. The voices had also convinced her that her thoughts might leak to others; thus, to protect others, she further tried not to think about the voices. Turning to the reaction of helpful others, we found that her husband had repeatedly tried to assure her that her suspicions were unfounded and that the voices were all in her head. He further encouraged her efforts to ignore them. Her psychiatrists also offered a similar message that the elaborate plots she imagined were untrue and that the voices were hallucinations which would eventually go away if she ignored them and kept taking her medication.

In our attempt to learn more about the voices and Pam's suspicions, we discovered a number of things. Pam was about twenty-seven years old when we first saw her. Her problems had started about two years ago. Pam was an attractive, African-American woman who had recently married a bright young man who was an electrical engineer and who was white. Pam had a beautiful singing voice. Not only had she sung at weddings and similar social events, but she had also sung professionally. She had worked with a producer in New York City and made several demo tapes. We learned that she had been molested by an uncle during junior high school years, and yet she was so strongly blamed and punished by her mother when she told her about it that Pam had gone to live with a relative in a neighboring state where she finished high school. It was still hard for her to be at family functions, but she had moved back to town after finishing two years of college. Her problems first started shortly after she and her new husband had moved into a small home. She was working as a teller in a bank.

Pam said that she had been feeling a sense of harassment and racial discrimination within the bank in general, and with her position personally. When she complained to her supervisors, this was denied; yet she then felt even greater scrutiny and discrimination toward her by her superiors. The voices first started after she went to the local employment offices and returned with a brochure on equal employment opportunity and workplace discrimination which the voices told her to place on her desk. When she did this, she said that you could hear a pin drop in the bank. Everyone was tense, and from that point on, she knew that someone would follow her when she went out for lunch. She noticed one of the board of directors following her on the way to the employment office, and the voices told her to go to a phone booth and call the employment office rather than go there. At that point, the voices told her that she was a psychological genius, that she was correct in thinking that the bank was out to get her. This fact was soon confirmed when her supervisor called her into the boardroom one day. There was another man there, and Pam said that she was presented with a paper alleging that she was "paranoid" of two-thirds of the people in the bank. She heard the man say to her supervisor before he left, "I told you that she would never sign." The voices were running rampant. Pam did refuse to sign any papers and she lost her job.

Pam's husband was supportive of her in filing a grievance with the office of unemployment services, but Pam hadn't told her husband of the voices. She was home more now, and she had loved their new neighbors and neighborhood. One day, Pam noticed the same man from the boardroom at the bank talking to Mr. Taylor across the street at his front door. Soon thereafter, the voices started in about the neighbors. The voices told Pam that she was in danger, and to be careful that her thoughts might leak and jeopardize her and those she loved. Pam withdrew more. The voices said that Mr. Taylor was a playboy; the Thompsons belonged to the Ku Klux Klan; Ms. Johnson was a witch who practiced voodoo and burned candles. The paranoia increased. When Pam became pregnant, she wouldn't eat the food some of her neighbors would bring by. She stopped eating food prepared by her mother as well. After the baby was born, Pam stopped going out completely. She stopped driving. She never sang.

By this time, her husband, the psychiatrists, and Pam herself felt that the solution to this problem lay in ignoring the voices. However, she heard them through the medication and she couldn't understand why. Contrary to others' suggestions, we asked her whether she would not only be willing to pay attention to the voices, but do so very deliberately. The only way that she was going to discover more about these voices was to pay attention to them. She agreed not only to keep a diary of what they were saying, but also when and where they were worse and when they were better or absent.

To Pam's surprise, she sometimes found that when she deliberately listened for the voices they were not there. At other times, Pam found that when she was quite active, the voices were also silent. When she was either out on her own or with her husband, the voices were at their worst. They were particularly bad when she and her husband were in a restaurant recently. The effect of the voices was always to shut her down and cause her to retreat. As we analyzed the times the voices came on, a consistent theme emerged. They appeared to be at their worst when she seemed to be anxious about taking action on issues or when she was taking a direction forward in her life. We hypothesized that, whatever the origin of the voices, their effect was to shut her down. They tended to retreat when she took them on directly and was active.

Based upon this speculation, we started designing tasks together to test this hypothesis. The voices became a signal to look for the issue or action to be addressed and then to attempt some action on it. She was to look for two signs of success. The first indicator was if the voices got worse. The idea was that frustrating the goal of the voices through action might at first cause them to escalate to try and shut her down. An increase in the voices might be a sign that she was beginning to frustrate them. The second sign was if they went away. If they began to retreat, then Pam knew that her action was removing the potential problem area, and that there was little else for the voices to play upon. In this stance, she would win either way.

One instance of this happened when she and her husband went out again for dinner. The voices started again. After a moment, Pam leaned forward and said to her husband that she hoped their waiter would accept them as a mixed-race couple and serve them as any others. He agreed, and they discussed their experiences of discrimination as the voices faded for her.

Through the process of her troubles, Pam's husband had tried to help her. His help, however, often made Pam feel discounted and misunderstood. He, on the other hand, had become more frustrated and isolated from her himself. His attempts to reassure her that she was safe, and his urging that she ignore the voices had only isolated her more from him. In an attempt to regain his support, draw them closer, and redirect his concerns, we met several times with him and with he and Pam as a couple. We urged his support of her homework, and that he acknowledge the reality of her fear and her courage in the face of it. Although we were unsure at first if he understood our position, we were soon reassured that he did.

Pam reported that, with nicer weather, and with the windows of the house open, she could hear the neighbors talking outside on the other side of the bushes. Although she couldn't quite hear them, she had told her husband that she felt that they were probably talking about her and their family. This time, instead of reassuring her that this was all in her head, or instead of getting frustrated and yelling at her, her husband had supported her as he never had before. He said that he couldn't be sure himself, but he knew of a way that they could both check this out in the future. As an electrical engineer, he put his knowledge to work. He connected their stereo system to a small microphone in the bushes between the houses. Any time Pam felt that the neighbors might be talking about them, she could turn on the switch and check it out for herself. She had, in fact, done this once and heard that the neighbors were actually talking about their son's little league baseball team. After that, Pam didn't feel that she had to check as much, but she felt reassured not only by her ability to be able to do so, but even more by her husband's support. She couldn't have asked for a better husband, nor we a better co-therapist.

Over a four-month period, Pam made remarkable strides. The more action she took, the less she heard the voices. When the voices did come on strong, she either looked for the issue to take action on, or noticed whether she was taking action which might have been frustrating any force aimed at shutting her down. She was driving again, and she was out job hunting. She was also now entirely off medication. Furthermore, she was singing again. One important marker in her progress was that she had sung at a family wedding. At the reception, she spoke up to a family member whom she felt had made a crack about her mixed-race marriage. She not only felt good about herself for doing this, but she also noted that, though the voices had a lot of material to work on, they were silent. What was even more exciting for her was that she was back in touch with her accompanist and they had gotten some very encouraging responses from some new jazz-oriented demo tapes sent to New York. Both she and her husband felt that they were back on the right track.

The final piece of information that we learned from Pam during a later session was that she had experimented with a fair amount of speed, or amphetamine, during college. Noting for her that the use of this drug had been known to cause some people to start having altered experiences such as hearing voices, we suggested that this might be why she heard them. If this was correct, then she might always be predisposed to hear voices under certain conditions. As we saw it, however, they seemed to be a useful sign for her. Some people, when under stress, had headaches; others clenched their teeth; still others felt butterflies in their stomach. She simply heard voices. From this perspective, the voices had become her friends. Whereas once she had secluded herself and become suspicious of others in response to the voices, Pam now used them as a sign to engage with her life and move on.

Pam's husband got a position with another company in another city, and they moved their family shortly thereafter. We all predicted that the voices would come forward again, but Pam now knew why they did, and what to do about them. We received a phone call from Pam a few months later. She confirmed that the voices had increased when she and her husband first moved, but they were now pretty much gone. She was settled into a new home with new friends, and she was both working and singing again. Whereas she thanked us for our help, we continued to thank her for teaching us so much about honoring our clients' views and resources.

What we learned from Pam and her husband, and others like them who struggled with what could be described as delusions and hallucinations, was to respect their struggle and to affirm their world view as valid for them and those around them. We saw how people become powerfully drawn into vicious cycles of well meant attempts to resolve their dilemmas, only to find their problems further escalate. This same attractor pattern became clear not only for the identified client, but also for family and friends, as well as for therapists (compare, Fraser, 1997, in preparation, for a further discussion of attractor patterns and chaos in human relationships). We learned how apparent reversals in these patterns, often appearing paradoxical from many perspectives, tended to resolve or dissolve these problems (Fraser, 1984). And, most important, we learned a humility for our own perspectives as only one point of view. We found once again that when we respected the wisdom of our clients' views and experiences, and helped them build upon their strengths, we were able to move with them toward significant shifts in their lives along positive new paths. I owe a debt to this client, as well as other clients who have helped to shape and inform my work ever since.

REFERENCES

Fisch, R., Weakland, J. H., and Segal, L. (1982). *The tactics of change: Doing therapy briefly.* San Francisco: Jossey-Bass.

Fraser, J. S. (1983). Paranoia: Interactional views on evolution and intervention. *Journal of Marital and Family Therapy. 21*(3), 265-279.

Fraser, J. S. (1984). Paradox and orthodox: Folie ç deux? *Journal of Marital and Family Therapy. 10*, 361-372.

Fraser, J. S. (1989). The strategic rapid intervention approach. In Charles Figley (Ed.), *Treating stress in the family.* New York: Brunner/Mazel Inc., pp. 122-157.

Fraser, J. S. (1995) Strategic rapid intervention: Constructing the process of rapid change. In J. Weakland and W. Ray (Eds.), *Propagations: Thirty years of influence of the Mental Research Institute.* Binghamton, NY: The Haworth Press, pp. 211-235.

Fraser, J. S. (1997, In preparation). *Crisis, chaos, and brief therapy.* In M. Hoyt (Ed.), *The handbook of constructive therapies.* San Francisco: Jossey-Bass.

Lemert, E. M. (1962). Paranoia and the dynamics of exclusion. *Sociometry. 25*, 2-20.

Watzlawick, P. (1976). *How real is real?* New York: Random House.

Watzlawick, P. (Ed.) (1984). *The invented reality.* New York: W. W. Norton.

Watzlawick, P., Weakland, J. H., and Fisch, R. (1974). *Change: Principles of problem formation and problem resolution.* New York: W. W. Norton.

A Bitter Pill

Phoebe Snover Prosky

A father approached me for help with his two adult sons, one of whom—the protagonist of this story—had been in a state mental institution for the better part of ten years where he was diagnosed as being schizophrenic and was subsequently heavily medicated. The other son had an alcohol problem.

We began the work with a session attended by the father and his two sons. This part of the family lived in our state. There were other adult children in the family; they and the mother lived in other states. The next step involved my contacting all the other family members by phone, talking to them about their views of the situation in their family. It appeared that the family had divided, and the fragment I had begun therapy with was seen as down and out. The other family members were professionals in various fields. Their understanding of the situation with the hospitalized son was that it was beyond hope; they had ceased trying to contact him in the last couple of years.

I arranged a telephone conference call with all but the mother, who was quite alienated from the father and chose not to be included. In this meeting, the son, who had been given up for lost, told his brothers that he was sorry he had been rough with them when they were little. They immediately accepted his apology and said that there had been nothing more than normal sibling wrangling. This son expressed that the call had been very enjoyable for him and asked to do it again. Subsequently, I held an all-sibling conference call and then a couple of calls, finally, with the parents alone, as the mother became interested in the process as it had proceeded. Within the span of these calls, I saw the original three family members a few times. The work took place over a period of about a year.

During this year, the family became better connected. The diagnosed son looked better and better, and participated increasingly in family activities. At a point in the work, the father decided to move to another country and felt things had improved so much that he might take this son with him. The son agreed to the project, and on their way, they made a surprise stop at a function at which the rest of the family was gathered. The family was reunited for the first time in many years. (The other son, although not present, had regular contact with other family members.) The father and son continued on their trip. They found a physician who would work with the son, gradually reducing his medication.

The incident which is the subject of this story occurred on one of the trips which the father and son had made back to this country to renew their visas. On their return trip, they had stopped overnight with others of the family and were preparing to leave for the airport. The father reached into their bags and took a pill for his diabetes, asking his son if he had taken his own medication. The son reached into the same bag and pulled out the same bottle—the antipsychotic medication. The father was taken aback that he had taken the wrong medication. The two proceeded to the airport for the first leg of their connecting flight. The father remembers placing their tickets on the counter, then passed out. When he again became conscious, he was in a wheelchair boarding the plane for the second flight out of the country, surrounded by attendants and his son. He recalls being very confused and drooling.

His son, by now on one-tenth of his original dosage of medication, had finished the paperwork for the international flight at the ticket counter, gotten his father a wheelchair, and seen them onto the first plane. He then arranged for the transfer of his father onto the connecting flight. The father reported feeling disoriented for the following two days on arrival at his home.

Some months later, on a visit to their country, I saw the father and son and heard this story. The father could not get over the experience he had with the incorrect medication and was incredulous that his son had been taking ten times the dosage he had accidentally taken. He said he had developed a new respect for his son. The son said he wanted me to know that he appreciated that first conference call we had had in which he had been able to apologize to his brothers. He cited that exchange as the foundation of his continuing recovery.

It has long been my experience that, for many, difficulties which bear the name "psychosis" can be effectively approached with family therapy, restoring the person who has been diagnosed to functioning without medication. This situation provided yet another example and further inspiration for myself and my clients who wish to work in this way.

The Extra Mile: Therapy in a Truck Stop

Adrian Blow

Jenny and I did not connect easily at the beginning. Sometimes, joining is a natural process where the client is friendly and responds willingly to questions I ask. The conversation usually flows at an easy pace. But not this time. Jenny was different. She reported her story in a verbose manner, with little affect. Her sentences were strung together, and it seemed as if she allowed me no more input than the occasional nod or grunt. It turned out to be one of those tense, awkward sessions. I felt as if I had contributed little to the fifty-minute conversation.

Jenny's problem was being prone to panic attacks. Every time she drove long distances on her own, she would have one. If she was with her ten-year-old son, she was prone to have one. However, when she drove with an adult, the attacks miraculously vanished. She could drive the fifty miles to therapy each week as long as a friend accompanied her. There was just something about driving alone on the open road.

When a panic attack would "pounce" on her, Jenny reported that she would sweat all over, experience rapid breathing, and tremble, as well as feel dizzy and nauseous—in short, it was an absolutely awful experience. She would invariably need to call someone to her rescue. (Thank goodness for cellular phones!) Soon, she became too terrified to travel anywhere. She would go out of her way to avoid situations or activities that would trigger a panic attack.

As time went by, I began to look forward to the weekly sessions with Jenny. Her problem fascinated me. As I gained her trust, a healthy therapeutic relationship developed. There appeared to be many contributing factors to the panic attacks. Jenny had grown up in an emotionally impoverished environment where the highest levels of emotional connection took place around negative messages of "You are not good enough," "You must try harder," or "Don't you think it's time you went to Weight Watchers?" Jenny had a history of bad relationships with men—two failed marriages and a series of shallow, short-term relationships. She failed time and again to lay down suitable boundaries in these relationships. The more she was used by men and allowed her personal space to be violated, the more anxious she became. Yet, when these men were not present, she felt alone, unwanted, and became concerned that she might be left on her own for the rest of her life. It was apparent that these men played a large role in her life and that she had somehow, in a complex way, organized the panic attacks around these relationships.

My treatment with Jenny was multimodal. I worked to externalize the problem as being separate from her, and to create space for change. I would ask, "How do panic attacks deceive you?" and "How do you and other significant people in your life contribute to their survival?" I worked to educate her to set healthy boundaries in her intimate relationships. I would ask, "What would happen if you just said 'no?'"

I worked to reconnect her with her family on an emotional level. I conducted family sessions with her immediate and extended family, and worked to enlist them in her battle with the panic attacks. I used strategic techniques and prescribed the symptom. By consciously instructing Jenny to enact the same cycle that produced the symptom, the meaning of the behavior was changed. Instead of being out of control, Jenny was following my instructions, and was thus in control of her attacks. If she did resist, that too would be positive change. I instructed her, saying, "I want you to go out and drive on the open road, and I want you to have a panic attack." And then, just in case she had one, I gave her instructions on how to ground herself in the present, breathe deeply, relax, and then continue with her journey. This she tried on occasion; it seemed to work, but the fear of the attacks kept coming back. Overall, Jenny would do any homework I gave to her sporadically and find many "good reasons" not to try. Panic attacks had her paralyzed; they tricked her over and over again.

I tried these and other interventions, and they appeared to help to a point. Jenny built healthier relationships with men. She reconnected with her family on many different levels, and she started to feel better about herself. However, the interventions did not appear to help Jenny meet her immediate goal of driving alone on the open road. She became convinced that she would never be able to do this again. The key intervention with Jenny came about unexpectedly. She called me on the phone and stated that she could not make it to our session. She had no one to drive with her. I asked if she would mind if I met her halfway for a session. After a little prodding, she agreed. I spent the next hour on the computer and prepared her a certificate. On it was written, "Victory over panic attacks certificate. In recognition of Jenny for standing up to panic attacks and in achieving a major victory. This day, Jenny has had a driving experience 'panic-attack free.'" I signed it and placed it in a folder.

With her consent, I brought a fellow therapist along to keep me company (and to maintain an ethically appropriate boundary) away from the office. We arrived at the rendezvous point a little late for "session" and found Jenny waiting. A confident smile adorned her face. She looked as proud as could be. We went inside a truck stop (of all places), purchased some Cokes, sat down in a booth, and proceeded to process the task that she had just accomplished. I reached into my folder and produced the certificate of achievement. I gave it to her. She read it, and for a moment, she smiled. Then tears filled her eyes until they overflowed and spilled down her cheeks. They were tears of joy. She was happy that someone had noticed—someone had acknowledged a victory in her life.

I only saw Jenny for a few more sessions before I moved to another state. I never heard what became of her or if the victory was permanent. Yet, I will never forget that day in the truck stop. At our last session together she had a folder in her hand, and she unexpectedly presented me with a certificate of my own. The words on it read, "Certificate of Appreciation. To Adrian Blow, your confidence and support will be remembered daily as I continue living life to the fullest!! Thank you Lord for this special angel." She signed it. This time, it was my turn to fight back tears. The most significant intervention in my mind was the relationship. It was professional, but it contained a crucial message—"I care, and you are valuable. I am more than prepared to go the extra mile (or twenty-five miles)."

The Jockey Who Couldn't Frown

A. Elaine Crnkovic
Robert L. DelCampo

This is the story of "Larry," a thirty-six-year-old racehorse jockey with a long history of alcohol and cocaine dependence and depression. Larry was admitted to the chemical dependency unit of a local psychiatric hospital. In the hospital, he was enrolled in a three-week, intensive inpatient substance abuse program, which he completed. During that time Larry saw me (AEC) twice each week for therapy.

Larry was the youngest of three children and the only son of a father who, Larry believed, demanded perfection in the extreme. As an example, Larry said that when he won eight out of nine horse races at the age of twenty-five, his father's only comment was "Why didn't you win the ninth one?" Larry's father was an active alcoholic and did not allow the expression of emotion at home. Larry spent much time cracking jokes and attempting to remain the center of attention in any group, especially when he was at home. He did this, for example, in the presence of his family to relieve the tension that would build whenever his father was intoxicated. However, he also felt unaccepted by his family of origin. As a consequence, Larry became attracted to groups that would afford him some sense of belonging. With his natural curiosity and need to belong, he very easily became active in a peer group that frequently teetered on the brink of breaking the law. For example, his driver's license had been revoked numerous times due to his driving while intoxicated. He continued to drive in these circumstances because his friends did not have driver's licenses either and the entire group

---

This case was facilitated by the first author, under the supervision of the second author.

wanted to party. Larry was the one they could convince to take the risk of driving without a license. In addition, Larry was facing criminal charges resulting from thousands of dollars worth of bad checks that he had written "just to see how long I could get away with it" in order to supply the alcohol for he and his friends' parties.

When Larry was growing up, if his father arrived home from work in an angry mood, the children automatically withdrew from him, became angry with each other, and bickered among themselves. If the father was happy, the children were also happy. Their feelings seemed to mirror their father's extreme ranges. In addition, Larry learned that anger was not allowed to be openly expressed by the children, because they received severe beatings whenever they bickered. Larry survived by convincing himself and everyone else that he was happy all of the time. Consequently, using illegal drugs such as cocaine and abusing alcohol became a way for him to numb out those feelings that he believed were inappropriate to experience, such as sadness and anger. Larry told me that when he was high, he felt as if nothing in the world mattered, that he was perfectly safe. Tests such as the Substance Abuse Subtle Screening Inventory (SASSI) indicated that Larry was severely depressed and possibly suicidal. Despite this, he consistently maintained a smile and continually cracked jokes!

When I first met Larry, I was a bit uneasy because I tried to speak with him about those areas of his life that caused him pain and what he could do to alleviate that pain. However, Larry avoided these issues with a passion, and I was unsure of my ability to make him become serious about our discussions. As I learned more about Larry, I discovered that he was fearful of becoming serious with anyone because he thought he would be hurt by that person. It was several days before he understood that he could joke around as much as he wanted out on the unit, but that it was important to be serious in therapy sessions. This occurred when he began to trust me. He realized that I would not divulge his "secrets" to others and that I would not use his feelings to attack him. In fact, I always tried to show acceptance of whatever emotion Larry experienced at any given time.

My main goal was to help Larry to develop different, more socially appropriate relationships with his horse racing group—other jockeys, trainers, grooms, etc. I tried to get him to realize that any personal emotion he experienced was valid and that he would need to keep the racing group in perspective so that he would not take on the group's feelings as he had done in his family of origin. Fortunately, three other members of the racing group were in the hospital during this same time, so Larry was able to practice interacting with them while not taking on their feelings. One way that helped him to accomplish this was by writing a list of rules that he expected himself and his peers to follow. One rule, for example, was "I will go to bed even when you want to stay up and talk, I will not feel obligated to keep you company." He shared this list with the group during group therapy. To his surprise, he received positive support from his cohorts.

Larry and I talked about various life situations. I always made a point to challenge his idea that unhappy feelings are not valid. Larry smiled and laughed as he disclosed that some of these life situations were frightening. I felt some concern about his response, since his smiling did not match the fear he was relaying in his words. I was not sure that he truly understood what he was feeling at times. I asked Larry to close his eyes and "see" his inner feelings. I did not think that he would do this because he was only beginning to trust me. He also seemed to need to portray himself as a rough and tough cowboy. However, he humored me! Larry stated that he saw red and felt a large hole inside that was extremely hot. When I asked him if a smile adequately reflected these feelings, he agreed that it did not, but could not model a more fitting expression. I asked him to open his eyes. When he did, I frowned, trying to model a facial expression that would match his feelings of fear and sadness. Then I asked him if the frown was more befitting of what he was feeling. He agreed, but was unable to form a frowning expression upon his own face! I could not believe what I was seeing and hearing, but I took him at his word.

I decided that I needed to become very directive, so I asked Larry to relax his face. I literally manipulated his facial features into a frown with my hands. When I let go of Larry's face, he immediately reverted to his ever present smile. However, after a few more minutes of manual practice, Larry was able to manipulate his own face into a frown, and then to actually frown without manual assistance.

I felt a sense of success with the intervention because it seemed that with his nonverbal and verbal communication in synch, it would be more difficult for Larry to ignore or suppress his true feelings.

Upon creating his first independent frown, Larry broke down into tears. He cried for several minutes, then shared that he felt overwhelming relief just to know that such expressions of emotion were all right and that he could begin to really be himself without fear of rejection. To me, this was a sign of progress, since I believed that Larry had not been "himself" for many years. He had been living in a type of denial which he had just begun to overcome.

Once he was able to express a more complete picture of himself by expressing a broader range of feelings, I tried to focus on Larry's relationships with others, such as the members of the horse racing group. I felt this was necessary because Larry had some serious resentment toward the group due to some of them trying to control him and tell him what to do, as his father had done when Larry was a child. I believed that Larry's peers could only control him as long as Larry allowed them to. I expressed this belief to him, and then gave him some information regarding assertive behavior and communication. Eventually, he was able to become more assertive with a domineering friend who reminded him of his father. He also became aware of and expressed many different emotions as he experienced them.

Larry completed the three-week, intensive inpatient program at the hospital and was discharged. He returned to the racetrack. He still found it difficult to fully express himself, but was gaining confidence daily. Relapse is a part of the disease of chemical dependency, and Larry's was no exception. Two weeks after discharge, he was arrested for shoplifting and was returned to the hospital. Although I felt somewhat disappointed, I tried to be careful to point out the gains he had made since his discharge and help him see the positive aspects of his situation. As an example, he was no longer smiling constantly and was able to talk with me about the relapse more seriously than he had the first time he came into the hospital. An older male peer had suggested the theft and cajoled Larry into "proving his courage." When we discussed this situation, Larry was able to admit that it would have taken more courage to decline the offer. I saw this as real progress, and told him so in very positive ways. I hoped to build his self-esteem a bit, thereby reducing Larry's risk for relapse. Since he was able to take responsibility for his actions and discuss the matter without joking, I considered this to be a great step in the right direction.

During his second stay at the hospital, which lasted a week, we focused on actions to take in the event of further relapse, as well as relapse prevention. For example, Larry realized that new and unfamiliar situations triggered an urge to use cocaine. He decided that for the time being, he would take his sponsor or a recovering friend with him to investigate the next track at which they would be racing. In addition, he began listing the names and telephone numbers of people that he could call for support in the event of a craving or an actual relapse. Finally, he outlined a plan of specific people to call and places to go if he began to use alcohol or drugs again. Upon discharge, Larry again returned to the racetrack, where he was to follow up with an administrator who was also in recovery, and who had come to visit him in the hospital.

Years of family abuse had taught Larry that he was not good; therefore, his-self esteem was painfully low. Growing up in a strict, patriarchal, authoritarian home inhibited Larry's natural desire to question authority in everyday situations. As a result, he found it necessary to express this frustration in inappropriate ways. Larry's emotional growth had been stunted since he began using cocaine and alcohol during early adolescence. As a result, at thirty-six years old, he was still trying to develop a personal identity. Once he began to establish healthy interactional skills and started respecting his judgement in social settings, he was able to express himself more honestly. The racing group had their own twelve-step group that was sensitive to the issues that they faced every day. Fortunately, Larry was able to become involved in this group. He obtained a sponsor who made himself available for support and nurtured Larry's newly found ability to make his own choices. Larry was now empowered to be able to do some healthy growing in an atmosphere of acceptance and trust.

Working with Larry introduced to me the obsession of many cocaine addicts and alcoholics to constantly take serious risks. He seemed to have a desire to push himself to the brink of death on a regular basis, while almost hoping that he would fall over the edge.

This glimpse of constant testing of the limits has helped me to more fully understand the urges and drives of certain types of substance abusers. This case taught me what a little bit of caring and ingenuity can accomplish for a therapist. As I began to understand the real Larry behind the jokes and laughter, I developed a deep respect for him. Such respect was for both the little boy who survived a life of pain and never quit and for the man who was now bravely walking through the uncertainties and additional grief of rejecting old coping styles in favor of recovery.

I believe the therapy was successful in this case, not only because I was willing to try anything, to the point of even directing his facial features, but also because Larry did not balk at my unusual requests. Larry really did not know where he wanted to start working. I was able to see where he was in his social groups and help him move toward a more healthy position. Such a concrete approach helped us both map out a plan and measure progress. Though I cannot predict the likelihood of another relapse, I can say with much certainty that Larry has a better idea of what to do should a relapse occur. Also, I believe he will be able to see problems evolving much sooner. In the meantime, he has more support than ever before, and he is now allowed to be himself. I many ways, he is just beginning to live. Much like a developing child, he has an exciting adventure before him.

How Caron Kept Her Feet Moving

Silvia Echevarria Rafuls

Caron was a twenty-nine-year-old woman when I first met her as an inpatient in a midwestern psychiatric hospital. She was admitted for severe depression which had led to her second suicide attempt in two years. Caron was paralyzed from the waist down as a result of a spinal cord injury she sustained at age fourteen when she fell off a horse. I was assigned to see her for inpatient psychotherapy. She had been seen one year prior for depression following her first attempt. However, Caron had not followed through with medication or treatment. Thus, she ended up in a worsened state of desperation and hopelessness that led her to overdose on the very medication that was prescribed to help her in the first place.

Caron had a way of rebelling and making her point, and she had done it again. She was abrasive and crude if she had to be, that is, if it would help get her point across. She was not so sure about seeing yet another therapist, who she doubted could be helpful in the first place. Generally, consistency was not her forte, but why should it have been. Nothing or no one seemed to last or stay around long enough to be relied upon for any great length of time. She believed people grew tired of her after a while and although she did not let her paralysis stop her from regular activities (e.g., driving, working, going to school), she did think her disability and the special needs related to it led others, including her own family, to stay away. Thus, the issues of mobility, independence, and autonomy were underlying many of our conversations about her current state. How much help to ask for and how much to depend on others was a constant struggle for Caron. On the one hand, she was so proud of herself when she succeeded in doing for herself; on the other, there were times when she really needed help in order to survive. This was especially true when she had to go to her parents for money, for mechanical help with her car, or for help with household problems.

Caron's parents did not have much in terms of economic resources, but did try to assist her when she asked. Caron, however, believed that everything had its price. She strongly desired an emotional and interpersonal connection with her parents that they were not able to provide her because these were issues they struggled with themselves. In one family session, for example, Caron confronted them about specific incidents during her childhood that she felt were abusive and neglectful. Her parents' inability to validate these experiences as such resulted in crushing disappointment and hurt for Caron. Despite this, she still needed them. Her disability and poverty made sure of that, and so, she would go back to her parents and get from them what they could provide—occasional, nonemotional, tangible help that required only small talk, some of their money, and some of their time. That was the best they could do.

Independence and autonomy were thematic throughout therapy. Ironically, the same freedom of movement that Caron desired to have with her legs, she also needed to have in terms of independence, self-confidence, and self-reliance. The dilemma presented itself in terms of when to ask for help and when not to ask for help, and furthermore, when either one of these were decided, she needed to avoid the trap of extremes (e.g., becoming too clingy or taking too much risk). It was in those traps of extremes that she would become confused and get very angry with herself and those she felt had trapped her. This would immobilize Caron, and it was then that she became most depressed (and suicidal), since life felt so pointless and senseless.

In therapy, however, it was clear that moving on in her life, getting ahead, and being able to care for herself were of paramount importance to Caron. Situationally and contextually, her depression made a lot of sense. How could I not recognize the poverty-based existence under which she had to live and the hopelessness which set in when she felt rejected or when educational and employment doors shut her out of her future-oriented vision? Caron tried, and sometimes it was only her humor that barely got her through.

My focus in therapy with Caron could not overlook the fact that some degree of control over her own mobility, her own freedom of movement in terms of possibilities, were very important in our conversations about change and difference. Having just received sixty hours of training in Ericksonian hypnosis during this time, I became a believer in the power of storytelling in terms of presuppositional thinking and language in therapy. In some cases, I utilized the expertise of master storytellers when I could not think of a story myself. With Caron I came to use Bill O'Hanlon's (1992) *Keep Your Feet Moving* story in audiotape form.

The story is based on a Buddhist Tibetan ceremony for enlightenment that occurred once every one hundred years. The ceremony consisted of entering the room of 1,000 demons through a door that remained unlocked. Once you were in, you were to walk around the room and come out the other side through another door. Although the instructions were simple, the catch of course was that you had to walk through your greatest fear (i.e., the thousand demons). The two most important pieces of information that were given before entering were: (1) "remember that this is all in your head, it's illusion, 'maya'," and (2) "keep your feet moving." Did you hear that? Keep your feet moving! Initially, I struggled with just how insensitive it might have been to present movement of feet to a paraplegic client. However, after some reflection, it seemed to make a lot of sense as a metaphor to use in therapy, especially with the feelings of immobility and entrapment that Caron experienced.

What came of this story after presenting it to Caron was that it offered us a tangible way of conversing about her moving on and her mobility in terms of change (i.e., how much she could end up doing for herself and doing with others that would get her ahead in terms of goals she had for herself personally and educationally). As clients often do, she adapted and added to the metaphor by envisioning herself at the bottom of an ocean. When she felt most assured and secure, she seemed to move with ease and could swim up for air and relief, thus keeping herself alive (and kicking). When she felt most dragged down, least secure, and most dependent, she felt buried in the sand and thus, unable to keep her feet moving. We talked about this every week. It was a very effective way of assessing her state of depression and keeping the focus on her feet moving, staying afloat, and being able to get to the surface (regardless of how brief that was).

Caron ended up being able to manage her depression rather well for the next year and a half, despite some very challenging medical complications and housing problems. She improved in terms of taking her medications and certainly kept up with therapy. After eighteen months of knowing Caron, I took a job in another state and had to face ending my therapeutic relationship with Caron. I will admit that this was not easy for several reasons. The first, of course, was that she had previous issues related to rejection, abandonment, and relationships not lasting. Second, I would miss seeing Caron. I was very inspired by Caron's resilience and the progress she had made.. Deep down I also feared that my leaving would upset all of Caron's progress and would set her back completely. Rather than staying within this egocentric frame we sometimes put ourselves in as therapists, I decided to perceive this as a challenge (for both of us). For Caron, to see how she would be able to deal with the transfer and follow-up as we were able to do eighteen months prior, and for me to not take on any more responsibility beyond providing her a well-thought-out and organized plan of transition for ongoing therapy. We decided it would be okay to correspond (as "nontherapeutically" as we could possibly do so).

A few months after my move, I received a Christmas card from Caron. She was able to move on with the other therapist to whom she was transferred. This was measurable success. She was willing and able to sustain a therapeutic relationship with two therapists in two years time, rather than shutting herself out from possible resources as she had done before. Her financial struggles were still real and some of her hopelessness was still founded in her health-related complications associated with her paralysis. The difference was that she could focus on ways to bring her feet (and legs) out of the sand and envision how much difference that could make in her life by helping herself, while also maintaining connectedness and trust with others as she allowed people into her life. Although emphasis has been placed on therapist continuity in this story, it does not imply that Caron should have an endless dependence on therapists. Instead, the connection to a therapist gave Caron the chance to experience trustworthy connectedness that eventually was leading her toward a network of support which she could keep balanced with a sturdy dependence of self as she tested out her independence and mobility.

Caron has been a tremendous inspiration in my life. I use her as an example in many of my classes, and will never forget her strength and resiliency. It is always fascinating to me how strength and resourcefulness are so easily dismissed and overlooked by so many of us, especially clients that I have worked with, as well as others that I have known personally. Despite some of the greatest odds in life, Caron was able to move on. This has been instrumental in strengthening my belief that this realization needs to be an essential part of our work. It is the language that facilitates awareness of our clients' strengths and motivates them into action somehow, as part of the therapy which we share in with them. I might add that this has also impacted my teaching and supervision as well. For that, I will always be grateful to Caron. I hope you will be too.

BIBLIOGRAPHY

O'Hanlon, Bill. (1992). *Keep your feet moving* (audio tape). Omaha, NE: Hudson Center for Brief Therapy.

DEVELOPING
THE SELF OF THE THERAPIST

Coloring Within the Lines:
The Tale of a Buddhist, Lesbian Family
Therapy Professor

Janet L. Osborn

A few years ago I heard a song written about the oppression and eventual demise of a woman due to her refusal to conform to the dominant culture's beliefs about what her behavior should be and its attempts to make her conform. The refrain, sung with great commanding urgency was, "paint by numbers, color within the lines." The song created a powerful framework in which to place my own and others' oppression. In a sudden moment of insight, I understood that the lines are drawn by those in the dominant culture, to whom seeing color outside the lines can be uncomfortable. It can spell danger, as well as elicit fears and questions such as: What if everyone were to color outside the lines? Would our family, country, or world fall apart?

Out of this fear can come the demand that everyone color within the lines. Yet, some of us, due to different culture, class, and/or sexual orientation, color outside the lines simply by living our lives. First we learn to deal with the demands by trying our best to color within the lines and hiding the places where we don't or where we choose to color outside the lines. Eventually, we may come to a

209

place of coloring where it feels natural for us to color outside the lines and deal with the consequences, letting the dominant culture confront its own discomfort.

I was recently reminded of this song and the framework of coloring within the lines when my colleague was asked to show his work at a conference. He was told at the last minute that he could not show what he had planned about oppression because it was too graphic. Oppression is graphic. Horrors such as the Holocaust, slavery, segregation, apartheid, fag and dyke "bashing," and the Japanese war camps are examples of the atrocities of oppression. However, daily life brings its own graphic reminders. Utterly inspired by my colleague's recent censorship experience, I decided to write my own family therapist tale. As this tale is my own, I cannot speak about any other experiences of oppression than mine as a lesbian family therapist and professor.

Living the majority of my life with lesbianism as a significant part of my self-narrative, I often color outside the lines. The resulting oppression that I have experienced and witnessed has given me a deep appreciation for the oppression my clients may be experiencing. I have watched friends be disowned by families after "coming out" as lesbian or gay, some of whom were dying due to HIV infection. While working for the New York State Department of Health AIDS Antibody Counseling and Testing Program, threats against lesbians and gays were routinely received on the information and crisis hotline. At that time, the entire program staff throughout New York State was gay or lesbian. Gays and lesbians across the country did their own prevention programs, with money donated by the lesbian and gay community. However, callers to the hotline made the assumption that being a health care provider meant being heterosexual. Since the advent of AIDS, violent crime against gays and lesbians has increased dramatically, including murder (National Gay and Lesbian Task Force, 1991). For example, a Metropolitan Community Church (a national Christian church for lesbians and gays) in California burned, due to arson during a church service, killing twenty-six people. Gay bashing (beating up gay men for sport) and drive-by shootings in gay neighborhoods have also increased.

Much of the oppression and heterosexism is more subtle and experienced on a daily basis. For example, lesbians and gays rarely see themselves portrayed in television shows and, when they do, it often does not fit with their experience. The lone lesbian or gay is shown within the dominant heterosexual culture, and the lesbian/ gay culture s/he also lives in is rarely shown. Additionally, lesbian and gay relationships are given fewer rights than those in the dominant culture. Lesbians and gays cannot marry, which keeps them from such benefits as joint tax returns, family health insurance, and parental rights to nonbiological children. Such limitations have far-reaching implications for them even at the time of death. Many wills are contested by family members when assets are left to lesbian/gay partners, including custody of nonbiological children. The language used to refer to couple often excludes lesbians and gays as well. For example, the very name of our professional organization, The American Association for Marriage and Family Therapy, is exclusionary, as gays and lesbians are not permitted to legally marry. One of the most blatant examples was the title of an article that a friend brought to my attention because she knew it would have an impact: "Human mate selection." Fine title, except that it was exclusively about heterosexuals.

This kind of hatred and negation has had a tremendous impact on me. While I was never completely secretive about my sexuality, the experience at the Health Department was so compelling that I could no longer remain closeted, hiding my true colors. I began to notice much more fully the oppression of gays and lesbians and to speak up about this. Initially, I think that this part of my narrative made me less open to other views. I became focused on the oppression of lesbians and gays not noticing other types of oppression. Over time, however, this experience has helped me to define my own beliefs and priorities. In order to teach about lesbian and gay families and homophobia in a nonreactive way, I have been pushed to become clear about my own values.

I was recently told by a student that she was in awe of my ability to stay "nonreactive" when the class was discussing views on lesbian and gay families. I felt so pleased that my ten years of Buddhist practice was paying off. Outwardly, I apparently appeared "nonreactive," which is the Buddhist way. This way is to accept the learner where s/he is and make an impact from there. I struggle between this way of life (that is so precious to me) and the inner rage I feel when I hear students (who know I am a lesbian) say that they think lesbians and gays should not have children. Others say they ("us" to me) should be "allowed" (allowed by whom, I wonder) to have children, but we should adopt only. After all, there are so many children in the world who need good homes. I hear these things coming from the students whom I feel such a commitment to impact and I wonder, "who are they?" Where did they get the idea that because they are heterosexual, they can decide that lesbians and gays are unfit parents or at least unfit biological parents? There appeared to be little recognition by some that as they said "they," they were saying "you." You, Jan Osborn, faculty member, should not be allowed to have children. Maybe part of my ability to stay nonreactive and raise points for discussion comes from a place of shutting down, of looking away. The truth too painful to face head-on.

After these particular two weeks of classes, the faculty began interviewing for perspective students for next year. One interviewee managed to say that he felt that homosexuality was inherently wrong and that he was not homophobic, all in the space of ten minutes. I told some of my colleagues from another University about it, and generated discussion about what admission criteria should be in terms of conservatism. Again, we raised the question of accepting the students where they are and hoping to have an impact on them. We all agreed that most Marriage and Family Therapy programs would accept a student who stated in an interview that homosexuality was inherently wrong. Clearly, we will accept students who believe that lesbians and gays should not be allowed to have children. I asked, "Do you think we would accept students into our program who felt African Americans, Hispanics, Asians, and Jews were inherently wrong, and should not have children or should adopt because after all, there are a lot of African American and Hispanic children in need of good homes?" One of my colleagues just said "Wow." We accept a different level of oppression, depending on who is being oppressed. What student or interviewee would speak those things to an African American, Hispanic, Asian, or Jewish faculty member even if s/he thought them?

But, without the pain of facing these opinions head-on, we make no impact. When I heard my colleague's story of censorship, I was outraged. He had been asked to show who he was and then was told, "You can't them tell them that." My "reactive" initial thought was that if I were him, I would want to say, "Forget it then; find someone else to speak at your conference." However, even as the thought was forming, the Buddhist part of me said, "But then no one will hear you." I was reminded yet again that the fight against oppression has to be fought within the frame of what can be heard: uncomfortable but not too graphic—fought just outside the lines.

I was then reminded of some of the times I made an impact. I was welcomed into the field of marriage and family therapy by the woman who would become a beloved mentor saying with great enthusiasm, "Oh, and you're a lesbian, too" (in addition to my other assets such as a nursing background, etc.). I told her that I'd never had my lesbianism met with such enthusiasm before. Her hope was that I would have an impact on other students. I did. There were three doctoral students with whom I became connected. We went through all of our classes together, and were counselors in residence together as well. We were perhaps an unlikely foursome: one Jewish, heterosexual woman; one Hispanic, heterosexual woman (though she didn't like to identify that way); one Mormon, heterosexual male; and myself, a Buddhist lesbian. The Mormon male and I got off to a rocky start. He was bothered because he thought that I raised the lesbian/gay issue all the time. Well, I suppose he was right. But, I just couldn't stay quiet when I noticed things such as our sexual history that asked only one question about homosexual sex, and it was sandwiched between "Have you ever been raped?" and "Have you ever had sexual fantasies of children?" He began to understand my vigilance after the following incident.

The counselor in residence director was showing us posters that were available for the offices. There was one poster of a beautifully written poem about the Holocaust. It begins, "First they came for the Jews and I didn't stand up." It continues for fifteen lines or so in a similar fashion, naming various other groups and ends with, "When they came for me, there was no one left to stand up." I said that while I thought it was beautiful, I struggled with it because lesbians and gays were not listed. Exasperated, the Mormom male shouted, "Not everything is about lesbians and gays!" To which I answered something along the lines of, "No, you are quite right, not everything is. But, the Holocaust impacted gays and lesbians greatly, while, of course, not to the extent it did Jewish people. Suspected gays were made to wear pink triangles instead of yellow stars of David. They also were murdered, not for being Jewish, but for being homosexual. For some people all over the world, homosexuality still justifies murder. This is why gays and lesbians wear pink triangles, lest we ever forget the murders which have gone before, and those yet to occur. This poster forgets us." Well, the director and some of the other counselors looked worried that it would be a long year. The man quietly said, "I'm sorry, I didn't know." He never hassled me again for speaking out, though I'm sure he tired of it at times. I also answered his seemingly endless questions about lesbians and gays, the most famous one being, "Jan, how come I never see a lesbian in a dress?" What other answer is there but, "Because when you see a woman in a dress, you assume she's not a lesbian"?

With all this said, I am left with the struggle of how to be a Buddhist activist, coloring where my nature directs me, without alienating those who color differently than me. People laugh when they hear me say this, but I don't think that one precludes the other. I remind myself that if I were not open and available, the students would not feel comfortable in telling me their true views, and no dialogue would occur. No impact made. I am truly happy that the students feel they can share their ideas with me regardless of the pain. Furthermore, Buddhism is about life-to-life connection. The impact is made through connection to other people. I believe that the healing of oppression occurs on this level. One of the women in the doctoral foursome and I experienced this kind of healing with each other. Through our ever-growing friendship, I have come to have a much more profound understanding of her experience as a Jewish woman, and she has come to understand my lesbian experience similarly. We have shared the similarities and differences of our oppressive experiences, as well as the profound joy in who we are. To have someone from outside the circle of experience step in and say, "I support you. I'm in this fight with you" is profoundly healing.

My hope is that this story makes it a bit easier to understand why some of us can be hypervigilant and "see oppression everywhere." It is everywhere. We are all oppressed on a number of lesser levels everyday. Driving in Chicago during rush hour is oppressive; being asked to do one more thing at work is oppressive, and on and on. But, when we are also oppressed in major ways such as not being able to provide adequate health insurance to our partners, or fear we'll never see our children again if our partner dies because we live in a state which does not recognize us as co-parents, and get spit at on the street for holding hands with our partner, these small oppressions are reminders of the larger, deeper oppression. The daily injustices are graphic reminders, and I find myself unable and unwilling to allow them to continue without standing up. My experience assists me in understanding the oppressive experiences my clients face, while holding the hope for them during their struggle to a place of strength. It is on this level of daily life-to-life connection that I believe I make my greatest impact. Thus, if I have an impact on one student in each class and help her/him feel proud of who s/he is, or assist them to understand another point of view, I've won by doing my job well and maintaining my Buddhist integrity by continuing to color irrespective of the lines.

The Kaleidoscope of a Retiree

Grace Luther

Retirement! At the end of May 1996, I will become an ex-university professor of marriage and family therapy. Regret, relief, curiosity about the future, and satisfaction with the past tinge my thoughts these days. It's easy to say, "I'm out of here"; it's difficult to say, "Goodbye."

Every retiree has a kaleidoscope of memories, colorful images that tumble together and then separate to form another image. Mine have been shaped and reshaped through twenty-four years of teaching, supervising, and performing therapy. I view them now with hindsight, the mirror of the past tempered by wisdom, time, and experience. I share these few with a chuckle and much awe of and respect for our human and godly spirit.

REAL THERAPY: TRUSTING THY CLIENTS

I was a doctoral assistant at the rehabilitation-education center of the University of Illinois. Many students with disabilities were attracted to the university by its outstanding support for them. As a therapist in their counseling center, I learned about "real" therapy.

Because of the extent of their disabilities, I sometimes honestly wondered if they would ever gain and succeed in a decent job or sustain normal relationships. An example was Ginny, who struggled to hold onto a connection with her parents. Her parents supplied everything she needed, but didn't want to be near her. She had severe cerebral palsy. Jerry and Ann Smith, confined to wheelchairs by spinal injuries, were raising a toddler and pursuing graduate studies. Amid a jumble of walkers, braces, and special equipment for parents and baby, they were trying to live a normal family life in a minuscule university apartment. Another example was Ryan, who was blind, passionately in love with running instead of walking (without his cane), and dating girls. He'd come in wounded from his latest run-in with a telephone pole or a recalcitrant female, decidedly discouraged by his lack of physical and social prowess.

I soon learned it wasn't my listening skills or technical proficiency as a therapist that they wanted. They wanted me to trust them. Through them, I saw true grit which helped me to counter my pessimism and prejudice with optimism, openness, and hope. I learned to discover and trust the spirit in each of my clients.

PET POODLE THERAPY

On one side of the room, two girls, ages ten and twelve, sat close together. Daddy and Stepmother sat facing me on the sofa. A fleecy white cloud of miniature poodle balanced itself on.the woman's lap. From time to time, Stepmother looked deep into its eyes as she petted and coddled it. The puppy returned the gaze, shook the pink bows on its ears, and licked her caressing hands with a tiny darting pink tongue. I was mesmerized by that tongue.

For two sessions we tried to open communication in the family, to find some threads of warm feelings between the children and the stepmom. They were like frozen puppets, responding stiffly to my encouragement to talk to one another about their thoughts and feelings. As they left the second session, the girls finally petted the dog in a constrained manner, the stepmom looked on coldly, and the poor dad tried to connect to all with a long-winded reminder that they'd never become a family unless they loved one another. The atmosphere was dismal at best.

As the family entered the next session, I noticed their mood had lightened. I wasn't sure what had happened, but something did. One never knows exactly what precipitates change. I also noticed that the poodle wasn't there.

"Where's the poodle?" I asked. The response was a trickle of giggles followed by a gust of laughter. Even the stepmom smiled. I sat amazed, watching their now lively faces and listening to the bits and pieces of the story as it emerged.

Stepmom applied her makeup using a mirror over a bathroom sink. Next to the sink was a commode. Ritualistically, the lady would lower the lid of the toilet and invite the poodle to hop up on it to watch the beautifying process. This day, she forgot to lower the lid. The puppy leapt up unexpectedly and landed in the bowl. Laughingly, the girls described the generous spray of water on the walls, the floor, and Stepmom. I noted their delight in relating that the poodle had to stay home because it was so wet. Right then and there, I established pet poodle therapy for dissolving triangles. I banished the poodle from further sessions. We spent a lot of time that day talking and laughing about the pet. Best of all, by the time the session ended, chairs and sofa were in a circle and their occupants had begun to talk to one another. Is it ethical to exclude pet poodles from family therapy?

SOMETIMES THERE ARE FAILURES . . . OR MAYBE NOT

Joan was a fiery volcano; Ted was an icy glacier. In Joan's family of origin, folks expressed their feelings in spontaneous eruptions. In Ted's, no one had feelings. Joan and Ted had found each other delightfully refreshing during their courtship. The storm began on their honeymoon and gathered intensity over the following years. By the time they reached me, Joan was still convinced she could help Ted get in touch with his feelings. He had concluded that she was mad because of her loud outbursts of emotion, especially anger. To prove her mentally ill, he dragged her to their family physician, two psychiatrists, and to a psychologist who gave her a battery of psychological tests. Their unanimous conclusion was that she was not mentally ill. Their unanimous recommendation was marital therapy.

Joan and Ted both declared that they wanted to improve their relationship. Having that amount of professional validation of her sanity, I began to explore their issues: communication, expressing feelings, and building intimacy. After several sessions, they announced they needed no more counseling and quit. I thought the therapy was a failure, for I judged that they did need more—much more. I was sure I had failed them and grieved for weeks.

A year later, I saw Ted at a neighboring church. I found out that he and his wife had divorced. He still maintained that she was mentally ill and believed he was much better off without her. "Self," I said to myself, "sometimes there are failures in therapy . . . or maybe not."

SUPERVISION—CATHOLIC STYLE

Two years ago, our academic department was housed in temporary quarters during extensive remodeling of our office building. Imagine a former cafeteria, divided into midget cubicles by movable partitions, now housing three separate university programs and the undergraduate admissions office. The two-story height of the ceiling and the thick padding on the dividers deadened most of the sound, but not all. I was especially concerned and careful about preserving confidentiality, so I usually did supervision elsewhere.

But one day, I goofed. I had to do quick supervision of a student who played part of a tape of a couple session. The male voice on the tape was describing his wife in racy and pejorative sexual terms, with plenty of foul language to enhance the conversation. Suddenly, a voice boomed from the other side of one of the partitions, shouting, "This is a Catholic University and we don't want any of that kind of talk around here!"

I just didn't realize how perverse my supervision had become. Furthermore, I made a firm resolution to thenceforth practice only "Catholic" supervision in my little cubicle.

UNBRIEF THERAPY

I believe in brief therapy. I teach brief therapy. In fact, I think I'm getting better at brief therapy. But some clients claim unbrief therapy—like Linda.

My earliest notes about Linda go back to 1988. She would drop in to see me sporadically, mainly with questions about the Catholic Church, which she labeled disdainfully, "The Church." She wondered about her fantasies of church walls breaking down. It wasn't until we got to the "blob on the floor which was either herself or her son" that her story began to flow. She had been spiritually and emotionally abused by a priest, her spiritual director. Two of her sons had been sexually abused by him. She felt betrayed, humiliated, and especially guilty about allowing her sons to be around him.

That was eight years ago. I am still seeing her, though much less frequently. Linda called forth from me such strong emotions and all the wisdom, courage, patience, and therapeutic skills I could muster. At that time, she was struggling with church officials to get them to believe her story and with the priest's congregation to get them to pay for therapy for herself and her sons. She was furious that the man was allowed to continue his ministry and endanger others in another part of the country. Her fury spread to every priest and inflamed her to besiege Church officials with letters, telephone calls, and threats of lawsuits.

The priest's abuse was only the crust of her issues. Under the crust was a husband who was bisexual, given to "making it" with guys as well as Linda, and on the verge of full-blown AIDS. Linda agonized over whether or not to leave him, what to tell their four children, and how to deal with prejudices among medical and insurance professionals.

In 1992, her husband died a slow, painful, and humiliating death. Most of the time, Linda had cared for him at home, a distasteful activity which affected the whole family negatively. Though the younger children didn't know their father had AIDS, they witnessed the stressful and frightening process. The emotional tension erupted openly after his death. Linda become distraught and depressed; the family became disorganized. One child had to be hospitalized for emotional problems. Some in her family of origin, wanting to help, rushed in to renovate her whole house and take over her finances—which Linda resented, but couldn't stop. Many of her friends vanished. Linda tried to start a business, and it failed. Someone from her parish harassed her sexually, and Linda began to recall her own experience of being sexually abused as a child.

Sometimes, I personally questioned Linda's incredulous stories. How could all of these things be happening to one woman and her family? Was I really competent enough to be working with her? I sought supervision and tried to involve other professionals with her. She kept coming back, by herself or with one or more members of her family. I worried that I was fostering dependency between us. I fretted and fumed—and prayed.

For Linda, life is calmer now. She no longer wails, "When will all this end?" Gradually, I discovered validations for her stories. Months after the incidents took place, I met a man who told me he knew I was seeing Linda and knew about the sexual harassment. In fact, he claimed to have stepped in to stop it!

Linda's children have also moved beyond those traumatic incidents. Two have graduated from college and married; one is entering college this fall; the last is doing very well in high school. Linda is blossoming in a secretarial position, and is studying to become a medical transcriber. I've often wondered what brief therapists would have done with all of this.

It's time to lay my kaleidoscope aside for awhile. Maybe someday I'll pick it up and do what so many other retirees threaten to do: write a book. Maybe not. Maybe I'll just spend my retirement doing what I like to do best—be a therapist who has learned to trust her clients. I learned much more in the past twenty-four years—too much to put in this story. I will tell you, however, another great lesson I stumbled upon: "Trust thyself."

Counseling Your Parents

Howard W. Stone

It's a long way from South Dakota to Arizona, even farther than the sum of the miles. Martha and Stanley Andresen made that trip, and there was no turning back. The two of them moved to Mesa, Arizona, from a small town near Sioux Falls, South Dakota. Both were born and raised in the southeastern part of South Dakota and, except for vacations, had not left that area for sixty-six years.

The Andresens liked the conveniences of a larger city, with its shopping, transportation, entertainment, and services. All of their family and friends still lived in South Dakota, but they looked forward to making new friends—and they loved the warmer climate.

Six months after moving, they arrived at my office door. Martha had called their minister back in South Dakota, and he referred them to me. She initiated the visit. "This move hasn't been what we expected, but we can't go back now. We sold our place," she stated. She went on, "Stanley is quiet, moody, and irritable most of the time. He hardly ever talks to me and when he says something, it's just to criticize. He blames the move on me. He's just generally hard to live with."

As their tale unfolded in the first session, I suspected that Stanley was not acting all that differently, but in the past, Martha had shrugged it off and spent her time with family and friends in their community. In Mesa, she had few friends, and relied upon Stanley more than she would have in the past.

Theirs had been a traditional marriage in a traditional small town. Stanley was newly retired. He had always complained about South Dakota's bitter winters: "We ought to move to Arizona when I retire, and get away from this cold." When retirement came, Martha took him at his word. Even though Stanley began to drag his feet at the end, their house sold faster than expected. Suddenly, they were on their way west.

For some reason, I could not seem to get anywhere with this couple, even though I am from the Midwest and knew the type of community they described. Like their children, I am a third-generation Scandinavian.

After three sessions, I decided to staff the Andresens' case. I reported at the case conference that I was very frustrated with the Andresens, saying, "They don't seem to be working very hard at the changes they need for adapting to their new home." I was so confounded by Martha and Stanley that I considered referring them to another counselor on our staff.

At the case conference, my colleagues asked the usual questions. Several of them pointed out what they saw to be wrong with the marriage, and how it might be handled. One staff member, Benjamin, listened quietly before he spoke up.

Benjamin: Where are your folks from?
Howard: Minnesota.
Benjamin: Where is this couple from?
Howard: South Dakota, right next door to Minnesota.
Benjamin: What did your dad do?
Howard: He recently retired from the post office.
Benjamin: What did Stanley do?
Howard: He retired from the post office six months ago.
Benjamin: How would you describe your parents' personalities?
Howard: Well, my father is very quiet and shy, and says very little to anyone. He has spent most of his life depressed and having migraine headaches. My mom is the one who runs the family. She's the dominant one who kept us kids in line.
Benjamin: How would you describe the personalities of these two people?
Howard: Definitely Martha's the one in charge. She has always been the one to speak for the family, to the kids, to friends and neighbors, and she does most of the talking in our sessions. Stanley prefers to sit on the sidelines. If he has anything to say, it seems to reveal a sad world with little hope and plenty of irritation. He's clearly a depressive.

Benjamin: How would you describe your parents' marital system?

Howard: It's a traditional marriage. Dad was always the boss technically, but the rules were expressed and enforced by my mother. She was the parental voice of the family to us kids and to others in the world.

Benjamin: How would you describe Stanley and Martha's marriage system?

Howard: They also have a traditional marriage, just what you would expect for people their age in a small town in the rural Midwest. Even though technically Stanley is the boss, Martha's the one who speaks for the family. [Pause.] Wait a minute! Are you suggesting . . . ?

Benjamin: It sure sounds like it.

Howard: You're not saying that I'm counseling my parents, are you?

Benjamin: There sure seem to be a lot of similarities between what you've told me about your parents over the years and this couple. Both couples are from the Midwest. All four of them are children of Scandinavian immigrants, and very religious. Both men have recently retired from the post office. Both men are quiet, shy depressives. Both women have been the leaders in the family. It sounds to me like this couple and your parents share many common characteristics. It also sounds like Martha and Stanley are very much like the personalities of your mother and father and have similar marriages.

I was stunned. It seemed so obvious, so clear, that a student in the first semester of an undergraduate marriage and family class would be able to see it easily. But I had not. In fact, I had been surprised at the way this couple frustrated my attempts to help them. It took someone else to point it out to me.

Counseling with Martha and Stanley went smoothly from then on. A few more sessions—which focused on communication and on helping the two of them become more involved in their new community and church—resolved what had brought them to counseling. We had not dealt with those problems in their relationship that I also perceived in my own family—those were Howard Stone's issues. Freed from the impulse to "fix" my parents' marriage, I was able to help Stanley and Martha begin creating a new life in Arizona, such a long way from their family, friends, and way of life back in South Dakota.

Certainly, I would never attempt to counsel a member of my own family. With Martha and Stanley Andresen, I discovered that I also should not counsel the *problems* of my family of origin when I encounter them in another family.

Trapped in Groundhog Day

Rudy Buckman

If I ask myself: "Which description is more likely to invite a healing response?" Is it reflexive?

—K. Tomm

In a recent movie Bill Murray finds himself trapped in a seemingly unending cycle of Groundhog Day, repeating the same experiences over and over with no relief in sight. To escape, Murray's character had to change so that his relationships with others were altered sufficiently to allow new experiences and a new future. Similar to Murray's character, I've recently had a very interesting experience in which Laura, a client, and I have been trapped in our own version of *Groundhog Day*. This experience of becoming stuck and eventually unstuck in Groundhog Day has profoundly affected me, the client, our relationship, and some of my ideas about therapy.

Laura and I have worked on and off for about three years, with gradual, but consistent resolution of issues that brought her to see me. I trace the beginning of feeling stuck to about a month ago, when Laura told me that she wanted to marry a man she has had a stormy relationship with for about three years. Her concern was that, just as she had in her first marriage, she would ignore warning signs that this relationship would turn out to be as hurtful as her first marriage. Consequently, we developed a plan that encouraged her to go into this relationship with her "eyes wide open," so she would be well aware of what she was getting herself in to.

While we followed this plan, I noticed her becoming more and more frustrated, angry, and disappointed in me, which became so intense she began to say things like "Why am I coming here?" and "Rudy, are you trying to piss me off?" This theme of very high expectations of others, their failure to live up to them, and her emotional reactions had become very relevant in discussions with me and her AA group. However, as the intensity of our discussions increased, I became very concerned that she might become so disappointed or angry that she would emotionally cut off, as she had with others in her life. Also, I became aware of feeling frustrated and unsure about how to proceed, and for some strange reason, I was actually perceiving her face to physically change so that she looked very similar to one of my sisters.

Growing up, I was very fond of this sister and had considered her to be my legitimate mother, since she had cared for so many of my physical and emotional needs. However over time our relationship deteriorated, as had many others in my family, due in part to anger and disappointment over family members' not living up to rigid family expectations. I never knew quite how to handle our estrangement, and our relationship ended without resolution when she died of cancer about three years ago. This lack of resolution, languishing like an undigested lump in my psyche, remained a reminder of my emotional entrapment.

What was I to do? Laura and I were not editing and rewriting a story, but had cast each other into a here-and-now Groundhog Day psychodrama that could have tragic consequences for both of us. I wish I could say that I easily stepped outside this drama, but I didn't. With great difficulty, I used some of my reflective habits of mind to review and pay close attention to our entanglement.

In reflection, I came to understand that the more I tried to help Laura—the more she pointed out how unhelpful I was—the more she became frustrated, angry, disappointed, and said things such as "I don't even know why I coming here"—the more I'd see my sister's face, feel frustrated and torn about whether to protect myself by withdrawing, trying harder to help (more of the same), or becoming critical of her. This conundrum was very sticky, and I had great doubts about my ability to become unstuck and explore new territory. My thoughts swirled with ideas from Freud (transference/countertransference), Kohut's and McGill's ideas about transmuting internalizations in therapy, to the philosophy and practice of aikido, which teaches how to transform conflict by joining with the attacker so conflict is transformed through an unusual kind of cooperation.

During the fourth session since I'd noticed our entrapment, our relationship had once again turned in upon itself, much like an emotional tornado, and I wondered if my unfinished business would continue to blind me to other ways of handling the situation. It was as if I could see in my mind's eye our relationship being strained and destroyed by our old interpersonal habits of self-protection and isolation, becoming another undigested lump of unfinished business. In the midst of feeling impotence and despair, a part of me began to center itself around a deeply felt need to reach out, to join with Laura, to invite her into a united front against what seemed like our common fate. As I followed this centered part of myself, Laura's world seemed to open up to me. How deeply she desired to feel close to others; how angry, frustrated, and disappointed she had felt as relationship after relationship had not brought much satisfaction to her life; and how she must feel as trapped as I do.

This was a different path with possibly a different future, but I began to wonder—Should I continue? Will I like this new future? Could it be worse than what I already experienced with my sister? Mustering my courage and proceeding, I said, "I've really let you down, haven't I?" She seemed to eye me suspiciously. Was she having the same doubts and concerns as I? We both seemed to pause, sensing the possibility of something new occurring between us, but unsure about how to proceed. She finally replied, "What do you mean?" As I listed several of her own examples of how I and others had "let her down," she cast her eyes downward. Uh-oh— where was this going? Were we forming a united front or was our relationship unraveling further? She looked me square in the face, eyes filled with what seemed like a new understanding and acceptance of herself and replied, "Yes, I'm good at putting a lot of expectations on others, aren't I?" Our intimacy demanded straightforwardness and I said, "Yes, and when we don't live up to your expectations, what do you do?" She said, "I feel like I do now—disappointed, frustrated, and angry and like the only thing I can do about this is to get away from the person."

During this conversation, the emotional field between us gradually changed to one of more openness and vulnerability. Every fiber of my being seemed to be saying, "Yes, this is a good path, a path with heart, a heart less protected and freer to open itself to another person's experience." Continuing on this path, I told her how much I appreciated her willingness to bring her high expectations, disappointment, frustration and anger into our relationship. She seemed surprised, and asked why. I replied, "So we can find a new way of handling this situation, you know, rather than cutting off from each other."

While discussing what this new way might look like and how she would investigate the effects of her high expectations, frustration, and anger on her relationships and sense of competence, a sense of healing came over our relationship. We had challenged the hold of Groundhog Day on our lives, and something new had occurred between us. Not only had our relationship been salvaged, but it also had been enriched and strengthened. Consequently, I no longer see my sister's face superimposed upon my client's face, and feel deep in my being that I have taken another important step in resolving an issue of great importance in my life. Laura continues to attend our meetings and reports that through this experience, she has really come to grips with how destructive her expectations have been on her and her relationships. In fact, she has recounted several experiences which illustrate how much her relationships have improved.

As I previously stated, this experience has profoundly affected me. Obviously, I learned a great deal about myself, about becoming stuck and unstuck in therapy, but what has really affected me the most has been the sense that I was participating in something larger than myself, such as an odyssey or spiritual journey. A journey similar to the one taken by Dante in the *Divine Comedy*, in which Virgil, who personifies poetic insight, leads Dante through the labyrinth of Hell to God. I was lost in old habits and powerful emotions, but found a way of becoming more human, more compassionate, and more capable of aligning myself with some egotranscending principle, such as service to others. This is how I make sense of this part of me that was so centered, so willing to reach out to another human being.

Joseph Campbell, in *The Power of Myth,* seems to capture the essence of my experience when he discusses the birth of compassion. He believes, as is the case in so many healing traditions, that compassion "is the healing principle that makes life possible" (p.112) and that this idea is "reflected in the medieval idea of the injured king, the Grail King, suffering from his incurable wound. The injured one becomes the savior. It is the suffering that evokes the humanity of the human heart" (p.112). Campbell goes on to say, "The big moment in the medieval myth is the awakening of the heart to compassion, the transformation of passion into compassion. That is the whole problem of the Grail stories, compassion for the wounded king. And out of that you also get the notion that Abelard offered as an explanation of the crucifixion: that the Son of God came down into this world to be crucified to awaken our hearts to compassion, and thus turn our minds from the gross concerns of raw life to the specifically human values of self-giving in shared suffering" (p.116).

Consequently, I feel thankful to have had another opportunity to learn about compassion and its role in healing. Doing so has also made me reexamine some of my theoretical ideas about therapy. For example, I'm much more concerned about making contact with a client from the first moments of our meeting. Verbally and nonverbally, I have a greater sense of wanting to reach out and begin forming a compassionate interpersonal connection. This has made me reread and appreciate even more the theories that emphasize the value of a therapeutic relationship and the advantages of working with the relationship itself.

While my narrative/postmodern assumptions emphasizing the self-reflexive nature of therapy enabled me to be very aware of both Laura's and my own reactions, I think its focus on meanings and descriptions through language may marginalize the body's felt or emotional experience. In this experience with Laura, the focus on here-and-now emotions, rather than meanings and descriptions about emotions, seemed to be a key in finding a way through this labyrinth. It was as if my emotions became a wise and experienced guide (Virgil?) that not only led me to reexperiencing my entrapment concerning my sister, but also "had a sense" of how to navigate a way through my current inertia with Laura. This has encouraged me, much like the Griffiths do in *The Body Speaks* (1994), to invite clients to feel their emotions more fully in their bodies and then follow the emotions to binding interpersonally constructed meanings. At that point, a therapist can use a variety of methods to deconstruct binding narratives and write nonbinding narratives.

Finally, I've come to appreciate and sometimes even welcome the experience of being trapped in Groundhog Day. These experiences are like walking on the edge, like treading the boundary between what is known and what is unknown. Of course Joseph Campbell says it best: "Very often, one of the things that one learns as a member of the mystery religions is that the labyrinth, which blocks, is at the same time the way to eternal life. This is the secret of myth— to teach you how to penetrate the labyrinth of life in such a way that its spiritual values come through" (p.115).

REFERENCES

Campbell, J. with Moyers, B. (1988). *The power of myth*. New York: Doubleday.
Griffith, J.L. and Griffith, M.E. (1994). *The body speaks: Therapeutic dialogues for mind-body problems*. New York: Basic Books.

Ben's Revenge:
Portrait of One Therapy Process

Leslye King Mize

Ben had to wait a long time. I was a young therapist and had not figured out about how to watch the clock. When he was finally sitting on my couch, it was very clear that he was irritated. Very quickly however, the story he began telling emerged with a great deal of bizarre and shocking detail. Was he trying to see how he could shock me? Was he testing me to see if I would hang in there? Stories of abuse, incest, multiple marriages, and multiple children for this twenty-four-year-old man were common factors in his tale. He reported being currently married to a forty-four-year-old woman who was drunk all the time. He described himself as a man who had lived many lifetimes in his short years, and he wanted to work on the choices he tended to make. Finally, he described himself as a man who felt as if he didn't have the choices that everybody else seemed to have. He wanted to change this.

I saw Ben for a long time. Our relationship became very important to him, and he told stories of his life that he had never told anyone. The office, in some ways, became a steady place for him where he could come and feel settled, a place where he came just for him. After a while, he began to make some important life changes and left therapy, content that he got his needs met. From my view, he had made some important changes and especially talked about his desire to father in a different way. Looking back, what I noticed about myself is that I didn't trust the process or my own effectiveness in it. Had anything really happened? Could I just not see it? Why was I still afraid of him and my own effectiveness as a therapist? Was he just being a good little boy to please me? What was really going on between Ben and I? Why was I not talking to anyone about this case? What was I afraid of?

Two years after leaving therapy, Ben returned. He reported that he had really made some major changes, and overall was very excited about the way his life was going. He said he had a very successful pest control business, remarried to a woman he felt he admired and respected, was participating in raising two of his four children, and was even running for city council. He reported he was back in therapy because he was having panic attacks, especially when he had to go into some dark, underground places for his business. He also stated that his grandfather, who Ben had reported earlier in therapy had molested him from the time he was six to eighteen, also suffered with panic attacks and was practically housebound before he died ten years ago. Even though his grandfather molested him, Ben reported still loving him deeply and feeling like he was the only person in his life that had really been there for him. Ben tended to minimize the molestation in his stories and maximize the connection. When I had tried in the earlier therapy process to focus on how the molestation might have effected his life and his relationships, Ben would just sluff if off, laughing about how those things happen and that it was no big deal! In thinking about the therapeutic process and what would be some goals for change, I (this is an important pronoun to note—not "we") worked at developing some strategies to minimize the panic attacks and to develop solutions for when Ben was in the middle of one. However, I got a sense that he really didn't care. He just wanted to ask me questions about my life and what I did when I wasn't in the office. As I addressed the process, I talked about how that was really not comfortable for me and explained that, after all, I was his therapist and my job was to listen to him, not for him to listen to me. He continued to share that I knew all about him, but that he knew very little about me. We reached an impasse, and I told him that he really ought to think about what he wanted out of therapy.

During this period of therapy with Ben, I was given a diamond solitaire from my grandmother that had been given to my father. My father had adored this stone, and it had much meaning for him before he died a few years before. One story of this diamond was that it was given to my grandfather from his best friend as a symbol of their friendship for sixty years and their professional work together. I too, as my father, was fascinated with the story, as men giving men such wonderful gifts had not been something I had experienced before—especially in my family. So the symbol of the gift was extremely meaningful to me. I began wearing the diamond around my neck as a pendant, and wore it one time in therapy on a day that Ben was coming in. I felt that due to the history of the diamond, I would really be blessed. Ben saw the diamond around my neck, and could not keep his eyes off of it. It fascinated him. As our session went on, he kept looking at my neck and the diamond. He referred to it several times during the session. Needless to say, I never wore the diamond again in session, but even after I stopped wearing it, Ben kept asking me to wear it again.

The next week, after the diamond session, Ben brought his current wife with him, which I had suggested would be a great idea. He introduced me to her as the woman who knew him better than anyone else in the world. It seemed to me that the entire time, he minimized his connection with his wife almost to the point of humiliation. She was a shy, reserved woman who did not say much and kept her head down. I tried very hard to engage her in the process, but she participated very little. Early in the session, I asked her if she would act as a consultant with us concerning the issue of Ben's reported panic attacks. She said she didn't even know that he had them. She said she thought he wanted her to come in because he was not happy in the marriage and wanted out. I remember putting myself in her shoes. The way he talked about his and my relationship would have been very difficult for me had I been his wife. As I began to address those issues directly, not much happened as neither Ben nor his wife wanted to address their relationship or how I fit into the problems they were having. Finally, I just stopped, backed up, and let the session direct itself. After discussing the children and Ben's business, the two left and didn't come back for some time.

During this period of therapy, Ben found out what the back line phone number was. Ben would call this number, often telling whoever answered that he was having a panic attack and needed help. Finally, disgusted that Ben was not hearing my requests for him not to call on that line, I referred him to another male therapist in the clinic, Mike, who was also my spouse. In the past, Ben was fascinated with Mike, always asking lots of questions about him and my relationship with him. I avoided these questions. I remember rationalizing that my clinical reason for referring him was that I thought someone else might be more effective in working with him at this point—especially a man. However, I now think that I was feeling angry and frustrated that Ben was not taking me seriously as his therapist, and that my relationship with him was more for him than just therapy. I never brought it up though, and neither did he.

Mike saw Ben for a number of sessions. He helped Ben design a plan for working with the panic attacks through cognitive behavioral relaxation techniques. Later, they would both report that it was very effective work. Ben would barely speak to me in the clinic, however. After his weekly sessions with Mike, if my door was open, Ben would stand at the door staring at me. I would say, "Hi, Ben," and he would just barely smile and walk off. I always felt uneasy and tried to minimize the experience.

A year or so after Mike and Ben terminated their work together, Ben called wanting to know if we would use him for pest control services. He had pushed us before on this issue, but we had explained to him that using his services might interfere with the therapy process. Mike and I both made it our policy not to use the services of our clients until a substantial length of time had passed. Ben claimed, upon this request, that a substantial amount of time had surely passed, that he was doing quite well, and that he wanted us to use his services, as it would show we had faith in his abilities. I was extremely uneasy, but we did. He would spray our home and the office.

After two or three months, I noticed that my diamond necklace was missing. I was heartsick, but felt that I had just put it away somewhere and that it would resurface. For several months, I struggled to remember where it might have been left. It never occurred to me that it might have been stolen.

When we called to have pest control service not long after, we discovered that Ben had gone out of business. I did hear from him again, however. He called me to ask if I would turn him in to the pest control board for suspecting that he had stolen something very valuable to me! There was a silence over the phone, and I asked him if indeed he had stolen my diamond. He laughed and hung up. That was the last time I ever heard from him again.

Looking back over this incredible tale, I have all kinds of insight and awareness that was certainly not clear to me at the time. My instinct to do therapy briefly was important not to brush aside. I also realize what a critical mistake it was for me not to trust my uneasiness early on and consult on this case, even if I had to stumble to clarity. I know now that somehow, I had some abstract shame over his attraction to me. Those "unprofessional" feelings of mine were somehow like the experience that women may feel when they have been assaulted—that somehow I had brought the experience on. My encouragement here and lesson to myself is to find the voice in the process and that Ben's participation and behavior were his experiences, not mine. Finally, the issue of attraction to one's therapist may not be addressed as clearly as it should be in the literature, and it's challenge as a therapeutic dilemma constructed.

Stories That Touch Us

Geddes Macallan

If you press me for an opinion, I can give you a quick and dirty one: therapy is a joke. But before you assume too quickly that you know exactly what I mean, let me tell a little of my story. To begin with, you might consider me a prime example—a poster child, really—of that mass-produced result of our advanced Western culture: a confused person with a bent toward giving up. What you see is a garden-variety example of the emotionally challenged walking wounded, who has spent years snatching defeat from the jaws of victory, getting close enough to claim success, but finding a way to shoot himself in the foot, or higher. I am a little frightened, a little sad, a lot moody, and well enough aware of it all to know the constant companionship of pain inside. In short, I'm quite a target for the burgeoning therapeutic industry.

You see, I said I wanted to change. And there have been no lack of resourceful, well-trained and good-intentioned helpers who delighted at the prospect of making a "therapeutic intervention." They patiently listened as I described my history. They took copious notes and spent hours charting the contours of my emotional road map. I read the books they suggested. I took the medicine they prescribed. We played out guided imagery and comforted the inner child. I practiced in groups and did homework on my own. But after a rather large investment of their time, no small amount of work on my part, and a not insignificant accumulation of therapy-related indebtedness (which I am now proud to say has been paid in full), the disappointing truth was that I was still conducting my life the same frustrated way. The world continued to be a less-than-friendly place. Perhaps with all this, a jaded reading of the opinion I stated above would really just be a cynical and frustrated criticism of the counseling profession. But I did want to change. And I needed help.

I found a helper who would be perfectly frank. A trusted friend suggested I contact him. A brief phone call, a short wait, and I was sitting in a waiting room, nursing enough discomfort to nudge me into taking the initiative to be there, but dubious enough about the process to wonder if change, other than changing therapists, was possible. I quickly learned the answer to that question was up to me. Not even halfway through the first session, two things were apparent: (1) the therapist was there to help me do for myself, and (2) humor was as important to him as it was to me. One-liners (I just miswrote "one-loiners"), infamous movie scenes, "have you heard the one about. . . ," sitcom gaffs, fifth-grade potty humor, and philosophical absurdity—we laughed, we blushed, we smiled, we hooted, and, somewhere in the process, we connected. I felt respected, understood, and liked. Hard to believe all that developed partly from the retelling of an ancient Groucho Marx punch line, "Well, I love my cigar, but I take it out occasionally." For a little while every couple of weeks, I did not need any help. And the feeling was good enough to want to experience it in the real world.

The trouble was that the real world was not so hospitable; at least it did not appear to be from my point of view. I was convinced that whatever I attempted was just too much for me to succeed. The harder I tried, the more frustrated I got, and the more creatively I worked at screwing things up worse. I just could not succeed. The combination of potential and failure was depressing. So we embarked on a path to face my worldly problems head-on. No pep talks. No grand strategy for self-improvement. No excuses or gimmicks. The plan was very simple: if I could not get over the bar, lower the bar. Eventually, after digging a ditch and nearly burying the bar, I stumbled over it. Maybe it was not pretty, but I succeeded. Success felt good.

By this time I was ripe for doing things in a new way. Achievement in and out of the sessions began to build confidence. Perhaps my problems were not more than I could handle. Could it be that I was capable of taking care of myself? It was time for a new image of how things worked. It happened on a Saturday morning. The previous week, we had talked about getting free of imaginary limits. One story particularly captured my imagination. It is said that when Indian elephants are small, they are trained by placing a chain attached to a small stick around one of their legs. Even the small stick is too heavy for the baby elephant to move. So, the elephant learns to stay in one place. Later, when the elephant grows and would be capable of moving the small stick without much more than a flick of its toenail, it continues to be controlled by the old chain and small stick. The elephant does not realize its own strength. It is held captive by the negligible actual weight of the stick. What really keeps the elephant in one place is its own recollection of the stick. Imagine how absurd it is for a small stick to prevent the huge elephant from moving. The elephant has no idea what it is capable of doing, but it acts as though it was powerless.

With this on my mind, I went for a walk in a park near my home. There were hills, budding oak trees, and lots of little creatures rustling in the leaves and underbrush. The exertion of physical exercise usually had as good an effect on my thoughts and feelings as it did on my body. The general notion of breaking free of limits played itself out in several areas of my life as I walked, thinking about vocation, intimacy, parenting, traveling, and creating. But I kept running into a dead end. There was some sort of demand that whatever I did had to be "good enough." Regardless of whether or not it was the first time I tried it, or did it when I was tired, or was doing something in a new way—a paralyzing expectation of perfection took all the life and fun out of things. There were only two ways of approaching things: the "right" way and anything else. So, weary of body and weary of mind, I returned to my apartment to get cleaned up. As I was getting into the shower—perhaps there is something about cleansing, baptism, or just being naked and vulnerable—it hit me. It is not that I am locked into only one certain, correct way of doing things. The fact is that any choice is possible, even the choice not to choose. But the important point for me was this: in any given moment, you cannot not change what happens next. It was not a choice between "doing" something or "not doing" anything: dieting or overeating, exercising or being a couch potato, thinking or watching TV, or working or being lazy. Those were *all* options among an infinite number of options. I cannot not change what happens next. And that is a very empowering, energizing, and freeing way of looking at things. There is no single "right way" which must be discovered and followed or all is lost. There are merely a number of options that can be chosen and attempted. Life becomes a big experiment with no meaningless outcomes. It all matters.

Armed with that new way of looking at things, born out of all the preceding meanderings of body and soul, I began to approach the important things in life without the chain and stick that had once held me captive. When the paralysis began to creep back, my mantra became, "you can't not change what happens next." You cannot imagine what good news that was. It was as if a tremendous gift had been given to me. It seemed as though I was given my life to use and invest as I wanted to. I felt like the beneficiary of someone's extravagant, gracious action. I felt respected, understood, and liked. What I increasingly realized was that I was both giver and receiver. I changed.

It was not easy for me to be honest, open, or to change. It took a radical experience of grace to break through. That felt similar to some other moments that had been freeing and life-giving moments such as when I physically revealed myself to someone and made myself vulnerable, as they did to me. Sex had that sort of honesty and surprising character of gift. Or like the sense of being caught off guard and vulnerable when a well-timed punch line was delivered in a classic joke. I lost my balance for a moment, was outside myself with a view of the "big picture," and in that instant of freedom, was somehow myself in a way most moments did not contain. It was the sense I had when I saw my daughter for the first time, seconds after she was born. Or like the awareness that settled over me as I held the hand and watched the chest of the ninety-seven-year-old man cease his breathing, an activity he had repeated about twenty times a minute every minute of every hour of every day since the country doctor had slapped him on the butt almost a hundred years earlier. Life, death, sex, grace, and humor seem like pieces cut from a common—or uncommon—cloth. Humor is in some pretty good company. From this point of view, it is with a sense of reverence and honor that I repeat, therapy is a joke.

Alcohol—I Somehow Remember . . .

Jürgen Hargens
"Mrs. Green"

INTRODUCTION

This is a somewhat unusual story—it has been written by two people. I thought that all too often, "client voices" belong to the realm of "unspeakable theories and unknowable experiences" (Conran and Love, 1993). As "alcoholism" can be seen as a field of controversies, of theories that seem to contradict each other, of approaches that seem to be based on myths (Berg and Miller, 1995), I thought it might be interesting to tell you a story about just this and to give you at least two stories—the story of the so-called professional (i.e., the therapist) and the story of the so-called client (i.e., the expert for drinking and not drinking). The first story "Alcohol Is Just a Remedy for Thirst, Isn't It?" is told by the therapist and the second story, "Just Letters . . . and Something More . . ." is told by "Mrs. Green," the client.

ALCOHOL IS JUST A REMEDY FOR THIRST, ISN'T IT?

This is a story about alcohol—at least when looking at the face value. But before starting, I have to make three remarks.

The work is still continuing and thus, I asked my *Kundin** to give her perspective on the story and she agreed to do so. This means

---

Kundin is a German word which literally means "customer." The adjective *kindig* also means "being an expert," "knowing," etc. Thus, we talk of clients as *Kundin* because they are "customers" in using our services, as well as being experts in knowing what they want and how to get it. We openly use this term, explaining these two aspects, and our *Kundinnen* (plural) usually like this idea.

that you can read two sides of the story. Each side has been written without knowing the other side. I read her story after I finished my story and vice versa. I am very excited about the similarities, differences, and comments. For me it is one of the rare moments to give public voice to the Kundin.

I have to confess, too, that I am very familiar with alcohol because my father drank most of his life—and most of his drinking was daily. All of a sudden, he gave it up when he was in his mid-fifties—without any treatment, without any professional support. He quit one day and he never did it again. I think this has made an impression on me, supporting my belief in the competency of people: People do what they want to do!

And third, I had written a book review for the local newspaper about a book which related the family history of Thomas Mann, a famous German writer. The book was written by Marianne Krüll (1991), a female sociologist who traces the influence of the women in the Mann family. As you can imagine, it was a *different* book and the review ended with a reference to my being a family therapist.

About two years after that publication, a woman called asking for an appointment. We met in October 1993 for the very first time. She said that she wanted to work with my partner* and I because we were the people who could help her. Asking how she knew, she referred to that book review! Meanwhile, in March 1996, we are still meeting together in therapy, but differently, having had twenty-two sessions together. The interval between sessions was about a month; starting in May 1995, the interval increased from two to three months—deliberately planned to help the Kundin get what she wants.

The woman—I call her Mrs. Green (as green is the color of hope and of life)—had problems with alcohol, but she wanted to continue drinking because she liked to sit in her room, reading and drinking wine. She just wanted to stop getting totally drunk. She felt forced by her surroundings—the family, the colleagues, the friends—who wanted her to totally stop drinking. We never questioned her goal;

---

*At that time, Jürgen always worked in a team of two, and Stefanie Dieckmann was the other therapist.

we tried to talk about what *she* wanted to do and how *she* thought she could use alcohol the way she wanted.

In between sessions she had *prelapses*. I prefer the term prelapse instead of relapse in order to make it clear for myself that the Kundin had *not gone back* (to drinking) but *gone forward* (to manage drinking *differently* with *different* experiences). She was found drunk by a co-worker, who asked me to call her. I did. So, what could I do on the phone? I just asked, "What do you want me to do?" and she replied, "Just hearing your voice makes me feel better and gives me hope."

She came to the next session and we talked about her prelapse. This had not been the only prelapse. There were two or three of them, and we never questioned her goal of continuing drinking as she wanted to do. We asked her what *she* thought we could do for her in this very session—we never addressed the prelapse unless she did herself.

She once came in telling us that she had to go into the clinic because the people and her employer forced her to do so. She hated it, but she did not know how to avoid it. So we had an interesting session about what she thought she could do—going into the clinic, undergoing a treatment which she thought was bad for her. We ended up painting a picture of Mrs. Green as *different* from other people—and as a *curious* woman. We asked her how she thought this different approach was informed, and what its practice looked like. Finally, we came up with the idea of doing field research: she could go into the clinic as a participant-observer, studying how the professionals realized an approach that was so different from what was good for Mrs. Green. Thus, she could go there not as a patient but as a scientist. We also came up with the idea of her writing a book about all this. She liked the idea. She went there and she had to tolerate this ambivalence. (By the way, she took notes, she is still taking notes, and *her* book is still in progress.)

By chance, we set up a meeting in fall 1994, exactly on her birthday—and she loved to come! The theme of that meeting was very fascinating: we talked about whether the diagnosis of "drinking" fit or not. Looking back, I think this theme could be seen as a wonderful birthday present.

suspect nearly half of (hu)mankind is convinced and which has so many absurdities that it should be obvious for everybody. I cannot tell in these lines what I really think about it. Just two things: I believe that the anonymity of self-help groups is very important for their success. Conversely, it is accepted that most people in the workplace know about it (the alcohol problem) in order to better control the alcoholic. And nobody has any reservations if my husband is strolling through our neighborhood looking for our friends, asking them not to offer me any alcohol. In other words, within the circle of people who are expected to help me (the self-help group) I am anonymous, and within the circle of the other people, I am a public person. How can I express my gradually becoming mad and not simultaneously confirm my alcohol problem?

In these moments, I always thought of my therapy in Meyn and the conversations that took place there, and often I also thought of insulting rounds of long-term hospital treatment that were filled with contradictions.

During the sessions in Meyn, the look forward became more and more important. I had totally lost sight (though a lot of other people reminded me) that my time of living was limited and that I had to become active if I wanted to achieve something. Of course, I am allowed to drink myself to death, and for a long time, the benefit of my drinking behavior did not compare with the damage. But I could not keep from drinking, though I was able to examine it. I simply acted before I turned on my senses. And today, I know that I cannot restore this condition with wine—I just stop. In former times, I had pushed on with high-proof hip flasks or big bottles, encouraged by patterns of control—and hide-and-seek-games with my husband. And there is, of course, a mere physical problem—to be ripe for the hospital.

Without really wanting it, I had to drink myself into a "ripe" condition four times so that I had to be hospitalized. I used alcohol to retreat from therapy, to tell the therapist, "Not me!"

In Meyn, I not only felt good, I started to realize how strong I am, and gradually recognized myself. I feared my own strength. To admit it could become dangerous for my surroundings. This I knew because I had learned very early.

So sometimes I reached such emotional highs (e.g., long-distance traveling, going to an attorney) that it became necessary to kind of "trip myself up" and come back down. But it was just these repetitions that gave me self-confidence, and I practiced this pattern over and over again.

In just the third session in Meyn, Mrs. Dieckmann and I thought—independently of each other—that I would never drink again—I felt so good. But just thinking this had to be followed by a setback.

For a long time, I surely knew—and it became more and more clear—that I would have "functioned" quite differently in my marriage and my family without these continuous feelings of guilt and meekness. I acted in a way in which I could expect even less of my husband because it is my feeling that he cannot deal with a strong woman. We would have had to separate very early and the family would have been broken.

I really cannot tell how this got gradually lost in Meyn. It just happened, and it is still happening. Some things I see through what "happened with me there." One thing I know for sure—if Stefanie and Jürgen would have tried to take my individual and original thinking out of me as so many people tried to do, I would have preferred to get mad!

My future plans are tempting, but definitely realizable if I stay healthy. And the (unpunished) success of my recent trip gives me certainty.

Mrs. Green

P.S. Basically, I am currently endangered—I realized just after our last conversation. It started with thoughts of uncertainty about who I really am and whether I should slip into and hide in my cocoon.

REFERENCES

Berg, Insoo K. and Miller, Scott D. (1995). *The Miracle Method. A Radically New Approach to Problem Drinking.* New York and London: Norton.

Conran, Tom and Love, Joyce. (1993) Client Voices. Unspeakable Theories and Unknowable Experiences. *Journal of Systemic Therapies,* Summer 1993, 1-19.

Efran, Jay S., Lukens, Michael D., and Lukens, Robert J. (1990). *Language, Structure, and Change. Frameworks of Meaning in Psychotherapy.* New York: Norton.

Krüll, Marianne (1991). *Im Netz der Zauberer. Eine andere Geschichte der Familie Mann.* (In the web of the sorcerers. A different story of the Mann family.) Zürich: Arche.

Achelra and the Big Experiment:
A Story of Collaboration and Connection
with a Scared Eleven-Year-Old

Susan B. Levin

The following story describes a therapeutic relationship between
Achelra,[1] her foster parents, myself, and the Children's Protective
Services (CPS) caseworker who was responsible for her. The first
sections contain my reflections on struggling to be respectful, collaborative, and nonhierarchical with an eleven-year-old child who
did not really want to be in therapy, and who really did not want to
talk about her past sexual abuse. The second section contains a brief
transcript of a conversation I had with Achelra and her foster
mother about their experience of therapy, after about three months
into the process. Finally, the last section takes a quick look at some
theoretical issues that were raised for me through this process. I do
not believe that there are many answered questions about these
issues, but hope that they generate further discussion.

A COLLABORATIVE STRUGGLE

Once upon a time, Achelra was faced with a tough problem. She
had a therapist (that's me) who also had a tough problem. Both of us
had a CPS caseworker who wanted us to do something we both
thought would be very, very hard. I thought it would be hard because
the caseworker wanted me to get Achelra to work on things that
Achelra did not want to work on. And as I am a collaborative therapist,[2] giving Achelra a problem to work on that was not what she
wanted to do was very, very difficult for me. Achelra thought it
would be hard because she did not want to think, talk, or feel about

having been sexually abused by her father.[3] Achelra tried to convince everybody that she had already talked about it in a counseling group,[4] and therefore, didn't need to anymore. Despite both Achelra's and my attempts to convince the caseworker (even Achelra's foster parents[5] tried to tell him that she was doing fine) the mean, old, grumpy caseworker[6] thought Achelra needed more help with this history, and Achelra's attempts to convince others that she was okay were signs that she was avoiding and denying the problem.

So . . . I met with both of Achelra's foster parents, and we agreed to work together to explain to Achelra the caseworker's position. It was difficult for Achelra to understand why the caseworker wanted her to "do this again." Her foster mother and I tried to explain, as best we could, what the caseworker's thinking seemed to be. We explained that he thought that Achelra would have problems in the future if she didn't work on these things now. We discussed with Achelra the analogy of healing wounds, and how if you cover them up too completely, they won't heal . . . that wounds needed air and medicine and to be carefully watched to make sure they were healing. We told her that many people believed the same thing about emotional wounds, and that we thought that her caseworker had the same idea.

Achelra agreed to *try* to talk about what happened, but confessed that she was very afraid of how hard it would be. She also reported that she thought it would be easier for her to talk to me alone. We discussed and explored what Achelra meant by "easy" and "hard" as it related to her talking about her experiences, and we also discussed what the caseworker might think we should do about making it easy on Achelra. We had an interesting discussion concerning these ideas, as learning to get through the hard things seemed like a good experience, yet purposely avoiding making it easier on a person in distress seemed almost sadistic. We also discussed the question of how to know if something would be as hard as expected. This brought the idea that maybe Achelra would find that talking about it would not be as hard as expected, and she could experiment with ways of checking that out.

With Achelra's help, we eventually came up with a number of ways for Achelra to experiment with finding out how hard it was for her to talk about what happened. Initially, this occurred with her choosing to talk with me privately, while her foster mother waited in the reception area. Achelra walked in, sat down, and jumped into a rapid, monotonous report of the incidents she remembered. This first "report" allowed little room for questions, and after she was done with her "report," Achelra explained that her idea was to "get it over with as fast as possible." Our conversation in the next session was based on our reflections of that "plan," how it worked for Achelra, and what the next part of the experiment would be. We discussed how hard the previous session had been in comparison to her expectations, and Achelra reported which part was the hardest (telling about her father having intercourse with her). Achelra decided the next step was to find out how hard it would be to tell her foster mother the same things she had told me, with the option of stopping if it became too hard. We developed a signal for Achelra to use if she felt like stopping, which called for her to scratch her right cheek with her finger.

In keeping with an open and experimental attitude, we started the next session with her foster mother finding out different ideas Achelra had about how to tell her story. She chose to start by writing a letter to her foster mom, stating what happened. Achelra seemed relieved at having this possibility for communicating, and literally hid behind a huge pad of paper while she wrote the letter. Achelra chose to have her foster mother read the letter silently. We talked about whether she could sit near her foster mom while she read it, and what might happen when her foster mom read what happened to her. Achelra wrote in the letter that she could hug her, that it might be hard and might make her cry. Following the silent reading of the letter, Achelra decided it was okay for part of the letter to be read out loud, and identified sections that she did not want anyone to verbalize.

THE "SAID" AND THE "UNSAID"

This led to a discussion of Achelra's ideas about the words being verbalized. Reporting that it was not really *that* hard to have written about it, upon review, Achelra said that it would be really hard to say it out loud. So . . . next session was spent exploring ways to say it out loud that were less hard than others. Achelra seemed to become very interested in this in terms of a real, scientific experiment, which she had recently learned about on a field trip to a science museum. Based on her new scientific perspective, Achelra developed a hypothesis, three experimental conditions, and signs of "hardness." Achelra's hypothesis was that it would be "hard" to read her letter (especially paragraphs two and three) out loud with me and her foster mom listening. She decided to experiment reading the letter from across the room, half-way across the room, and sitting next to her foster mother, while measuring "hardness." Achelra's measures for hardness were: stumbling, pausing, hiding her face, racing through the reading, using a soft voice, and crying. After each reading, she rated herself. She also had her foster mother and myself rate her. Achelra seemed surprised (as were we) to conclude that distance/proximity was not as important to ease in verbalizing her story, as was repetition. Achelra found that each time she read the letter, it got easier. We related this to practicing— the more you practice difficult things the easier they get.

Sessions continued to be oriented toward discussing whether there were further experiments that she was ready to take (with finding out how hard it is to talk about what happened to her). Achelra predicted hard challenges such as talking with her biological mother about the sexual abuse, talking with her foster father, and being able to trust men. During this period, Achelra reported for the first time that her fourteen-year-old brother had also sexually abused her prior to the family's separation. Again, conversation focused upon what it was like for her to talk about these things, and whether it was as hard for her as she anticipated.

TALKING HELPS

In preparing to publish this story, Achelra has reviewed several drafts. She has reported that therapy helped her "overcome my feelings and emotions" and that "talking about it over and over again helped." The following is a transcript of a conversation between myself, Achelra, and her foster mother (FM) about therapy, and whether or not it had been helpful.

Sue: How would you describe what happened in therapy to a friend?

Achelra: It helped me overcome my feelings and emotions. Practice talking about it, over and over again, helped . . . . I'd go to therapy again if I was doing really bad and feeling really bad and had too many flashbacks and got just plain sick. Therapists should be very sweet and helpful and kind. They should strengthen me. I felt stronger when I read the letter [she wrote to her foster mother about the sexual abuse], when you were rating me, and I was rating myself.

FM: It's interesting. I think we got off to a slow start. Some of the games we played, when we played hangman, trying to get started, not talking about real problems. I didn't know how to help the therapist, whether to push Achelra. It's a learning process, having not been through it before, to decide, hey, we're not going anywhere here.

Achelra: I thought the slow start was fun, I kind of miss that part. I wish we could do both.

FM: The slow start led to us being more relaxed; maybe it would have been a little too clinical.

Sue: What do you think has been the hardest part of therapy so far?

Achelra: Trying to tell what my dad did, for the first time. I didn't feel like you'd understand; you and my foster mother were totally different people, and I didn't know you very well. Having to get to know a whole new therapist, starting over. Going through this again.

FM: Trying to get Achelra to open up because I have difficulty with that myself. A lot of the things that I would keep to myself are the things I am encouraging her to talk about.

Achelra: That's not good; that's what my mom did and she ended up with [multiple] personalities.

Sue: What do you think has been the easiest part of therapy? What was the most helpful?

Achelra: Reading the letter I made, telling about what my father did, and talking about it with practice. Practice made that easy. Playing the games was easy, except I was hoping you wouldn't bring up what happened. Practicing was the most helpful. What was helpful was getting through to my mind that I had to do it. I knew I couldn't hide and not say anything for a whole hour, I had to say something and just get it out.

Sue: What advice do you have for therapists who are stuck with the problem of what to do when the client doesn't want to talk about something, and the caseworker (and others) think the client should?

Achelra: Say it's for the client's own good to talk about it because it won't stick with them for the rest of their life, you can lose a lot of the memory and still have a little bit, it won't bother you so much. They should have fun so the client doesn't think it's boring; making it fun is enjoyable . . . playing hangman with what happened . . . combining games and what happened.

THE CASEWORKER'S STORY

What has not been addressed yet is the caseworker's understanding of Achelra's participation in therapy. As a member of the therapeutic system, and the person who referred Achelra to therapy, the caseworker's concerns contributed a major part of the agenda that was constructed for therapy. The caseworker, who had fairly regular contact with Achelra, her foster family, her birth mother, and her siblings, was pleased with the reports he got regarding the therapy process. However, the caseworker left CPS before Achelra finished therapy, and a new caseworker entered the therapeutic system, with her own ideas and concerns. Achelra continued to practice talking about her "hard-to-tell story" and seemed to have a new understanding that when things seem hard, you should experiment with ways to handle them; you will usually find some ways that you are comfortable with.

THEORY: A PROFESSIONAL STORY

Psychological theory holds that sexual abuse and trauma will interfere with psychological development and health if not treated. Many people believe that individuals suffer in silence because they are in denial or cannot face the pain of confronting the issues. Social constructionism and narrative theory take a different look at how personal narratives develop through relationship. Additionally, some feminist and collaborative perspectives have introduced the notion of "voice" in relationship to identity. For individuals to be able to talk with others to make sense of their lives as a part of the construction of meaning is critical to the self (Levin, 1992). Some propose that trauma is a condition in which meaning-making processes are interrupted (Lifton, 1982; Frankl, 1979).

There are many reports from survivors of trauma, whether from child abuse, domestic abuse, war or other violence, of feeling they could not talk with anyone about their experiences. It is interesting to consider the possibility that this is the result of a social situation—the lack of a concerned audience—rather than a sign of an individual defect (weakness, denial, avoidance, lack of trust). Children who are abused are afraid to tell, as they expect their parents to be their only caretakers and may feel threatened by the perpetrator, or fear rejection by the nonabusing parent. Women who have been battered report telling others about their experiencing abuse and find that they often jump to advice, telling them to leave, and responding as if they must be crazy to want to stay in the relationship.

A HUMAN AUDIENCE

Finding the right audience is often difficult, and it may not be that just any concerned individual or therapist could be one. For Achelra, though her caseworker was concerned and willing to be an audience, he was not the right person for Achelra to start with. As Achelra so strongly put it, she needed practice in order to be comfortable with talking about her experience and be able to expand her audience. It is also important to recognize, however, that in some ways, I was unwilling to be her audience. Out of concern and respect for Achelra, and a recognition of her fear, I did not carry an assumption that she needed to talk about her sexual abuse experience in therapy. This highlights the interaction and reflexivity inherent in "being an audience." One cannot serve as an audience unless invited to do so. It is my contention that had I been the person to "push" Achelra to talk about being sexually abused, I would not have been the right person for her to talk to. If you are the director of a play, you cannot also be the audience, can you?

What happens when people do not find an audience, when one does not have the determination to try to find someone to talk to? Achelra's caseworker was right, from my perspective, to "force the issue" of her talking more about her abuse, but not for the reasons he believed. Achelra came to learn that there are people in the world she could trust, that her experience does not have to be hidden because no one wanted to listen, that telling someone about it might not make them see her differently, and that being connected to others is what being human is all about.

Equally significant was Achelra's surprise at finding that she could orchestrate ways of working on her "problem" (the difficulty in telling about her sexual abuse). This experience taught her that problems become solvable by searching out options, making small steps, and practicing them.

SUCCESS STORIES

There are many ways to look at my story about Achelra, what happened between us in therapy, and what the outcome was. That we might call therapy a success here could be questioned, and what was successful about it could have many interpretations. My ideas about the results of our work together, as reported above, clearly reflect my theoretical bias toward collaborative, option-generating, flexible therapy. That it could be called a success is only based on one way of looking at it; Achelra, her foster parents, and her case-worker(s) were pleased. I continue to struggle with the initial question of being in a position of working with someone on a problem that he or she does not want to work on. When this someone is a child in a non-powerful position in a family or protective system, his or her opinion is often overlooked. We as experts "know" what is right, what is healthy, and what should happen to help the child. There must be many children, I assume, who would not respond to the situation as Achelra did. I believe a careful ear, a warm heart, and an open mind can keep us from causing harm in therapy to those who are entrusted to us to be healed.

Finally, to underline a "success" of Achelra's experimentation, it should be noted that a very uncertain eleven-year-old, who started off almost refusing to participate in telling her story, is fully aware [and has given consent] that I am sharing *our story* in a big way, through this publication.

NOTES

1. Achelra is the name chosen by my client to disguise her identity, as she actively participated in helping construct this story, and is fully aware that it is being published.

2. Doing therapy from a Collaborative Language Systems approach invites therapists to understand their clients as the expert on their experiences, knowing more about the problems at hand, than we do. We are therefore humanized, and are not the possessors of the "truth" or the "magic" needed to fix people.

3. Achelra's father was in prison during the period in which therapy took place, for the sexual abuse to which he admitted.

4. About six months prior to our meeting, Achelra had gone to a group for girls who had been sexually abused, that met during an eight-week period.

5. Achelra was in her second foster home after a one-year placement in another home fell through. Achelra and her three siblings were all placed in different foster homes.

6. Achelra's caseworker really isn't mean, old, or grumpy, but rather very concerned about Achelra and trying to do everything he can think of to make sure that she heals from her abuse experience. His idea that she was in "denial" is extremely common in the helping professions when someone disagrees with his or her treatment plan.

REFERENCES

Frankl, V. E. (1979). *The Unheard Cry for Meaning*, First Edition, New York: Simon And Schuster.

Levin, S. B. (1992) *Hearing the Unheard: Stories of Women Who Have Been Battered*. Dissertation abstracts.

Lifton, R. J. (1982). Beyond psychic numbing: A call to awareness. *American Journal of Orthopsychiatry, 52,* 519-529.

LEARNING AND SUPERVISION

A Blessing

Howard W. Stone

Carter showed up at seminary in August wearing cut-offs, tennis shoes, and a muscle T-shirt. He was in his early thirties, blond, tan, and handsome, with a winsome smile.

Carter had been born into a well-heeled East Coast family and went to the right Ivy League university. After graduation and a two-year stint as a stockbroker, he "dropped out" and moved to Berkeley, California. His life alternated between Telegraph Avenue and the beach . . . days of sand, surf, and sun, and evenings of meaningful conversations in coffee houses and sidewalk cafes.

Somewhere between the beach and the coffee houses, Carter found faith. It was not the New Age/Zen/Eastern-inspired religion of many of his companions on Telegraph Avenue. It was not the hellfire-and-brimstone religion of the Bay area's street corner evangelists. He started attending a Presbyterian church in Berkeley, and after some time, realized that he needed to make some changes in his life. There had to be another purpose for his days.

Carter felt called to the Christian ministry, and so he sold his surfboards and his wet suits. He left the beaches and the sun of California for seminary in north central Texas, where I teach. A week after arriving in Texas, he sat in my Introduction to Pastoral Care and Counseling class. Carter looked as if he'd be more at home on a surfboard than in a seminary classroom. He was cool and laid back. He had the best suntan in the room. I soon discovered that he was also a good student.

Most of the students at our seminary serve local churches as assistant ministers while going to school. At first Carter declined to work in a church; he was not certain whether he wanted to be a minister and chose to tend bar at a downtown hotel instead. Later that year, he accepted a position as a youth minister in a suburban congregation. He saw it as a way to find out "if this ministry thing is my bag or not."

Early one Monday morning, Carter caught me in my office. I was busy preparing for an afternoon class, but within seconds his story pinned me to my chair. He said he had not slept since Saturday. He looked exhausted.

Ben, aged thirteen, was a member of Carter's middle school youth group. He played on the church softball team. Carter had talked with Ben briefly at youth meetings and ball games, and knew that his home life was somewhat chaotic. Ben did not get along well with his mother; his father moved in and out of the family's home; Ben never knew if his dad would be at home or not.

With a ball game coming up in a couple of days and in need of a good infielder, Carter stopped by Ben's house to say hello, let him know that he had been missed at several recent events, and that he was needed at the game.

No one answered immediately, but the front door was ajar. Carter stepped partway in and called out Ben's name. Someone Carter did not know showed up at the door. Carter introduced himself as the assistant pastor of their church and asked for Ben. After a little uncomfortable quizzing by this unknown person, Carter was ushered into the home.

Carter quickly learned that Benjamin's mother had committed suicide only a few hours before. The police had been there and gone. The county coroner had left with the body only moments before. Ben's father, William, was there along with Ben's older and younger sisters and several other relatives. Everyone was in shock; they sat in the living room saying little. There Carter stood, dressed for youth ministry, in his khaki shorts, golf shirt, and tennis shoes.

Carter told me that his first impulse was to apologize for being there, excuse himself, and tell them that he would come back later, "but I knew that as a minister, I was supposed to stay with these people, to help them in any way that I could to begin to deal with this terrible loss that had just happened."

After greeting the assembled group, Carter went over to Ben and asked him what had happened. Haltingly, Ben told the story, with the others in the living room filling in the spaces. Barbara had been drinking for three or four days. Part of the time she was in a stupor, and the rest of the time, she screamed at Ben and his sisters. She was primarily angry at her husband, William, who had left the family once again. William had stopped by to see the children. He and Barbara argued. She went into the bathroom with her husband's pistol, and shot herself in the head.

Ben asked Carter to follow him, and before he could think twice the two of them were opening the door to the bathroom. The floor, walls, and ceiling were splattered with blood and particles of brain tissue. The lights in the bathroom had been left on, and the heated brain tissue on the light bulbs had begun to stink.

Carter stumbled back into the living room with Benjamin. He asked if a minister had been there yet and they said no, he was the only one. Carter asked if they would like him to call the senior pastor at his church. They answered (to his dismay) that his presence would be enough.

Never before had Carter been at the scene of a death or with a family in grief. No one in his immediate family had died, nor had anyone in his acquaintance committed suicide. His mind was reeling, trying to figure out what a minister ought to do at a time like this. Finally, he had the nerve to ask if they would like a prayer. Several people said, "That would be fine." Carter told me, "I have no idea what I said in that prayer. I just remember the sheer terror I was experiencing in a situation where so little makes sense." After the prayer, he sat with the relatives in their stunned silence. "Most of the people were looking vacant, hardly saying anything. All of the time, I was in shock. I didn't know what to do, and wished I wasn't there. What does a minister do when someone has committed suicide? What do you say to a thirteen-year-old boy whose mother has just killed herself?"

After a period of time, Carter realized that the smell in the bathroom was filtering into the living room and everyone was uncomfortable with it. No one wanted to clean it up. No one wanted to see it. And yet, they wanted it gone. Carter asked if they had a bucket and a scrub brush.

"I took the scrub brush and a bucket and some soap, and I started with the ceiling and then the walls, and finally the floor. I had to empty the bucket in the toilet a number of times to get rid of the blood and the bits of brain. The hardest part was scrubbing off the baked material on the lights that had heated up and now stuck like glue. I had trouble keeping my breakfast down. I kept wanting to vomit, but I knew it would not be good for them to hear me doing that."

After he finished cleaning the bathroom, more relatives arrived. Carter excused himself and left. "I wandered around aimlessly the rest of the day doing my work almost as if I wasn't there."

The funeral was to be on the day following Carter's visit to me. As we talked, he wept. He spoke of his feeling of incompetence and a sense that he had not done what he should have done. Finally, he looked up from his lap, tears streaming from his eyes, and said, "I didn't know what else to do. I just took a bucket and scrubbed the bathroom. Did I do right?" I had been silent throughout the entire tale. When he asked, "Did I do right?" I looked at him and replied, "Yes, you did." After a moment he said, "Now, I will be able to sleep."

The story was so compelling that I had listened without comment. But when he stopped and looked straight into my eyes and said, "Did I do right?" I knew why he had come. He needed my reassurance that he had ministered to this family in a proper way. In fact, I was in awe at the way he responded in this agonizingly difficult situation. He had come a long way in a short time, from life on the beach and in the coffee houses of the Bay Area to this poor family's house in north Texas. I merely answered, "Yes," but for Carter, it was like a blessing, a word of affirmation.

I saw Carter several days later, and he told me the senior minister had performed the funeral and that he assisted at the family's request. He was sleeping again—haunted by the events, but sleeping.

Uncritical warmth and unending supportiveness, whether in counseling or in supervision, serve little purpose. In time, the counselee or supervisee cannot take them seriously. But there are moments when people have experienced the horror of life and seek a blessing. In those situations, we can offer our benediction—saying, in effect, "In the midst of the horror and the tragedy and the brokenness, you did all that anyone could ever do. You did right."

A Trilogy of Changes
Initiated by the Amazing Brainiac

Shelley Green
Justyna Ford
Kathleen M. Rhodes

INTRODUCTION

This chapter tells three stories—one about a family changing, a second about how this change altered a team of new therapists, and a third about how the therapists' learning changed a supervisor. The case that provides the foundation for the first story was seen early in the first semester of a masters-level practicum by a team of student therapists, and was the first session ever seen by the co-therapists, Justyna Ford and Kay Rhodes. Shelley Green, the supervisor of the team, was behind the mirror during the first and second sessions, consulting by phone, and entered the room to talk with the family at the end of the second session.

This particular story has had great impact for each of us, and for our work together as a team. For Justyna and Kaye, as well as the other team members, the timing of the case was critical. Because it occurred early in our time together, it became in many ways a guide for how we would like to work—briefly, respectfully, playfully, and effectively. It encouraged us to challenge our initial perceptions, to work hard to understand how clients (and we ourselves) are doing the best we can at the moment, and to look for the ways our clients' solutions are working well for them, without assuming those solutions cannot evolve.

The authors would like to thank our team members—Rose Flavin, Carol Griffith, Hagit Meshulam, and Staci Wor—who helped make this story possible.

For Shelley as well, the timing was important. To watch fledgling therapists not only excel, but arrive at a sophisticated understanding of change in a few short weeks made it possible to use a new kind of shorthand during the remaining weeks of practicum. The team's understanding of clinical cases and the therapists' ability to work effectively seemed to be in fast forward for the rest of the semester. It was and continues to be a delight.

All three of the stories related here are important to us, but before the ones about the therapists and the supervisor can make sense, we must tell what happened to the family. It has now been six months since we met the family, and the story that follows is told from our careful review of the tapes and our collective sharing of what "happened" as we now understand it. Following this family's story, we will tell you about our own accompanying changes—first the therapists' and team's, then Shelley's.

THE FAMILY'S STORY:
WEANING THE AMAZING BRAINIAC

Twelve-year-old Michael, his mother (Barbara), and father (Al) came to our clinic desperate to receive help for Michael so that his mother could avoid, as she said, "going crazy." The two therapists, Justyna and Kay, entered the room for the initial session. As the three family members sat huddled together on a small sofa intended for two, Michael leaned on his mother's shoulder and periodically cried quietly. Barbara stroked his arm and hair; Al looked somber. They described agonizing, exhausting nights in which Michael and Barbara stayed up until 4 or 5 a.m. attempting to complete Michael's homework assignments. Generally, Barbara only learned of the assignments the night before they were due, and the pressure was on for her to help Michael finish. A frustrated Al arose each morning at 3:30 a.m. to get to his job at a bakery. He rarely shared intimate time with Barbara, and he expressed worry about her lack of sleep and the pressure she assumed. Barbara described Michael's problem as one of low self-esteem and great self-doubt. She noted that while she had always helped him with his homework, the problem had intensified this year as he entered seventh grade and received more involved assignments. Also this year, Barbara had returned to work full-time, so the demands on her took a great toll. She described through tears, "I'm tired; I'm so tired of being the one who pulls him through school. I don't have the strength to be up all night with him." Throughout this discussion, Michael offered silence when asked for input, and continued to whimper quietly while holding his mother's hand.

We learned that Barbara was a teacher, currently instructing adult learners, and loved her work. Thus, she felt compelled to help Michael, and wanted to, but did not believe she could continue her current level of involvement. Barbara also let us know that Michael possessed an extremely high IQ, and that he knew this; but she also thought he might have "some type of learning disability." Michael told us, amidst tears, that he needed help organizing his thoughts. As he exclaimed, "Everything's going through my head at once, too much stuff too fast, and I can't organize everything." He described his mom sitting with him and helping him organize his thoughts on paper. His toughest challenge involved getting started on assignments; he spent hours, his father said, "procrastinating."

The family described this "intensive tutoring" as a family legacy. Barbara shared that her mother did all her homework for her until she was in the eighth or ninth grade. Barbara had helped Michael since second grade, but she refused to "do it for him." Two weeks prior to this first session, she had decided she simply couldn't do it anymore and had refused Michael's pleas for help. According to Barbara, Michael began "to mope and cry and beg," and eventually went to his grandmother, who, true to her history with Barbara, simply did his assignments for him.

At this point in the session, Michael began to sob, telling us that his grandmother didn't let him do any of the work. He cried, "She tells me what to write so we can get it done. I don't get to do it by myself, and I want to. But I can't." As we discussed the differences in Barbara's and her mother's helping styles, it became clear that if Michael's grandmother became the "helper," Michael would soon be doing no work at all.

To our amazement, we discovered that at times Michael played the part of helper as well. He helped his little brother Stephen with his homework, and peers at school frequently called upon Michael for help. However, the family did not see this as significant. Michael's pattern was consistent: he waited until the night before a major project was due, then sobbed and begged his mother to help. She always came to his rescue, and they always made As on their projects. Since his grades were born directly from her efforts, withdrawal offered great risk. In addition, Michael faced a move to a new school next year, and if his grades dropped, acceptance into a good private school would be jeopardized. His parents worried that if he were rejected, he could not thrive in a large public school.

Although the younger brother, Stephen, did not attend, he was in many ways a catalyst for the first session. Al remarked that Stephen's sadness and feelings of being cheated resulted in their decision to attend therapy. As Al commented, "Stephen needs his mommy, and there's only so much mommy to go around. A couple of weeks ago, he began letting us know he feels cheated, and we know this isn't right for anyone." Michael began to cry again and said, "Sometimes I think everything would be a lot better without me. You wouldn't have to spend so much money, and you'd have more time for Stephen. I hog all the time and it's not fair." As he continued to cry, his parents reassured him, but reiterated their urgent desire for change. Barbara held his hand while she described their plight: "If I don't do it, it won't get done, and he'll sit and mope and cry, and he's so sad and I feel so sorry for him, and I love him so much." She felt her own disadvantage from her mother's attempts to help, and wished for his speedier independence. Yet, she continued, "We grew up knowing that that's what you do [i.e., helping]. But I'm very, very tired."

As both Al and Barbara made clear that they agreed something had to change, Michael laid his head in Barbara's lap and sniffled quietly; she stroked his hair and arms, and said slowly, amid her own tears, "He's humorous, he's bright, he tickles your funny bone when he's not crying." Michael's bar mitzvah was approaching, and they were very worried he would disappoint them, himself, and the rabbi. Al indicated that he had talked to Michael repeatedly about the need to study, but it didn't happen unless he locked him in his room, forcing him. Al declared, "We can't help him. He has to do it for himself." Michael and his mother hugged and kissed as the therapists left the room.

As our team met for a brief consultation, the therapists described being very touched by the family's closeness, but very concerned for Michael. He resembled a five-year-old boy in his manner of speaking, his fears, his tears, and his connection to his mother. We wondered what else in the family's relationships might be at stake if this homework connection were to come apart, as this had been a way of life for the family for two generations.

The therapists returned to the family and Justyna asked the family, "We would like to know, if you stopped helping him, and he didn't fail, what might you lose?" Barbara immediately responded that she would lose nothing, and that she would be incredibly relieved. As the family began to contemplate the idea, both therapists described how important this way of life had become to the family, and how disruptive change might be. They asked Al, Barbara, and Michael to each consider the changes from their own individual perspectives, and speculated that because they each desired this independence so much, it might prove quite difficult for them to imagine any potential accompanying losses.

During this discussion, Barbara encouraged Michael to share with the therapists something he told her during the break. He was insulted and offended by the therapists' assumption (indicated by earlier questions) that Barbara "does his work." He clarified that "Mom just helps me organize my thoughts. I try and do it from there. That's the hardest part." Justyna and Kay apologized, and thanked Michael for setting the record straight. The family left with encouragement from the therapists to carefully consider any potential losses that could accompany newfound independence.

At the second session one week later, Michael and his family, including Stephen, entered the room in a lively, animated fashion. Barbara and Al sat together on one sofa, touching frequently, and the boys on another. Michael appeared remarkably changed, and Al noted that Michael had accomplished a great deal during the week. As the family talked with the therapists, Michael was active and involved in the discussion, and his voice tone and affect were markedly different from the previous session. He fluently and confidently described the work he had accomplished, and he described doing it all independently. Both Al and Barbara were amazed by the changes he had made, and Barbara noted her lack of involvement in any of his assignments.

The conversation rather quickly turned to a discussion of how the two boys maintained their rooms, chores, and got along with each other. After several moments of this talk, the team phoned in, expressing curiosity about the change in direction. Justyna commented on this to the family, and Al and Barbara both agreed that things were dramatically different. Al enthusiastically declared, "I hope that this has stimulated him, given him a sense of accomplishment. I would like to find a way to somehow reward and reinforce his progress." Barbara, Michael, and Al described the "torture" Barbara had previously endured, and laughed as they described Barbara asking Michael, "What did we get on our paper? Did we get an A?"

The therapists congratulated them on their hard work in getting Michael to this point, and on their wisdom in realizing that it was time to let go. Upon hearing this, Barbara told us an important story from her past:

> When I was nursing him [Stephen], there came a point when I was no longer receiving any physiological benefit from that, so I said, "You know what? I love you; you're twenty-two months old; you're a great kid; look at how wonderful you're doing; and now it's time for the factory to stop." And he would come up to me and ask me, "Can I have some milk?" And I said, "No, it's still broken." How do you show someone it's broken? I had to put Band-Aids on [my nipples]! But it got to a point where he was able to eat enough food and there was no physiological and physical benefit left for me, so we were done, we were complete. . . . It was again my saying, "Certain changes have been hard for me," where I said, "OK . . . it's enough." And it wasn't a matter of being resentful . . . But "We can hug each other in a different way. You don't have to do that; you're big enough that you don't need that right now."

Kay asked if Barbara felt the same way now about Michael, as she was no longer reaping the benefits from her helping him. Barbara described that their relationship had become more of a burden than a pleasure, and that she couldn't enjoy helping Michael when he was being, in Michael's words, "vegetable boy!" She said, however, that she knew there was a "wealth of intellect" to be accessed, and she wanted to be a part of his success. As she and Michael were discussing his tenure as "vegetable boy," Barbara withdrew a list from her purse and told us, laughing, "I remember you asked what would I lose in this and that we should each think about it. I didn't remind anybody to think about the things they would lose; I wanted to think about what I would lose!" She then paused for a moment and said slowly, "We would lose time together."

As Al assured her that they would not lose time, but would in fact gain a different kind of time, Barbara went on to explain that her nature is to teach, and that her unique skill lies in challenging and working with students to draw information from them. She did not want to abandon her niche as an "engaging teacher." She told Michael she wanted to be his guide, rather than to shove him down the road, and expressed her fear that he might go "careening off the road." As she said, "I want you to find the road map." Michael responded, saying that that he believed he would "just stop to look at the map more often." He confidently shared that the map would guide him, and observed that before now, he "never really did anything." Kay asked him if this week he was clear that he had done more than had been possible in a long time, and agreeing, he rose and went to hug his father.

The team and therapists were subsequently amazed as Michael went on to describe in great detail and with supreme self-confidence his upcoming science project: "My hypothesis is going to be solar energy intensification by using magnification on the lens. With solar panels, a sheet of plastic and a box . . . I'm going to take a big magnifying type of plastic and a regular type of solar panel and I'm going to see what happens if I magnify it to the intensify the strength of the solar energy. Magnifying the light to see if it makes the solar energy absorb better and work faster. . ." At this point, the supervisor, Shelley, entered the room and began to comment on the changes in Michael, particularly noting the elaborate description of his project. Shelley asked if Michael would consult with some of the program's doctoral students who were having difficulty getting their ideas well-formed for their dissertations. Michael beamed and agreed, while his parents laughed.

Shelley then went on to say that the team had noticed that Michael seemed much older than when they first met him, and they weren't sure how that had happened so quickly. She commented on Barbara's concern that she and Michael might lose time together if things changed, and connected this to Barbara's poignant story of nursing Stephen. She turned to Barbara and said, "At some point with Stephen, you said, 'enough is enough. . . . get the Band-Aids!' It seemed to me when you were describing that, that you knew, developmentally, when it was time for that to happen. You knew it was time to get the Band-Aids, and you would have a new and different relationship with Stephen when that stopped. And it struck me that you knew, somehow, it was time to get the Band-Aids this week, too. I don't know how you knew, and not only did you know, but things happened! Michael knows what he's doing here." Barbara and Al agreed, and Barbara commented that prior to this time, Michael simply had not known he knew. She again said that what they had been dealing with for many years (since second grade) was low self-esteem. Shelley asked Michael how his self-esteem was doing at the moment, and he responded enthusiastically, "Better than before!"

Al noted that when one accomplishes something, self-esteem goes up; Shelley agreed, noting, "I think that's what we're seeing this week; he's seeing something in himself and you're seeing it too. And you don't want to think that now everything's fine and there's never going to be a setback, but on the other hand, we do want to respond to what we're seeing tonight because it's a very dramatic change in a very short time, which tells me he's got a whole lot of resources." Barbara turned to Michael and exclaimed, "Did you hear that? You've got a whole lot of resources! I know that there's this incredible ability there." Stephen looked up from playing with his toys and yelled, "The Amazing Brainiac!!!" The therapists and family dissolved into laughter, and Shelley told the family that the team believed they (the family) were now on a roll. She noted that the team wanted to respect both their accomplishments and their reluctance to trust the changes, and offered them the option of whether or not to return for more therapy. Barbara replied thoughtfully, "It's interesting you should ask us that because on the way over here tonight, I was feeling much better about things. I was thinking, 'do we really need to be here?' I figured it would be very beneficial for Michael to have a closure to this." Shelley reiterated that Michael seemed to be taking off on his own, at which point Michael rose to hug his mother.

The therapists continued to discuss Michael's progression toward manhood, particularly in light of his approaching bar mitzvah, and wondered in what ways the family would continue to notice Michael appearing more mature in the coming weeks. Barbara, recognizing her ability to predict the end of therapy, exclaimed, "Boy, I must be really intuitive! We really appreciate you all." As the session came to a close, Stephen asked if it was time for another break, and Barbara responded, "It's done time!" Stephen jumped up, yelling, and raced around the room, only to be intercepted by Michael, who picked him up and carried him out.

As the team said good-bye to the family, Barbara said that they would keep in touch and would bring by Michael's science project if we wanted to see it. Three weeks later, we received a phone call from Barbara, indicating that Michael had written an "incredible" book report for his English class, and that he had done the entire assignment on his own. She said that she was not staying up at night with him any more, and she was clear he could do well on his assignments on his own. We assumed the Amazing Brainiac was weaned and on his way. Soon Barbara would be able to remove the Band-Aids.

THE TEAM'S STORY:
TRUSTING THE CHANGES

We gathered as a team after the case concluded and asked ourselves what made the difference during those two brisk sessions. Neither party had any live experience in the therapeutic arena—we offered this family their first experience, and they presented us with our initial client encounter. And we connected. Together for the first time, we forged something entirely new. During the team discussion, Justyna described the advantage of our freshness, inexperience, and lack of preconceptions. The family encountered great curiosity, coupled with a lack of judgment from us. We didn't see how we could "fix" them. How were maiden voyage therapists like us going to fix anything or anyone? Perhaps this was our collective saving grace.

We understood how chronic this problem had become and how it permeated their entire system. We saw the family's ability to be significantly involved in Michael's life as an advantage, not something we should stamp out. Some of us saw a bright kid who became helpless in the process of being helped. Others in our group didn't perceive him as helpless, but did see his mother as being steadfastly, enduringly helpful.

During our team discussion, Kay said that upon her return to the second session, she could not believe this family's remarkable, bewildering progress. Not only was Michael a different young man, but his parents were connected again as well. Kay didn't know whether to trust it, and wasn't sure what to do with it during the session. None of us expected the family to change so rapidly and radically. We stared at each other in amazement—this case must be a plant! The change seemed to occur too fast; therapy seemed too brief.

How did this change occur? As "experts," we didn't tell this family that mom needed to stop it. We gave them permission to think and feel the same way and focus on the same things, but with a slightly different skew. We were playful and nonconformist, we coaxed them off-guard and engaged them. We took a leap of faith and, frankly, we weren't sure about the intervention we had been asked to offer, but we kept encouraging them to ponder it. We felt too overwhelmed to question our supervisor's strange, golden words.

After the first session, we learned that the therapists behind the one-way mirror had already grown weary of hearing this young man whimper like a small boy. But the two of us who found ourselves face-to-face with the clients remember feeling vital that evening, experiencing life in the room, and enjoying our time with this family. In the future, as difficult as a case may be, when things seem bleak, this case will inspire us and remind us that even when a family looks very, very stuck and very, very much at their wits' end, rapid change is possible.

The memory of this case has helped us to find our way through clinical entrapment many times in the past few months. It has helped us understand how to simultaneously be comfortable with stability as we offer change, and to know that our job is not to decide how or what the family chooses, but to respect the balance they find.

THE SUPERVISOR'S STORY: FAST-FORWARDING TO CHANGE

I have been supervising therapists for almost ten years now, and during that time, few client stories and few team stories have been as immediately transformative for me as this combined tale. The family's story has stayed with us as a team, and has certainly entered into our team conversations many times over the past six months. We have laughed about our own rather strange version of the "miracle question." As we presented it to the family, it went something like this: "We would like to know, if you stopped helping Michael, and he didn't fail, what might you lose?" Translated now into the formula question—"If you were to change X, and Y went well, what might you lose?"—it has become a way for us to always remember the wisdom in each family's current actions before we rush in to change them. Whether or not we ask it of the families, we consistently ask it of ourselves in regard to them. It is thus a form of shorthand to help us think creatively about the binds families find themselves in.

But beyond the question and its implications, what has stayed with me has been the incredible ability of two brand new therapists to enter into a warm relationship with a family in crisis, to look for and immediately see the strengths present in that family, and perhaps most important, to be willing to take an idea into the room that doesn't yet make sense to them and learn to fly with it. Justyna and Kay both said that they thought the idea was unusual, but they took the "leap of faith" and pursued it, probed it, and encouraged the family to do the same. In some ways, they had the same experience as the family, and they made use of that experience in a similar way. Kay observed that when the family returned so changed, she didn't know what to think or to do; she didn't trust it. But she watched, she listened, and she learned to trust the change.

After this case, these two therapists were changed. When they now enter the room with a new family, they know what to do. It might not be what I would do, but it makes sense and they have developed their own style of connecting. Initially, I didn't know how much to trust their change. Was their ability to be articulate truly evidence that they understood the theory, or did it just provide a pleasant cover for confusion? What I learned over the next few weeks was to watch, to listen, and to trust what I saw. As I did so, I found that each of the six women on this team has a unique ability to forge a therapeutic alliance; each works differently, but in many ways, each comes to a similar place. Partly because of this young Brainiac we met together early in our relationship, each of them knows how to respect the position of the families who come to us—to find the strengths, to access the logic of people's behaviors, and to create new meanings around those behaviors.

I'd love to think that each time I have the opportunity to work with a new team, a transformative case will find its way to us soon after we come together. Instead, I think I will look for the transformative lessons that come with each case and with each trainee, whether the family members (and therapists) change immediately and dramatically, or slowly and subtly. The lessons I learned from Michael and his family, and from Justyna, Kay, and their colleagues, have encouraged me to watch for the ways therapists learn about change from the families they see. It is now my impression that much of what these therapists know about being therapists came from the families. Similarly, almost everything I know about supervising I learned from trainees. Hopefully, I can learn and change as quickly as they can.

The Tale of the Ripple

Mallika Ruth Samuel

Dub . . . dubdub . . . dub . . . dubdub . . . , what in the world was *that*? Well, it was nothing but the beating of my heart. The palms of my hands were sweating, as few minutes of the viewing of my videotape had lapsed in our supervision class. I was anticipating a bag full of criticisms.

To begin with, I anticipated criticism such as, "a total lack of connecting or joining with the client." The second and the third and the fourth criticisms I felt were coming: absence of eye contact, a body posture that depicts a sense of closure, voice is too soft, too many silences and pauses . . . and on and on. When one takes a look at the above list, it definitely raises questions about the making of a competent therapist in the mental health profession. After all, these are the basic ingredients for successful therapy, right?

As I was anxiously reeling off this list in my mind, I heard the voice of my supervisor, say, "Well done." I just couldn't believe it. I thought, "Poor me, he is just trying to save me from any further embarrassment, particularly in front of my classmates." Or, I thought, "He is just using the usual adjectives . . . I wonder whether he really means it or not." I was suddenly awakened from these thoughts by the discussion the supervision class was having over my tape. What finally made sense was the fact that the evaluation of my performance as a student therapist was based on my ability to apply the principles that underlie the particular model I was using, not on my ability to mimic American ideas about "joining." He said, "Successful joining is determined by the *clients*, not by me." What a relief! This experience—being seen as competent by my supervisor and peers—is what I refer to as the "ripple."

My supervisor threw a pebble into my pond of learning that created a "difference" in the learning process and had led to subsequent changes which became evident in the therapy room. Believe me, ripple after ripple followed. What exactly was this difference? Now, just fantasize with me for a moment. Here is a female student in her early twenties hailing from the south of the subcontinent of India. Add to this a conservative upbringing, mingled with a supposedly timid personality that further colors this picture. Besides, attempting to study the family therapy in a foreign academic context was certainly an added stress! With such a backdrop, one has a double portion of struggles.

Going back to the effectiveness of that first ripple in my second semester of practicum . . .

"Your clients are waiting to see you," came the announcement from my fellow therapist as I hurriedly entered the office area. "I hope you don't get apprehensive, but based on their attire, your clients appear to be hardcore Texans," she said. This was enough to make my heartbeat accelerate again! On being briefed and reassured by my friend, I stole a quick glance at the reception room, and lo and behold, there they were—the "traditionally clad" Texan couple. The gentleman appeared to be straight out of the stories and movies I had watched on television about the "wild, wild West" (of America)—hat, boots, and all. To cap it all, their nonverbal behavior was all the more intimidating to me because I could sense "tension," not "problem," in the air. They sat away from each other, with the wife occasionally staring or glaring at her husband. Well, as you know, by now I could hear my heartbeat go all the more: dub . . . dubdub . . . dubdubdub. I also had all kinds of thoughts racing through my head. First of all, I had to pull myself together to greet and introduce myself to them, and then usher them into the therapy room. With my palms all sweaty, I felt I had to get myself to extend a firm handshake, which just didn't come spontaneously or naturally to me, given my cultural upbringing . . . It was then that I felt the stir of *the ripple.*

Suddenly, the focus was now more on the clients and less on me as a foreign student therapist. The individual "me" was intact, which facilitated creating a difference in the lives of my clients. But, by accepting and by being sensitive to my cultural context in supervision, I was able to enhance my sensitivity towards my client's cultural context. While reeling under the effect of *the ripple,* I advanced toward where my clients were seated, and the greeting and ushering was done with a sense of newfound confidence. It also occurred to me for the first time what it would be like on the other side of the fence: I considered my clients' perceptions of me. All along, the focus was on me; now what mattered most was being sensitive to my clients and ensuring that they feel comfortable and at ease. Once we sat down within the confines and privacy of the therapy room, the first session began. And when I write "began," I mean that it was a new beginning for me. So, in my shy, soft, voice and my wheatish, short stature, bringing whatever handicaps I perceived to have, I inquired:

Ruth: In what way can I be of help to you both?
Ray: She is going to leave me.
Rebecca: Oh yeah, and do you know why? He is having an affair!
Ray: You mean "had" . . .

Soon, with my ears strained to follow their Texas accents closely and carefully, I intervened with this question: "Tell me, please, prior to all this, what did you both see in each other that brought you both together in the first place?"

It was now their turn to tune in their ears to follow my southern Indian accent! Sure, I checked with them on whether they were able to follow me and I made sure that in case they didn't, they were free to interrupt me and to tell me so. Remember, this was part of being sensitive to my clients rather than moping over my own struggles. Going back to their answers to the above query, they each described characteristics that they valued and admired in each other and what their relationship was like before the present situation. I did not realize how time went by . . . until there was a knock at the door from another student therapist who needed to use the room! Now, it was my turn to receive feedback, which I used to dread . . . but this time, I posed the question with a genuine sense of curiosity:

Ruth: If I could do better in the next session when we meet again, what would I do?
Ray: Please do the same!
Rebekkah: I never realized how much good there was in the relationship!

Whoa! I thought, the traditionally clad Texans and the foreign, shy, timid, lack-of-eye-contact, soft-spoken-whatever student therapist did connect after all! . . . thanks to *the ripple*.

When time came for the second session, I again heard the voice of one of my fellow student therapists: "Your client is here to see you—he seems to have come in early." I turned around and asked, "Excuse me, did you say *he* is here and not *she*?" "Yes, that's right. Is something wrong?" Well, *the ripple* continued. This time, there was absolutely no sound of the beating of my heart. It was a normal heartbeat. I greeted the traditionally clad Texan gentleman with a firm handshake, and ushered him into the therapy room. He told me that he and his wife agreed that he was to come alone to work on his issues. In this session, we explored how he could again be the husband he was to his wife before the affair.

In the third session, they both came back together; this time I was eagerly looking forward to their visit. As soon as they entered, I strode toward them, giving them each a firm handshake and a loud and hearty "How are you both?" The session focused on their desire to live with each other and work things out. So, we turned our attention to how each of them could make this come about. Even today, I cherish the experience of that session because it involved delving in to the wealth of each person's unique resources which could harmonize to arrive at a workable solution agreeable to both. One portion was especially rewarding:

Rebekkah: He used to be such a sweet-natured man, and I want more of that.

Ruth: Give me examples of occasions when he was a sweet-natured man. In other words, what did he do that indicated to you that he was a sweet-natured man?

Rebekkah: Well, for example, he used to fix me surprise breakfasts . . . he used to take care of the children without me asking or requesting for help . . . he would always verbalize his appreciation for my good housekeeping . . .

Ruth: Now, on a scale from 1 to 10, where does he stand in terms of being a sweet-natured man, and where do you want him to be?

Rebekkah: As of now, it is probably a "5" and I want him to be a "7" to start with.

Ruth: Well [addressing Ray], how can you be helped to get to "7"?

Ray: I need her to let me know or remind me that she wants more of this . . .

By the end of this session, I had to be reminded again by a student therapist's knock on my door that the session had to come to a close. I was so totally into the process that the "me" did not occur at all. That was the last session I had with them, and as they walked out of the room hand in hand, I just couldn't help but ask this question: "Did you both perceive me to be different in terms of culture, etc.? Did it get in the way and, if so, how did you both overcome the difference?" They promptly replied, "Sure you looked different, but neither of us perceived any *real* difference. What mattered to us was that you did your job by making us see our relationship differently!!"

Thanks to *the ripple,* my individual style facilitated creating a difference in the lives of my clients. Also, by accepting and by being sensitive to my cultural context in supervision, I was able to enhance my sensitivity toward my clients' cultural contexts. In other words, the focus was now more on the clients and less on me as a student therapist. I walked into the therapy room experiencing a total sense of freedom to be "me" (a brown-skinned female from southern India with a soft voice, minimal eye contact, closed posture, and noticeable accent). All of this became negligible simply because, in that particular context, I was comfortable with myself. What mattered most was how we were working together to construct a solution. Despite encountering the traditionally clad Texan couple (and I mean Texan to the core!), the "me" wasn't an issue. The reason: my difference was valued in the supervision process, and therefore I was totally at home with the differences that existed in the therapy room. The moment this difference took place, the momentum of change was enhanced.

I had found a way to harmonize my individual style with the tenets of my therapy model, and synchronize with my clients' world views. This whole experience with this particular couple was edifying and unforgettable. As for me, I got caught up in a sense of profound respect and admiration as we unearthed each of their strengths. As time drew near for the conclusion of the final session, I was overcome with a feeling of happiness. It was for real—I had actually witnessed the effect of *the ripple.* I couldn't help but let the couple know as they left the room, hand in hand, that to me this was the "best session" I had had that semester. There continue to be more ripples, but I am forever thankful for that first supervision ripple.

What Do You See if You Look into That Word?

Tom Andersen

SETTING

The local therapist, who is present in the room, wanted the consultant (Tom) to talk with the client (Sheila). The local therapist himself wanted to sit back and listen to her speak.

PART OF THE TALK

Sheila was very upset when she was told that her mother had waited one week before she visited her mother (Sheila's grandmother), who had been admitted to a hospital two weeks ago. Sheila then told how it had been for herself two years ago when she had a throat inflammation and a high fever. In her heart, Sheila wanted someone to come to her, but she could not ask anyone to come because that was not part of what she was able to do—"If I am to receive help, that must be given to me. I cannot ask for it."

Tom: How do they . . . your family . . . see you? Do they see you as a person who should never ask for something . . . or do they see you as a person who deserves to ask for something for yourself? How do they see you?

Sheila: I am not sure . . . I . . . uhm . . . I don't think that they look in terms of that . . . I think that . . . you know . . . look at . . . I guess that the family I grew up in . . . we were supposed to be self-reliant. . . . A certain amount of self-reliance . . . independence was the big word in my family.

As she uttered the words "independence was the big word in my family," the pitch of her voice dropped slightly and a sadness came over her face. I thought I would learn more about the word "independence," but Sheila had to finish what she was saying before I could ask my question.

Tom: Self-reliant?
Sheila: What?
Tom: Independent?
Sheila: [nods] "Independent" was really the big word . . . and . . . You know I feel that I got the message there.
Tom: I am sorry . . . you feel that . . .
Sheila: I feel that I got that message there. . . . Right . . . and I feel that that was something I really incorporated into my life. . . . I have . . . no . . . As soon as they were not responsible for me, it became . . . there was no longer an issue. . . . I mean they don't talk of that any more, you know . . .
Tom: But it is still there.
Sheila: I feel like to . . . ask for . . . uhm . . . when I was sick, finally my sister called my mom and said, "You have to come back there. . . . You have to come to see Sheila. . . ." and my mom did come back . . . and . . . and I thought very badly about that . . . because then my dad was left on his own. . . . It was very . . . it was very awful. You know, I almost got the sense of . . . I was causing . . . I was causing . . . I was in my own crisis, but I was also causing people around me to have crises. It was kind of like a chain reaction. . . . Something bad happened here . . . something pretty awful. . . . You know everybody has a little bit of a share of that. I don't know how anybody else would handle that . . . uhm . . . . I mean in an ideal situation . . . I don't know. I mean . . . in an ideal situation, I guess I wouldn't be sick. In an ideal situation, I suppose that . . . actually I don't know what would happen in an ideal situation . . . how I would react to that . . . if . . . if . . . being anyone if . . .
Tom: How was that word "independent" expressed? Was it in the open or was it implicit, or . . . How was it expressed?
Sheila: Well, it was verbally.
Tom: Verbally . . . the word "independent"?

Sheila: Yes.

Tom: In the way you should be independent or independence in general? . . . or . . .

Sheila: We should be independent . . . . They wanted us to be independent . . . and . . . .

At this point, her shoulders dropped and she looked down at her hands, which she grasped in an attempt to support herself.

Tom: So how . . . along the route, when you came to be acquainted with the word and let that word be part of yourself. What do you see in that word if you look into the word "independent"?

Sheila: I don't like it. I personally don't like that word very much . . . partly . . .

Tom: Do you see things that . . . Say more . . . what don't you like when you see into the word or look into the word?

Sheila: Well, I see . . . talking about loneliness is so hard for me . . . you know I just . . .

Sheila puts her hand to her face and starts weeping.

Sheila: This was something I tried to not to think too much about. I guess the word "independent" does mean staying alone . . . and for me that has gotten to be lonely . . . being alone. . . . That's what the word . . . we used to talk about being independent and I finally said, "Don't use that word about me anymore . . . it is reinforcing something that I really don't like . . ." having to do everything myself . . . having to . . . I have always felt it has been forced on me . . . for me. What I would like to do is just . . . I don't think independence is a virtue. I don't think so at all. I mean staying alone . . . having to cope with things myself . . . I just don't . . . I don't think . . . I don't think I treat other people like that but I treat myself like that. . . . I feel that I treat other people as . . . I try to provide support at least when I can. . . . When it comes to me, I . . . it's like I don't seek support . . . instead of . . . Maybe I do. . . . I think about a year ago, I finally realized that thing, "independence" about me . . .

She raises her shoulders and neck, and the strength of her voice increases. The hands leave each other and they are moved to each of Sheila's sides, and the front of her body "opens up."

Sheila: I constantly used that word to describe me and I finally . . .
I am *not* independent. . . . *No*, I am *not* independent like you think
I am. I may have grown up with the idea that I should be, but that
is not what I believe in now. I believe that people should be
supportive. I believe in being cooperative . . . you know, always
strong all the time . . . so that it something that I feel I . . . It is
really worthwhile for me coming here and talking about things I
wouldn't talk about. . . .

Sheila was asked what her mother would see if she looked into
the word. "Virtue," she said. "And your father?" "Virtue," and she
paused and laughed and said, "That was strange because he would
see another kind of virtue than my mother." Her sister and her
grandmother would see it the same as herself.

Sheila was then asked what would happen if she went to her
mother and father and said, "Let us sit down and talk about what we
see when we look into the word 'independence'." "Are you crazy?"
Sheila asked, "They would think I was crazy!" But she went to her
sister two months later, and they had a talk about what they see
when they look into the word "independence."

TALKING IS SEARCHING THROUGH WORDS TO FIND MEANING

One can, when one follows the text, see how Sheila searched
through her repertoire of words to find the best word to express
herself. The spoken text, as it is transcribed, is very different from
written texts. Written texts have big letters in the beginning of a
sentence, commas, full stops, etc. Spoken texts have breaks and
pauses. Wittgenstein said that our language gives us the possibilities
but also the limitations for what we can come to understand (Grayling, 1988). The spoken comes first; then, by talking, we reach
meaning.

WORDS ARE INFORMATIVE AND FORMATIVE

What we say inform others *and* ourselves what we think. But the
act of talking forms the person (Andersen,1995; Bakhtin,1988). The

act of uttering, which includes all of Sheila's movements and words, forms her. When she first talked in resignation about the burden of the word "independence," her body dropped; as she talked in protest, her body rose.

WHAT THERE IS IS IN THE WORDS, NOT BEHIND THEM OR UNDER THEM

This was also something Wittgenstein thought: that we do not have the language in us, but we are *in* the language. We are in the language as the fish is in the water (Grayling,1988). As therapists, we should search for what is in the words, and abandon the Freudian idea that the words stem from an inner psychological "core." Harry Goolishian (1989) reminded us so often to "listen to what they really say, not to what they 'really mean'!"

WORDS TOUCH AND MOVE

When Sheila spoke, the words reached my ears *but* also her own ears. When she heard "independence," she was also moved. And the word "independence" seemed to move her more than the other words she spoke. When I saw her being moved, I was myself moved. And those moments in therapy where the client is moved by his or her own utterance and the therapist becomes moved by seeing the client become moved seem to be good points from which to continue the conversation.

However, some words are not touchable because they are too emotion-filled. Therefore I feel most safe to raise one or two general questions about the word to see if the client is able to stay with the word. As you have seen, Sheila was first asked how the word was expressed and then what the command in the word was. Sheila could respond easily on both the questions; therefore, I understood that she was ready to look into the word. Sometimes, however, words can be so tough on the person who is speaking that the word should not be dealt with. When a man said the word "suffer", he sobbed so strongly in pain that I determined to find a less moving word to talk about.

BEING IN THE WORLD IS BEING IN THE FLOW OF UTTERANCES

Utterances are words plus simultaneous physical activities. We become the persons we become as we utter how we utter. Life is a chain of uttering moments. As therapists, we take part in these uttering and moving moments. One nice part of the therapist's contributions is to be present and available to be moved.

REFERENCES

Andersen, T. (1995). Reflecting processes; acts of informing and forming: You can borrow my eyes, but you must not take them away from me! In Friedman, S. (Ed.), *The Reflecting Team in Action*. New York: The Guilford Press.

Bakhtin, M. (1993). *Toward a Philosophy of the Act*. Austin: University of Texas Press.

Goolishian, H. (October 4, 1989). Personal Communication.

Grayling, A. C. (1988). *Wittgenstein*. New York: Oxford University Press.

It's Show Time!

Raeline M. Nobles

Thirty minutes until show time, and it's spent reviewing notes, pacing the hall, and making sure (for the fourth time) that the equipment, chairs, and coffee are all in their proper places. Butterflies in my stomach flutter the light fantastic, sending a soft rush of adrenalin every time they rise to flight. Yes. There it is again. That warm, hot, cold, soft, sharp, dull, scratchy mix of excitement, tension, worry, nerves, and anticipation. It's a slightly scary thing. An edgy thing. A sweaty palms thing. It's the night I meet my new team of student therapists for the semester. It's a good thing.

After five semesters of supervising groups of graduate psychology students as they hone their skills with clients, I still experience the same thoughts and feelings before I meet my new team. Who will they be? What ideas and theories will they bring to the table? What are their expectations of themselves, of the team, and of me? How can I facilitate the creation of a cohesive group and still nurture a diversity of creative thought? What will I do differently this time? How can I do a better job? What will I contribute to their education and they to mine? How will I exemplify the theory, the philosophy, the understanding of talking with clients that I do believe in? Will I? How will I explain to the students (and to myself) the discrepancies and inconsistencies I only occasionally but inevitably exhibit? What can they and I learn from these? What will I do to help foster respect for families, the team process, themselves, and myself in spite of and hopefully because of these little faux pas? How will this team experience help us all become better therapists and more effective consultants? What challenges will our clients bring to us? What stories of insight, courage, despair, hope crisis, conflict, and love will we be privy to? What difference will we all make? What am I doing here?

These and countless other questions race through my head. I scramble to read my notes, check the equipment, and get another cup of coffee.

It's now twenty-nine minutes until show time.

Resisting Resistance,
or a Lesson on Cooperating (and Writing)

Jürgen Hargens

This is a story that told me a lot about structuring cooperation. For me, cooperating is at the heart of working "this way" and it is part of an even more important issue: respect. These two ideas function as some kind of basic guidelines in my work. I do not want to define or specify them. I think you have some ideas what I may mean by these terms, and I think this is just what you should keep in mind when reading my story and giving meaning and sense to it.

Stories are manifold with a lot of different intentions. From my perspective, in telling stories I cannot avoid becoming somehow "educational." I decide which story I am going to tell in which way—and thus, I surely have some intentions! I have selected this story because it reminded me of a basic point: How do I relate to my ideas when clients seem to not fit into this frame? I selected this story of working with an individual because it taught me about the difficulty of doing something different*—which may help in constructing something different that could make a difference both for my client and for myself.

I am working in the countryside in northern Germany. I belong to a group of therapists who work with sexual offenders as part of a little program sponsored by the country government. One day, I got a call from a colleague who was tired of working with one of his clients after having tried for more than a year. The client—I call him Mr. Brown—was sent by the court because he raped a woman. He didn't show up regularly, he didn't want to cooperate, and he was

---

*Doing "more of the same" is what we are used to doing. Setting a different frame may work as a context marker for a different perspective—valuing competency, strength, and resources.

unwilling and unmotivated—this was what the colleague told me. He asked me whether he could refer this man to me, and—God only knows why!—I said "yes." I usually say "yes" because I think it is important to support people who want to be supported.

Two months later—in August—I got an official letter from the court, informing me that Mr. Brown has been sentenced to come to me for therapy. Nothing more happened. One month later I got a call from the probation officer (I will call her Mrs. White), asking whether Mr. Brown has contacted me. I said he had not, and she went on to say that she would go after him. Only two days later I found a message on my answering machine from Mr. Brown, who urged me to give him an appointment just five days later. As he had no phone, I wrote him a letter, telling him that I was unable to offer him an appointment at the time he asked for and asked him to call me. I offered him two times when he could be sure to get me on the line. Nothing happened. As I have troubles with the mail sometimes, I wrote him another letter, informing him when he could get me on the line again about a fortnight later.

In this instance, I worked within the legal field, and as I had an "official" contract—doing therapy with Mr. Brown who has been sent for therapy—I was obliged to inform the court about the continuous meetings. Thus, I always sent a copy of my letters to the probation officer. That helps me to keep things open.

Only three days later, I got a letter from Mr. Brown in which he asked for an appointment, suggesting the next Tuesday. He described the way he had to go and the transportation he had to organize, as he was working and living on an island. He had to take the ferry, then take the train to next city, and from there he had to take the bus to arrive in Meyn—starting with the ferry at 7:30 a.m., arriving in Meyn at 11 a.m.

So we set up an appointment for the middle of October, and I invited both his former therapist and his probation officer. Unfortunately, the probation officer canceled her appearance just before the session. The therapist did show up. He didn't seem to be convinced that Mr. Brown would appear because of his former therapeutic experiences with him. To make a long story short—Mr. Brown arrived, we talked together, and some interesting issues emerged during the interview.

I set the stage for this interview by telling the other two people that I would like to use this meeting to get the best out of it—getting to know the experiences and revealing what the people have in mind about each other. This, I explained, is also my usual way of working—being open, reflecting in the open, and cooperating with the people. First, I asked the therapist about his experiences with Mr. Brown. He described his experiences, saying that the client hadn't participated in therapy. They had a lot of sessions over the year, but since the client did not show up regularly, he did not know what to do about therapy. Thus, the therapist decided to stop the therapy, especially because Mr. Brown was facing another trial. This was the point when he referred Mr. Brown to me.

I asked Mr. Brown about his experiences and expectations. He said that he disliked the scenario—we were all working against him; we had prejudices and he had no real chance of making himself known to me in the way he really is. He said I could not be neutral anymore.

My question was: "What do you want to do about this situation?"

Mr. Brown wanted to continue therapy, but stated that it should be the two of us. I agreed and told him about a basic rule: he is the one who is responsible for the meetings. I will end every session, and if he wants another meeting, he has to ask for an appointment. I will never do so. He agreed, asking for another appointment—and that was that.

What I have told you is the setup of the story. What follows is the story that taught me a lot about "resisting resistance," or about cooperating (and writing).

The next session came, but Mr. Brown did not show up. Thus, I wrote him a letter, sending a copy to inform his probation officer:

Dear Mr. Brown,

For a reason which I do not know and about which I do not want to speculate, you did not show up today for the agreed appointment. I have sent a copy of this letter to the probation office at _____ [city].

Yours sincerely,

About two weeks later I found a message on my answering machine: Mr. Brown informed me that he had been on holiday, thus, he did not receive my letter. He asked for another apppointment. I wrote him back:

Dear Mr. Brown,

I have your note that said you were on holiday and that you just got my letter in which I noted that you did not show up for our appointment on November ___. You asked for another appointment. My proposal is: Wednesday, December ___ [about fourteen days later].

I have sent a copy of this letter to the probation office at ___ [city].

Yours sincerely,

I am sure you guess what happened—Mr. Brown did not show up. I wrote another letter:

Dear Mr. Brown,

For a reason which I do not know and about which I do not want to speculate, you did not show up today for the agreed appointment. This is the second appointment that you have missed without any explanation. I know well that three times is a sailor's right, or the Bremen right.*

I have sent a copy of this letter to the probation office at _____ [city].

Yours sincerely,

Mr. Brown called, setting another appointment for the middle of January. At the beginning of January, I received a letter from the court, asking (1) How often has the client been expected to show up since the formal court decision of August? and, (2) How often has the client missed the sessions without excuse? It also said, "This is an urgent request!"

---

* This is a German saying. As Mr. Brown came from an island, I thought it might be a good idea to relate to a "sailor's right." I also thought that this reference might give the event a different frame/context.

I wrote a letter to the court in which I described what happened without any comments, just telling the dates, the dates of the letters, etc. Of course, I sent a copy of this letter to Mr. Brown and Mr. Red, Mr. Brown's new probation officer.

Mr. Brown did not show up for his next appointment, and I informed Mr. Red about this. This time I wrote a different letter. Mr. Brown got a copy of my short letter to Mr. Red, and I wrote to him as well:

Dear Mr. Brown,

We had agreed by phone that you would call me if you could not come today. This did not happen, for a reason I did not know. I have informed your probation officer.

As there still exists the court requirement of coming to therapy, and as we have been in contact for some time, I'd like to kindly ask you how the course of therapy is looking from your perspective. My questions are:

1. What positive changes have taken place since our meeting here in Meyn on October ___?
2. What changes have occurred that suggest that therapy shows success?
3. How did you succeed in making these changes?
4. Which changes should continue for/with you so that the court is convinced that you do not need any therapeutic support?
5. What ideas do you have about how I can be of further help?

I kindly ask you to send me your response as soon as possible, before January ___ [fourteen days later].

Yours peacefully,

Just three days later I received an answer in which Mr. Brown sent along the ticket for the ferry, indicating that he missed the bus to Meyn after having taken the ferry. He gave me the timetable and his letter ended:

I do not know what you had in mind with your questions, but something has changed. I am about to work part-time as a free-lancer in the field of computer printing.

If you have a date for January which might fit within the timetable, I would be very thankful.

You can guess which way my story is going! I wrote another letter:

Dear Mr. Brown,

I got your letter, and now I know that you missed the bus. It would have been nice if you had called—I would have known quickly and I would have been able to pass this information on. Thus, I could only answer the court's question of whether you had attended this last session with a "no" without giving any reasons for your absence.

I am pleased to learn that you have responses to my questions on how the course of therapy is looking from your perspective. I think this letter is not an appropriate way to go into further detail about this.

You asked for another appointment in January. I suggest Monday, January ___, at 11.00 a.m. If I do not hear anything from you, I assume that you will come. Otherwise, I am sure to hear from you.

I have sent a copy of this letter to the probation office at _____ [city].

Yours sincerely,

The same thing went on—another message on my answering machine, another letter, another call, and finally a date we agreed upon. As you can see, Mr. Brown now called *before* missing an appointment—a change!

So, we had a second meeting about three months after the first meeting. He really came! I complimented Mr. Brown for taking care of himself, doing what he thinks is important to do. I also told him that his behavior would have consequences, of course; I knew that the court had cancelled his probation and that he had applied to fight this cancellation. I said I could see that it might be good to come to therapy because of this situation, but I was not sure what I should or could do about this. So my question to Mr. Brown was: "How would you like to use our meeting?"

Mr. Brown said that he did not know. I replied, "I do not know either. So—what should I do? I think it would not be a good idea to just do therapy, because you know very well what fits you and what doesn't fit you. So I can only ask again: How would you like to use this meeting?"

He came up with some ideas. He wanted (1) to strengthen his self-confidence, (2) to somehow become accountable (because there was nobody else he could talk to), and (3) to work through the stories of those days when he committed his crimes.

I answered that I remember from our first meeting that he was very careful about how people interacted with him, that he was sensitive about prejudices other people had toward him. "How should I behave so that this will work out for me and for you?" I asked.

This was the beginning of a very exciting journey into his ideas about himself. I learned about his loneliness, his strengths, his hopes, his will to take charge, etc. We never spoke about his crimes, about his relationships to women, or about his sexual attacks on women. What I tried to do was just to follow his path—which does not mean to forget about his crimes or his attack.

He taught me about how carefully he took care of himself and the way he offered me his *unique way of cooperating*: by not showing up. It was up to me to cooperate with his offer. What I tried to do was to put my "most basic" guideline into action, *respecting*, which is not to be confused with *accepting*. I tried to respect his worldview and the way he acted upon this view. In this way, I focused on his strenghths—*he did a good job to take care of himself the way he did.* All of a sudden, his "resistance of not showing up" entered a different frame*: to carefully find out what fit best for him.* His "resistance of not talking about his situation" entered the frame of *testing when the ground is safe enough to try something new.* His missing sessions without excuse and asking for more sessions entered the frame *of willingness for change even after years of pain.*

From this perspective, Mr. Brown started to talk about some of his future wishes, his ideas of a better life, his hopes, etc. And this, in turn, led to discovering some small steps he had already taken and small successes he had overlooked. I do not know where the work is going—it is an ongoing work for us, a lesson in cooperating.

All Depends on Your Perspective

Janet L. Osborn
Laurie B. Levine

In my early therapy days, I (J.O.) was under what I now believe to be the mistaken belief that emotion was everything. Being the vocal woman that I am, others were also aware of this trait of mine. As a matter of fact, I was voted "the most likely to make a client cry in the first session" in our class mock elections. This story is about how this apparently played out in my style of supervision.

As doctoral students in Marriage and Family Therapy, we had the honor of supervising first-year master's students. One of the women I supervised (Deb) had a fear of eliciting deep feelings in her clients. She had great empathy and cried easily. Fearful that she would cry in session, she often avoided the feelings of her clients. This troubled her, as she too believed that she needed to get to her clients feelings (or at the very least not avoid them) in order to be helpful. We discussed what it would mean to her to cry in session. She believed that it meant she was a bad therapist, and that her clients may feel that they had to take care of her. I reframed the situation, saying to her that perhaps her empathy and ability to cry so easily with clients was a gift, and that she may serve as a mirror for what the client was feeling, thus sending them the message of "it is all right to have your feelings with me." She was willing to buy my reframe enough to ask me to assist her, via live supervision, with a female client with whom she felt stuck. She felt that there were deep emotions underneath the powerful stories the client related with relatively no affect.

The live interview was arranged, and the session commenced. I attempted to assist by calling in and bringing the two back to the feeling when they got off track. After the third or fourth call in (usually my limit for an entire session), Deb told the client that she needed to meet with her supervisor and would return shortly. When she came into the viewing room, she shared how difficult this was, because she was fighting with her own feelings and was afraid that the client would see. She wanted to go back into a cognitive mode, but also felt that she needed to do it differently. We spent a few moments with her own fears, and then reviewed ways to track the client that would lead the client more deeply into her feelings.

Deb went back into the session and was able to track the client in such a way as to access her feelings. The client sobbed about her current situation with her mother. She said that she had always felt as if she were the adult and her alcoholic mother the child, that there was no room for her feelings. Deb was able to sit with the client quite empathically without crying herself. She was also able to cognitively discuss with the client the work she thought they had both been avoiding. The client left, stating that although it was so painful to have her feelings about her mother, she felt hopeful for the first time that her life could be happier.

That's my take on what happened. My close friend and colleague (L.B.L.), quite by accident observed a different perspective. The following is her account:

In order to provide some context for my perspective on what I observed, in contrast to Jan, I was voted "least likely to make my clients cry." I clearly viewed the world through a cognitive lens.

With that said, I was working at a desk that allowed me to see the hallway between the therapy rooms, and as I waited for my own client, I witnessed the following: I was aware that Jan was doing a live session with her student. We were new supervisors at the time, so this was a reasonably newsworthy event. As I was working at the computer, I could hear the faint ring of the phone in the therapy room. This occurred several times in the first half of the hour, so I suspected that it was an intense session. Then, out of the corner of my eye, I saw Deb come out of the therapy room, looking flustered and overwhelmed, and enter the observation room. This confirmed my suspicions, and I went back to work. A short time later, she emerged from the observation room and headed back to the therapy room. She paused for several seconds in what looked like an attempt to brace herself for whatever was to lie ahead in the session. She sighed loudly, mustered the necessary energy, and finally reentered the therapy room. This further confirmed my suspicions and stirred my compassion for both Deb and her client.

When Deb and the client finally exited the therapy room, it was clear to me that my suspicions about the session being intense were inaccurate in that intense was an understatement. It was clear that the client had been crying (or actually sobbing) as her eyes were red and she had that bewildered, exhausted look clients get when they have experienced second order change. As I reflect on it now, Deb had a very similar look. As the two women walked past me, I had great compassion for both of them and thought, "Oh, guys, Jan must've gotten ahold of you." At that moment, Jan came out of the observation room without any traces of the bewilderment or exhaustion she helped create for her student and the client and we went to lunch. I was amazed.

The Expert Interview

Jamie Raser

I have been very fortunate to train and work at a place where there was always an interest in "cutting edge" theory and therapy. In my early days there, many of the "masters" of the field came to present, demonstrate, and discuss what they were presently doing and thinking. We often had small, intimate workshops by these people, just for the staff of the institute and a few friends. It was a wonderful experience because we could see close up and firsthand what they were doing, and talk to them about it later, perhaps over dinner or drinks.

One day we had a visiting "expert" from a different country who was quite famous for the style of family interviewing he and his colleagues were using. To demonstrate this interviewing style, one of our colleagues at the institute brought in a family she had been working with. The family consisted of a mother and teenage son. The problem was that they got along horribly and that the boy ran away several times a month. He usually put himself in dangerous circumstances when he was away, so the mother was very concerned and wanted him to stay put. The therapist admitted that she had not been successful at slowing the boy down or at improving the mother/son relationship. She needed some new ideas.

There was a small group of us behind the one-way mirror watching and videotaping the session. We had all read the visiting therapist's book and several articles about his technique and were all thrilled to see it demonstrated—by the master himself! As I mentioned, he was not from the United States; he had a heavy accent and was at times difficult to understand.

The interview lasted about one and one-half hours and was a classic, textbook demonstration of the expert's methods. Every detail of his theories and techniques was evidenced in this one session. The mother and boy were very attentive to the therapist, always looking at him, smiling, and nodding as though they, together, were interested in everything the therapist was saying. This was a videotape that we knew we could review over and over again and use to train other therapists. We all felt privileged to witness this event.

The colleague who brought the family in was not scheduled to see them again for about two weeks. We were all very curious about how the family had responded to this intervention. When the colleague finally came to report to us, we were anxious to hear the news. First of all, she reported that the boy had run away three times since the interview. This was quite a surprise to her, so she asked what they thought of the interview. The boy and mother looked at each other and grinned. "We didn't understand a word he said," announced the mother. Upon further exploration, they admitted that they understood about 25 percent of what he said, just enough to nod at the right times or give a brief answer to a question they thought was being asked.

None of us could understand this. The family was attentive, nodding, and seemed to go along with everything that was happening. It was a classic demonstration! It was an expert interview! Everything was perfect, except that the family couldn't understand a word that was being said.

From then on, I questioned "expertness" and "expert demonstrations" in general. The experience taught me how important it is to include clients' voices and let them lead the way. We therapists are not the experts on therapy. Neither are the "masters" and the textbooks they write. The only ones who can really judge how good the therapy is are the clients.

Index

Order Your Own Copy of
This Important Book for Your Personal Library!

TALES FROM FAMILY THERAPY
Life-Changing Clinical Experiences

_____ in hardbound at $49.95 (ISBN: 0-7890-0065-2)

_____ in softbound at $24.95 (ISBN: 0-7890-0450-X)

COST OF BOOKS_____

OUTSIDE USA/CANADA/
MEXICO: ADD 20%_____

POSTAGE & HANDLING_____
*(US: $3.00 for first book & $1.25
for each additional book)
Outside US: $4.75 for first book
& $1.75 for each additional book)*

SUBTOTAL_____

IN CANADA: ADD 7% GST_____

STATE TAX_____
*(NY, OH & MN residents, please
add appropriate local sales tax)*

FINAL TOTAL_____
*(If paying in Canadian funds,
convert using the current
exchange rate. UNESCO
coupons welcome.)*

☐ **BILL ME LATER:** ($5 service charge will be added)
(Bill-me option is good on US/Canada/Mexico orders only;
not good to jobbers, wholesalers, or subscription agencies.)

☐ Check here if billing address is different from
shipping address and attach purchase order and
billing address information.

Signature_____

☐ **PAYMENT ENCLOSED: $**_____

☐ **PLEASE CHARGE TO MY CREDIT CARD.**

☐ Visa   ☐ MasterCard   ☐ AmEx   ☐ Discover
☐ Diner's Club

Account # _____

Exp. Date _____

Signature _____

Prices in US dollars and subject to change without notice.

NAME _____

INSTITUTION _____

ADDRESS _____

CITY _____

STATE/ZIP _____

COUNTRY _____ COUNTY (NY residents only) _____

TEL _____ FAX _____

E-MAIL_____
May we use your e-mail address for confirmations and other types of information? ☐ Yes   ☐ No

Order From Your Local Bookstore or Directly From
The Haworth Press, Inc.
10 Alice Street, Binghamton, New York 13904-1580 • USA
TELEPHONE: 1-800-HAWORTH (1-800-429-6784) / Outside US/Canada: (607) 722-5857
FAX: 1-800-895-0582 / Outside US/Canada: (607) 772-6362
E-mail: getinfo@haworth.com
PLEASE PHOTOCOPY THIS FORM FOR YOUR PERSONAL USE.

BOF96